Staking their claims

Staking their claims

Corporate Social and Environmental Responsibility

in South Africa

Edited by

David Fig

UNRISD
UNITED NATIONS
RESEARCH INSTITUTE
FOR SOCIAL DEVELOPMENT

UNIVERSITY OF KWAZULU-NATAL PRESS

Published in 2007 by University of KwaZulu-Natal Press
Private Bag X01
Scottsville 3209
South Africa
Email: books@ukzn.ac.za
Website: www.uknpress.co.za

ISBN 978-1-86914-107-3

Managing editor: Sally Hines
Editor: Christopher Merrett
Cover design: Flying Ant Designs
Typesetting: RockBottom Design

United Nations Research Institute for Social Development

UNRISD is an autonomous agency engaging in multidisciplinary research on
the social dimensions of contemporary problems affecting development. Its
work is guided by the conviction that, for effective development policies to be
formulated, an understanding of the social and political context is crucial. The
Institute attempts to provide governments, development agencies, grassroots
organizations and scholars with a better understanding of how development
policies and processes of economic, social and environmental change affect
different social groups. Working through an extensive network of national
research centres, UNRISD aims to promote original research and strengthen
research capacity in developing countries.

Current research programmes include: Civil Society and Social Movements;
Democracy, Governance and Well-Being; Gender and Development;
Identities, Conflict and Cohesion; Markets, Business and Regulation; and
Social Policy and Development. For further information on UNRISD work,
visit www.unrisd.org.

Printed and bound by Interpak Books, Pietermaritzburg

Contents

Foreword by *Peter Utting*   vi

Acknowledgements   xi

List of contributors   xii

List of abbreviations   xiv

1   The context of corporate social and environmental responsibility   1
David Fig

2   Political economy   13
Andries Bezuidenhout, David Fig, Ralph Hamann and Rahmat Omar

3   The mining industry   95
Ralph Hamann and Andries Bezuidenhout

4   The chemicals industry   141
Shirley Miller

5   The food and drink industry   173
David Fig

6   The impact of Black Economic Empowerment   207
Roger Southall and Diana Sanchez

7   Responsibility from below in the era of AIDS   241
David Dickinson

8   Afterword: Getting below the bottom line   265
Edward Webster

Index   271

Foreword

A prominent feature of globalisation has been the dramatic increase in the size, geographical reach and cultural presence of transnational corporations (TNCs), large retailers and utility companies. As the economic power of big business has increased, so too have concerns about its impact on society and the environment. Such concerns are not new, of course. What is changing, however, is the way they are addressed. Traditionally, companies sought to enhance their social role by engaging in charitable acts, and governments and trades unions attempted to regulate corporations through various mechanisms that included penalties for non-compliance. Today, in contrast, softer regulatory roles are being assumed by non-governmental organisations (NGOs), industry and business associations, multi-stakeholder entities, and multilateral bodies such as the United Nations and the Organisation for Economic Co-operation and Development (OECD). Many TNCs and large domestic companies are adopting voluntary initiatives that aim to improve the social and environmental performance of companies in ways that are compatible with fundamental business objectives related to profitability and competitiveness, and as part of strategies of risk and reputation management. Such actions and approaches constitute what has become known as corporate social and environmental responsibility (CSER).

CSER is frequently defined in very broad terms: the ethical behaviour of a company towards society, greater responsiveness on the part of owners and managers to the concerns of a company's stakeholders, or voluntary initiatives that go beyond philanthropy and the minimum standards set by law. Often used interchangeably with notions of corporate citizenship, CSER tends to involve a range of initiatives associated with occupational health and safety, education and training, labour and other human rights, anti-corruption, and environmental management, as well as company support for community development projects. CSER is also associated with new management tools and institutions, such as codes of conduct, reputation management, socially responsible investment, life cycle analysis, product stewardship, triple-bottom-line reporting on social, environmental and financial performance, stakeholder dialogues, and public-private partnerships.

This book provides a comprehensive overview and assessment of the state of CSER in South Africa. It yields rich analytical insights into the historical and contemporary dynamics of CSER and its contribution to development. In chapter 2 the authors examine the origins and trajectory of CSER from a political economy perspective, which emphasises the interplay of different social actors and regulatory institutions, the politics of institutional and policy change, and the potential, limits and contradictions of CSER initiatives.

Such a perspective is crucial for overcoming six limitations that characterise much of the writing on CSER that has proliferated internationally since the 1990s. First, analysis in this field often remains narrowly focused on the description of best practice case studies and assumptions about win-win scenarios that tend to ignore tensions, counter-trends or contradictory practices related to corporate activities or CSER itself – practices that have perverse social, environmental and developmental impacts. Second, CSER is generally seen as a modern phenomenon, driven largely by actors and forces associated with contemporary globalisation, with CSER transmitted primarily via TNCs through global value chains or through other actors and institutions centred in the North. From this perspective, the specificities and dynamics of CSER related to local history and actors are often downplayed. Third, the analysis of why companies may be doing things differently and performing better, or of how to scale up CSER, sometimes ignores important drivers of CSER related to the broader societal, institutional and regulatory context. Fourth, critics of TNCs and CSER often dismiss the latter as window dressing or greenwash, without acknowledging the contribution of activism to progressive institutional change, or the fact that decent capitalism requires a complex mix of institutional arrangements that includes not only so-called hard law but also varieties of softer regulation. Fifth, both mainstream and radical perspectives on CSER often view either voluntary or legalistic approaches – or soft or hard institutions – as inherently superior to the other. Frequently ignored are the possible complementarities and synergies between these different approaches, and the potentially fertile ground for regulatory design and intervention that lies at the interface of quite different institutional and regulatory arrangements. Finally, raising social and environmental standards in developing countries may seem an obvious and desirable objective. However, this goal is often pursued without thinking through the developmental implications of CSER, such as the costs involved for small and medium-sized enterprises, and without the active participation of key stakeholders from developing countries in the design and implementation of CSER initiatives.

To address these limitations in the analysis of CSER, the United Nations Research Institute for Social Development (UNRISD), with the support of the MacArthur Foundation, launched a research project in 2001 that examined the implications of CSER for social, sustainable and economic development, as well as for democratic governance and business regulation. Studies were carried out in several developing countries, including Brazil, India, Mexico and South Africa. Research was also conducted on evolving patterns of business regulation and new institutional arrangements associated with the privatisation of regulation, as well as standard setting, company reporting, social auditing, monitoring, certification and social investment, which involve not only companies and organised business interests, but also NGOs, multi-stakeholder initiatives, international organisations and public-private partnerships.

This book shows that, in the South African context, CSER has less to do with conventional explanations related to business ethics, and that it involves far more than the transmission of ideas and management practices through global commodity chains, foreign direct investment and Northern or international actors. The analysis situates CSER within the distinctive history and features of state-capital-society relations in South Africa. Under different phases of South African political economy, CSER has been an instrument used by TNCs and organised business interests to position themselves in relation to the state and civil society. Under apartheid, for example, some TNCs tried to distance themselves from the political regime by adhering to certain labour standards. During the struggle for democracy in the 1980s, big business responded to societal pressures from trade unions and other groups to clean up its act. With the transition to democracy in the 1990s, CSER became an instrument to ward off the threat of regulatory intervention, as well as a response to the rise of environmental activism. And during the subsequent turn to neo-liberalism and technocratic governance in the late 1990s, CSER and public-private partnerships constituted compensatory mechanisms for the rolling back of the state.

Rather than seeing CSER as an inevitable win-win situation, the analysis examines both sides of the equation by describing the numerous advances that have been made in CSER practices and institutions while also identifying the costs and benefits accruing to different social actors and interests, and the associated trade-offs and contradictions. Like other UNRISD studies of CSER in developing countries, the overall picture that emerges is one of a gradual broadening and institutionalisation of the CSER agenda. It remains, however, not only fragmented and patchy, but quite limited in its transformative potential due to the policy, regulatory and political environment in which companies operate and which promote contradictory business practices. Some corporations, for example, have taken steps to improve labour standards in their core enterprises while simultaneously shedding labour, or expanding production by relying on subcontracting, which often implies a deterioration in labour standards. Furthermore, the core business practices or social institutions of some leading CSER companies may be inherently polluting or socially perverse, but such aspects may remain off-limits in the CSER agenda. As noted by the authors, mining companies, for example, generally have significant HIV / AIDS programmes but often fail to address one of the fundamental causes of the pandemic, which is the single-sex dormitory system for migrant workers. Similarly, some food companies have taken a lead in the CSER field but ignore issues of food security and hunger, including the affordability of basic foodstuffs, land redistribution, support for small farmers and the health effects of their core products. A unique feature of South African CSER programmes has been black economic empowerment (BEE), which aims to promote greater diversity of ownership. In relation to CSER, however, the authors reveal serious tensions with this approach as applied in practice.

How can CSER become an instrument that amounts to more than a band-aid for development, or one that essentially legitimises business as usual? Can it become an instrument for promoting a more transformative model of development? Answering these questions has been at the heart of the UNRISD programme on CSER and development. This and other studies suggest that what needs to change is not simply the scale and quality of voluntary CSER initiatives, but the policy, institutional and political environment in which CSER takes place. As in many developing countries, CSER in South Africa is constrained by the macroeconomic policy framework, a weak regulatory or deregulatory environment, the ideology of voluntarism and the politics of CSER, which is heavily dominated by organised business interests.

Moving from a disabling to an enabling environment for CSER would require what some refer to as a developmental policy framework – that is, one that is less fixated on economic stabilisation and liberalisation, and more on economic diversification, the promotion of small enterprise and redistribution that goes beyond current approaches to BEE. It would also require greater attention to the notion of corporate accountability, which implies that large companies should not only have to answer to different stakeholders, but also bear some sort of cost in cases of non-compliance with agreed standards. This implies not only a strengthened role for state regulation but exploring the potential for combining or articulating softer and harder regulatory approaches. Some of the more effective institutions for promoting CSER in South Africa operate at the interface of the voluntary and the legalistic. The voluntary guidelines of the *King Report on Corporate Governance for South Africa* that call for triple-bottom-line accounting have, for example, become listing requirements for the Johannesburg Securities Exchange. In relation to the politics of CSER, there is a need to build on what the authors refer to as the 'small renaissance in civil society's capacity to act as watchdogs and whistleblowers', as well as to forge stronger alliances within civil society, notably between NGOs and trade unions, and to revitalise the type of multi-stakeholder participatory policy making that was a feature of democratisation during the immediate post-apartheid years. Within this sort of policy and institutional context, CSER might become part of an agenda for transformation and poverty reduction, rather than a palliative for a pattern of development that continues to be characterised by high levels of social exclusion, inequality and environmental degradation.

Peter Utting
Deputy Director
United Nations Research Institute for Social Development
(UNRISD)

Acknowledgements

The Sociology of Work Unit (SWOP), based at the University of the Witwatersrand, Johannesburg, has been collaborating with the United Nations Research Institute on Social Development (UNRISD) in Geneva to conduct this research on corporate social and environmental responsibility in South Africa. The research team consisted of Andries Bezuidenhout, David Fig, Ralph Hamann, Shirley Miller and Rahmat Omar. We gained immense insight and inspiration from Peter Utting, deputy director of UNRISD and a leader in the field. Funding for the project came from the John D. and Catharine T. MacArthur Foundation.

SWOP's director, Eddie Webster, gave us wholehearted and invaluable support, and has contributed an afterword. SWOP's administrator, Khayaat Fakier, assisted our efforts with good-natured and professional attention. Anthea Metcalfe reliably and efficiently arranged our public workshop, while Shameen Govender and Thandeka Ndebele provided administrative support. Other researchers who contributed to earlier stages of the project include Dick Minnitt, Fiona Bizos, Nicola Acutt, Hesphina Rukato and Hilton Trollip. We received important editorial assistance from Karin Pampallis. We owe all a profound debt of gratitude.

Earlier drafts of some of our work were presented at UNRISD conferences in Geneva (November 2000) and in Manila (February 2002), as well as a SWOP workshop in Johannesburg in May 2003 when we reported back to our informants and other practitioners and academics in the field. In July 2005 a presentation on our project was made to the First Southern African Symposium on Corporate Citizenship, hosted by the University of South Africa's Centre for Corporate Citizenship in conjunction with the African Centre on Corporate Citizenship. I also benefited immensely from participation in the International Research Network on Business, Society and Development, whose secretariat is housed at the Copenhagen Business School.

A final word of thanks goes to Glenn Cowley, Sally Hines and Christopher Merrett at the University of KwaZulu-Natal Press for making this book a reality.

David Fig

Contributors

Andries Bezuidenhout recently gained his doctorate in sociology at the University of the Witwatersrand, Johannesburg on the political economy of the white goods industry in Southern Africa. He is a research officer at the university's Sociology of Work Unit. His research interests include comparative industrial relations in Southern Africa, industrial policy, changing patterns of casual labour, and trade union responses to globalisation.

David Dickinson is senior lecturer in industrial relations and HIV/AIDS in the workplace at the Wits Business School, University of the Witwatersrand, Johannesburg. Since 2000 he has researched various aspects of the response by South African companies to HIV/AIDS. His current research focus is on workplace HIV/AIDS peer educators.

David Fig is an associate of the Sociology of Work Unit at the University of the Witwatersrand, Johannesburg. He is an independent researcher on environmental policy, covering the fields of energy, climate, bio-diversity, trade and corporate accountability. He participates in the International Research Network on Business, Society and Development based at the Copenhagen Business School. He recently authored *Uranium Road: Questioning South Africa's Nuclear Direction* (Jacana, 2005).

Ralph Hamann is a senior researcher at the Environmental Evaluation Unit based at the University of Cape Town. He has formerly held research positions at the University of South Africa's Centre for Corporate Citizenship and at the African Institute for Corporate Citizenship, Pretoria. His PhD on corporate social responsibility in the South African mining sector was conferred by the University of Essex in 2004.

Shirley Miller is an independent researcher specialising in occupational health. For many years she worked in the South African labour movement, negotiating better environmental, health and safety conditions for chemical workers, and representing the trade union movement in a number of multi-stakeholder bodies negotiating new environmental and related legislation.

Rahmat Omar is currently engaged in research on call centres in South Africa. She is acting director of the Centre for Adult and Continuing Education at the University of the Western Cape. She worked for many years in the South African labour movement, and represented it on a number of statutory bodies, including the National Commission on Higher Education and the South African Qualifications Authority.

Diana Sanchez is a researcher for the Democracy and Governance Programme at the Human Sciences Research Council (HSRC), Tshwane (Pretoria). Her main area of research has been socio-economic transformation in South Africa. Previously she worked for the Colombian government and in the international NGO sector in South Africa. She holds a BA in government and international relations and an MA in social sciences from Uppsala University in Sweden.

Roger Southall is honorary research professor in the Sociology of Work Unit at the University of the Witwatersrand, Johannesburg. He was formerly professor of political studies at Rhodes University, Grahamstown, and is editor of the *Journal of Contemporary African Studies*. He is author of *Solidarity or Imperialism: International Labour and South African Trade Unions* (University of Cape Town Press, 1995) and has published widely on African and labour studies.

Peter Utting is deputy director of the Geneva-based United Nations Research Institute for Social Development, where he currently co-ordinates the Programme on Markets, Business and Regulation. Since the late 1990s, he has specialised in research on corporate social responsibility in developing countries and regulation of transnational corporations.

Edward Webster is professor of sociology and co-director of the Sociology of Work Unit at the University of the Witwatersrand. His current research interests are on organisational responses to the changing work order in the Global South and forms of livelihood strategies among the working poor in South and Southern Africa. His most recent publication is a co-edited volume with Karl von Holdt, entitled *Beyond the Apartheid Workplace: Studies in Transition* (University of KwaZulu-Natal Press, 2005).

Abbreviations

AAC	Anglo American Corporation of South Africa Limited
ABI	Amalgamated Beverage Industries
ACT	Apartheid Claims Taskforce
AECI	African Explosives and Chemical Industries
AICC	African Institute of Corporate Citizenship
AIDS	Acquired Immune Deficiency Syndrome
ALDP	Accelerated Leadership Development Programme
ANC	African National Congress
ARV	Anti-retroviral
AU	African Union
BAT	British American Tobacco
BAT-SA	British American Tobacco – South Africa
BBC	British Broadcasting Corporation
BCSD-SA	Business Council for Sustainable Development – South Africa
BEE	Black economic empowerment
BEE Com	Black Economic Empowerment Commission
BSE	Bovine Spongiform Encephalitis
CAF	Charities' Aid Foundation
CAIA	Chemical and Allied Industries' Association
CBE	Communities for a Better Environment
CCMA	Commission for Conciliation, Mediation and Arbitration
CDE	Centre for Development and Enterprise
CDM	Clean Development Mechanism [of the Kyoto Protocol]
CEO	Chief Executive Officer [Managing Director]

CEPPWAWU	Chemicals, Energy, Paper, Printing, Wood and Allied Workers' Union
CHAMSA	Chamber of Commerce of South Africa
CIAA	Confederation of the Food and Drink Industries of the European Community
CONNEPP	Consultative National Environmental Policy Process
COSATU	Congress of South African Trade Unions
CSER	Corporate social and environmental responsibility
CSI	Corporate social investment
CSO	Civil society organisation
CSR	Corporate social responsibility
CUP	Cambridge University Press
DA	Democratic Alliance
DEAT	Department of Environmental Affairs and Tourism [South Africa]
DJSI	Dow Jones Sustainability Index
DoL	Department of Labour [South Africa]
DRD	Durban Roodepoort Deep [mining company]
DSD	Department of Social Development [South Africa]
DTI	Department of Trade and Industry [South Africa]
EIA	Environmental impact assessment
EMCA	Environmental Management Co-operative Agreement
EMPR	Environmental Management Programme Report
EPA	Environmental Protection Agency of the United States
ERPM	East Rand Proprietary Mines
ETI	Ethical Trade Initiative

EU	European Union
FAO	Food and Agricultural Organisation of the United Nations
FAWU	Food and Allied Workers' Union
FMC	Food Monitoring Committee
FSC	Forest Stewardship Council
FTSE	an indexing company owned by the *Financial Times* and the London Stock Exchange
GDP	Gross Domestic Product
GE	Genetic engineering, or genetically engineered
GEAR	Growth, Employment and Redistribution programme
GEF	Global Environmental Facility
GEM	Group for Environmental Monitoring
GM	Genetic modification, or genetically modified
GMOs	Genetically modified organisms
GNU	Government of National Unity
GRI	Global Reporting Initiative
HIV	Human Immunodeficiency Virus
HR	Human resources
ICAEW	Institute of Chartered Accountants of England and Wales
ICEM	International Federation of Chemical, Energy, Mine and General Workers' Unions
IDC	Industrial Development Corporation [South Africa]
IDP	Integrated Development Plan
IEF	Industrial Environment Forum
IFC	International Finance Corporation
ILO	International Labour Organisation
IMF	International Monetary Fund

ISO	International Standards Organisation
IUCN	International Union for the Conservation of Nature and Natural Resources [commonly known as the World Conservation Union]
JET	Joint Education Trust
JSE	JSE Securities Exchange [formerly the Johannesburg Stock Exchange]
LED	Local Economic Development
MERG	Macro-economic Research Group
MIC	Mineworkers' Investment Company
MMSD	Mining, Minerals and Sustainable Development (project)
MMSD-SA	Mining, Minerals and Sustainable Development – Southern Africa
MNC	Multinational corporation
MPS	Management practice standard
NACTU	National Council of Trade Unions
NAFCOC	National Federation of Chambers of Commerce
NALEDI	National Labour and Economic Development Institute
NBI	National Business Initiative
NDR	National Democratic Revolution
NEDLAC	National Economic Development and Labour Council
NEMA	National Environmental Management Act
NEPAD	New Partnership for Africa's Development
NGO	Non-governmental organisation
NNP	New National Party
NOSA	National Occupational Safety Association
NUM	National Union of Mineworkers

NUMSA	National Union of Metalworkers of South Africa
OAU	Organisation of African Unity
OECD	Organisation for Economic Co-operation and Development
OHSA	Occupational Health and Safety Act
OSHA	Occupational Safety and Health Administration [United States]
OUP	Oxford University Press
P&G	Procter and Gamble
PIP	Practice in Place
ppb	Parts per billion
PPC	Pretoria Portland Cement
QIP	Quantitative indicators of performance
RCR	Recordable case rate
RDP	Reconstruction and Development Programme
SAB	South African Breweries
SABC	South African Broadcasting Corporation
SABCOA	South African Business Coalition on HIV/AIDS
SACOB	South African Chambers of Business
SACTWU	South African Clothing and Textile Workers' Union
SADC	Southern African Development Community
SADTU	South African Democratic Teachers' Union
SAFCOC	South African Federation of Chambers of Commerce
SAGA	Southern African Grantmakers' Association
SAIRR	South African Institute of Race Relations
SALB	South African Labour Bulletin
SANF	Southern African Nature Foundation

SANSOR	South African National Seed Organisation
SARHWU	South African Railway and Harbour Workers' Union
SASOL	Suid-Afrikaanse Steenkool- en Oliemaatskappy (South African Coal and Oil Company)
SAWIS	South African Wine Industry Statistics
SEIFSA	Steel and Engineering Industries' Federation of South Africa
SETA	Sector Education and Training Authority
SHARP	SASOL's HIV and AIDS Response Programme
SHE	Safety, health and environment
SH&E	Safety, Health and Environment Centre [SASOL]
SMME	Small, medium and micro enterprises
SRI	Socially responsible investment
SRII	Social Responsibility Investment Index
Stats SA	Statistics South Africa
STD	Sexually transmitted disease
SWOP	Sociology of Work Unit
TAC	Treatment Action Campaign
TNC	Transnational corporation
TRC	Truth and Reconciliation Commission
UNDP	United Nations Development Programme
UNISA	University of South Africa
UNRISD	United Nations Research Institute for Social Development
UPOV	International Union for the Protection of New Varieties of Plants
VAPS	Vaal Triangle Air Pollution Health Study

WBCSD	World Business Council for Sustainable Development
WCED	World Commission on Environment and Development
WSSD	World Summit on Sustainable Development
WTO	World Trade Organisation
WWF	Worldwide Fund for Nature

1

The context of corporate social and environmental responsibility

David Fig

Corporate social and environmental responsibility (CSER) has multiple meanings, settings and practices. As globalisation of capital gathers pace, so does the necessity for the documentation, debate and interpretation of the phenomenon. Current practices are too often presented at face value, with any progress measured incrementally. However, there is a need to raise more fundamental questions about their history and purpose.

This is particularly so in South Africa, where the powerful links between capital and state have tended to erase memories of past transgressions by business and diluted any proposals for redressing them. Post-apartheid South Africa has initiated the process of deracialising the ownership of capital, but the direct beneficiaries of this exclude most stakeholders. Inequality persists, reflected in the statistics of mass poverty and unemployment, and very few steps have been taken to redress ongoing environmental injustice.

Nevertheless, the pressures on business to behave responsibly have grown over recent years. Some of the impetus for this has come from external or globalised processes. In addition, a plethora of codes and charters, shareholder and consumer activism, media coverage and civil society campaigns are among the mechanisms which have persuaded business to take steps in this regard. Part of our task has been to understand how significant these steps have been in South Africa.

National-level studies are difficult to accomplish. Yet, for a number of reasons, this level of analysis remains important. South Africa is the locus of one of the world's most important mineral-energy complexes. The history of its extractive, manufacturing and service industries is intertwined with processes of racial and gender-based subjugation as well as class-based oppression. Capital under apartheid was ring-fenced and relatively immobile. More recently it has utilised the more liberal climate of globalisation to relocate to other jurisdictions or to spread its investments, particularly to the rest of Africa. South Africa's democratic constitution, while enshrining private property, has also opened opportunities for citizens to assert a range of basic rights.

Staking their Claims provides an analytical overview of CSER in South Africa, and goes into more depth by means of case studies of particular industrial sectors and cross-cutting studies on key issues. The overview, chapter 2, uses a political economy approach, that grounds CSER practices within recent South African history and explains their emergence in the 1970s and later. Andries Bezuidenhout, David Fig, Ralph Hamann and Rahmat Omar catalogue the array of voluntary initiatives that have been applied, analyse the factors that have influenced them, and discuss the meanings of CSER by dissecting some of the surrounding rhetoric. They end with an evaluation of the significance of CSER. The sectoral studies in chapters 3 to 5 focus on key elements of the economy: mining (Ralph Hamann and Andries Bezuidenhout), chemicals (Shirley Miller) and food production (David Fig). Each of these sectors contains a mix of local and international corporations. The case studies detail role players, activities and CSER initiatives, highlighting some of the key examples of partnership and conflict. We have also included cross-cutting studies, chapters 6 and 7, on the important issues of black economic empowerment (Roger Southall and Diana Sanchez) and of HIV/AIDS (David Dickinson).

Moving away from apartheid

A key challenge for South African business has been the ending since 1994 of formal segregation and racialised job discrimination. During the apartheid era a number of firms took heart from initiatives like the Sullivan Code to desegregate the workplace, and admitted black workers into semi-skilled positions. Some also took initiatives on urban reform at a time when the apartheid state was reluctant to acknowledge the permanence of urban black communities. However, the overwhelming structures of apartheid endured, including the migrant labour system, the racial division of labour, discriminatory salaries, poor social services, residential segregation and the perpetuation of ethnic homelands. Violations of human rights, including political and trade union rights, were commonplace. While the economy boomed, the benefits went mainly to the owners of capital and to the white middle and working classes. Businesses in turn contributed to the apartheid system through assisting in sanctions-busting operations, paying of taxes, receipt of state subsidies, and provision of services and technologies to the police and military apparatuses.

The economy centred on local manufacturing, and the export of minerals and agricultural produce, while growing international sanctions led to the subsidisation of local arms, energy, and other strategic industries. From the mid-1980s pressures for disinvestment by international firms grew and the era of growth drew to a close. The contradictions caused business to open a dialogue with the exiled African National Congress (ANC).

The ANC had as its guiding document the 1955 Freedom Charter, which argued for the nationalisation of the commanding heights of the economy, particularly referring to the financial and mining sectors. However, by the time of its unbanning in 1990, it no longer insisted on this economic approach, evolving instead a Reconstruction and Development Programme (RDP) that foresaw the economy being restimulated by expanded social expenditure. Even this vision seemed too radical for business to swallow. It realised that some transformation and accommodation of new priorities would be needed, but was nervous about the extent to which this might be necessary. At the same time, the ANC was moving towards much more orthodox economic positions. Within two years of taking office, the populist RDP was sidelined in favour of the Growth, Employment and Redistribution (GEAR) programme, which embodied the push for trade liberalisation, privatisation and deregulation. Unlike the RDP, the GEAR policy was never opened to democratic debate. In addition, the cautious approach to land reform meant a minimalist response to land claims.

These policies sent the private sector a strong signal that national-isation, wholesale redistributive measures and land appropriation were not seen by the ANC as necessary to the transition. The state backed business in combating claims for reparations initiated by certain sections of civil society on behalf of the victims of apartheid policies.

As a result, a number of cases of litigation in international jurisdictions collapsed without the support of the South African government. In addition, although the Truth and Reconciliation Commission (TRC) held economic hearings, no action was taken against businesses deemed to have profited from apartheid. In effect, business was absolved from any past wrongdoing in the pervasive context of reconciliation.

However, some challenges were imposed by the state upon business. Legislation was passed to extend employment equity, which favoured the designated groups of black people, women and the disabled, in an attempt to redress past discriminatory employment practices. Another set of measures taken were those loosely labelled black economic empowerment. These attempted to shift corporate ownership by insisting on the progressive acquisition of capital by individual black entrepreneurs or broader groups of beneficiaries. To advance this, the state introduced a system of sectoral charters and scorecards. Further legislation provided greater protection to workers, guaranteeing minimum wages to historically underpaid groups (such as farm and domestic workers) and outlawing unfair labour practices. Business has frequently complained about such measures, arguing that they contribute towards skills shortages, and hamper the flexibility of labour. Simultaneously, stronger environmental legislation has been met with misgivings about the reduction of local industry's competitiveness.

Despite these constraints, the business sector has witnessed the liberalisation and deregulation of vast parts of the economy, the significant loosening of exchange controls, and a degree of privatisation of the state sector (steel and oil-from-coal, for instance). Some industries have outsourced significant parts of their labour forces, or rely more on casual labour, piecework and home work to meet production targets. This has had a deleterious effect on the core workforce, including a large reduction in the number of trade union members and the ability of unions to service their membership. In general, therefore, business regards post-apartheid South Africa as a more favourable operating environment.

What is extremely problematic, however, is the failure of both business and the state to address the extent of extreme poverty in society. The situation is deteriorating with South Africa overtaking Brazil for the dubious distinction of having the highest Gini coefficient, the measure of the greatest extremes of wealth and poverty, in the world. While growth has occurred incrementally since 1994, it has been relatively jobless. South Africa has a very limited safety net for the unemployed. As a result, criminality and gangsterism have flourished.

The transition has also seen extensive evidence of corruption and malpractice amongst politicians (arms deals, travel scandals and revolving doors) and in the private sector (the cases of Brett Kebble and Fidentia). On the environmental front, while laws have been strengthened, there is still considerable evidence of corporate environmental abuse, a history of weak implementation of the regulations, and poor understanding of the goals of ecological sustainability in industrial planning.

What business has done

Our findings show that the lead businesses in the field of CSER are those which are perhaps the most globalised. They have extensive investments abroad, they have placed their major listings abroad, or they have signed on to international codes of conduct. Many of these lead businesses now produce sustainability or social reports, may consult different stakeholders from time to time, or have implemented quality controls in relation to health, safety and environmental management. In broader terms, business has strengthened its contribution to corporate governance through the series of King reports, commissioned by the Institute of Directors. Many of the firms that we researched have employed teams of people responsible for implementation of higher standards in these spheres, or the management of relationships with their stakeholders.

Our study shows considerable adherence to codes of conduct, where these apply. Many firms have voluntarily signed on to the ISO 14000 series, and to sectoral self-regulated codes like Responsible Care in the chemical industry, the Forest Stewardship Council certification in relation to timber plantations, or the Kimberley process to restrict the trade in conflict diamonds. Only a few firms are signatories to the UN Global Compact, whose principles are broader.

South African firms make considerable donations to social causes. This may be seen as offsetting the limitations of the state in areas like crime management, education, HIV/AIDS, conservation, and the arts. Sometimes, the philanthropy is linked to the company workforce, or targeted at consumers as a strategy to enhance sales. Some firms have adopted a foundation approach, whereby certain research or charitable institutions become direct beneficiaries. There is also considerable expenditure on sports sponsorship.

The gaps and contradictions

While there is certainly more conformity to emerging practices within the field of CSER – such as reporting, the implementation of voluntary standards, or targeted philanthropy – these practices often fall short of public expectations. This could be because while firms may be committed to better management of their social and environmental practices, their core business may actually be doing disproportionate social or environmental damage. For example, the electricity utility Eskom, which pioneered the Industrial Environmental Forum and is a keen member of the UN Global Compact, is simultaneously the country's largest polluter (CO_2 and nuclear waste). SAPPI and Mondi, which compete locally and globally in the paper and pulp sector, are well known for their sponsorship of environmental projects, but nevertheless operate very dirty paper and pulp mills. Despite certification of 900 000 hectares of their timber plantations (Forestry Stewardship Council 2007: 45), these companies continue to pay poverty wages and impact negatively on biodiversity, and water and air quality (Karumbidza 2005). British American Tobacco of South Africa may have won national awards for best CSER reporting, yet the company admits its product is harmful to consumers.

Increasingly, firms have realised their need to perform a role in the mitigation of the effects of the HIV/AIDS pandemic, but Dickinson shows in his study in this collection that the response has been 'slow, partial and erratic'. His review of a recent survey shows that almost half the companies with over 500 employees have yet to conduct actuarial risk assessments, while less than a quarter provide anonymous HIV testing, which gives more reliable feedback. Another survey indicated that three quarters of the canvassed companies had no idea of the prevalence of HIV/AIDS in their firms and almost two thirds had no strategy to manage the disease in their workplaces. This weak response to the pandemic is surprising in view of the high costs to employers of absenteeism, illness, high turnover of personnel, loss of skilled workers and the draining of benefit funds. The voluntary efforts of staff, which he terms corporate social responsibility (CSR) from below, often exceed the formal commitments of many firms.

As Southall and Sanchez show, companies that have gone some way towards implementing black economic empowerment (BEE) measures, have tended to be weak on CSER. The black business community also harbours contradictory views: one sees emergent entrepreneurs having a responsibility for capital accumulation and expanding black ownership of the economy; while another argues for reciprocity between them and the communities from which they have sprung. While their hold over capital is still fragile, and involves significant debt, black business may be resisting pressures to support broader community development. Some interpret CSER as part of the historical penance that white entrepreneurs have to undertake, absolving themselves from making a strong contribution. Hamann and Bezuidenhout confirm that opportunities for outsourcing within the mining industry have resulted in some emerging mining companies resorting to a reduction of labour standards. This point could be extended more broadly to other forms of labour flexibilisation[1]. The extent of casualisation in South Africa, resulting in wage reduction and insecurity, detracts from the advantages that CSER practices may be offering.

Other forms of economic liberalisation have also had a deleterious effect. For example, the clothing and textile sector has been opened to competition from Chinese producers. This has resulted in the erosion of many thousands of local jobs, and despite the implementation of temporary trade restraints, it is unlikely that these jobs will be reinstated. In the food sector, the liberalisation of agriculture has been a factor in the driving up of food prices. Other factors include perennial drought and the results of devoting scarce arable land to the production of crops for biofuels. Higher food prices are a key contributory factor to poverty, hunger and malnutrition. However, as Fig points out, higher food prices do not constitute a target for CSER interventions on the part of food producers. The impact of price inflation and resulting food insecurity may very well offset all the good intentions by CSER practitioners in the food sector.

At the level of environmental, health and safety regulation, South Africa is still relatively weak, or, in some cases, unwilling to act decisively against key firms. As a result, some sectors have felt the need for self-regulatory approaches. One such example, as Miller illustrates, is the chemical industry. The ferment raised by the Bhopal incident caused major chemical companies to initiate a system of raising environmental quality, which it calls Responsible Care. In addition, South Africa's framework environmental legislation, the National Environmental Management Act (107 of 1998), allows for co-operative agreements between stakeholders on environmental management. Miller has demonstrated that neither the Responsible Care approach nor the co-operative agreements have satisfied other stakeholders that they are an effective alternative to full state regulation. In the context of South Africa, as in many other developing countries where compliance with existing standards is still inadequate, voluntary initiatives are not really a satisfactory substitute for state-regulatory approaches.

Responsibility

South African firms have much preferred the term corporate social investment (CSI) to that of CSER. This reflects the business ethos – social and environmental interventions by firms are seen as investments with the likelihood of some kind of return in the form of reputation, enhanced markets or brand recognition. Erasing the notion of responsibility, however, assumes that there is no history of and hence no accountability for past abuse. Ignoring the past is no solution to the creation of trust and stakeholder confidence. The impacts of migrant labour, forced removals, land confiscation, job reservation and other workplace discrimination are considerable, flow across generations, and have yet to be redressed. By shifting the meaning of CSER, and dwelling on the more neutral concept of CSI, firms are negating any responsibility for such impacts. Under the concept of CSI, business and socio-economic development are seen as distinct, with development being quite external to business. Development is therefore seen as an add-on option rather than as an integral part of taking responsibility for restitution. Having missed opportunities like those offered by the Truth and Reconciliation Commission to explore such responsibility (Truth and Reconciliation Commission 2003: 727), firms operating in South Africa have not yet entered the confessional mode, let alone that of willingness to consider reparations.

Blowfield and Frynas, in their efforts to suggest a broad definition for CSER, place the notion of responsibility squarely at the feet of firms. For them CSER is:

> an umbrella term for a variety of theories and practices all of which recognize the following: (a) that companies have a *responsibility* for their impact on society and the natural environment, sometimes beyond legal compliance and the liability of individuals; (b) that companies have a *responsibility*

for the behaviour of others with whom they do business (e.g. within supply chains); and that (c) business needs to manage its relationship with wider society, whether for reasons of commercial viability, or to add value to society (Blowfield and Frynas 2006: 503, our emphasis).

In the case of South Africa, our understanding of the term responsibility should embrace historic and current responsibilities. The question of business accountability for the past has tended to be erased because of a strong and complex network of alliances between business and state established in the post-apartheid era. This has taken different forms, including private-public partnerships, ex-politicians moving into the business sector, multiple and overlapping directorships, sponsorships, and so on.

However, without a rendering of accounts, South Africa is ever more likely to be subject to the 'morbid symptoms' which Gramsci felt characterised political transition (Gramsci 1998: 276).

The research agenda

Our research was part of a broader initiative which hoped to understand CSER in semi-industrialised developing countries. We drew on many informants within the business sector, but nevertheless maintained a critical, independent approach to our subject matter. There has been much academic discussion of the need to strengthen a critical, independent CSER research agenda in developing countries (Utting 2003, Fox 2004, Blowfield and Frynas 2005, Prieto-Carrón et al. 2006).

For example, Prieto-Carrón and other colleagues in the International Research Network on Business, Development and Society identified four areas as part of an alternative critical research agenda on CSER and development in the global South:

- the relationship between business and poverty reduction;
- the impact of CSR initiatives;
- power and participation in CSR; and
- governance dimensions of CSR (Prieto-Carrón et al. 2006: 979).

These points implicitly contain the need to understand the relationship between macroeconomic policy and poverty as a context in which to examine the extent and impact of CSER.

Such an agenda has also been discussed for South Africa (Fig 2000, Sharp 2006, Hamann 2006). We think that this work has embodied some of these proposals, as well as covering some of the key concerns raised by Prieto-Carrón et al. In the case of South Africa, we have attempted to show that the effectiveness of CSER initiatives can only be understood and measured against broader national socio-economic policies. There are increasing trends towards deepening social inequality and income concentration, inadequate social services, economic liberalisation, food price inflation and labour flexibilisation. Against these trends, it would be difficult to see CSER practices making much progress in combating poverty.

Our choice of industrial sectors was taken in part to embody the progress made in CSER in South Africa, as well as to create some synergy with comparative national studies of Mexico and the Philippines. There is clearly room to research other South African sectors in depth, and to build on the work of Jeppesen and Granerud (2002), Luetkenhorst (2004) and Fox (2005) in their analyses of the CSER performance of smaller firms.

The work before you represents a collective effort of some importance, being a concerted attempt at a critical and systematic analysis of CSER in contemporary South Africa. Its purpose is to contribute to a broader understanding of interactions between business, state and society in a context of dynamic change in an emergent economy. We hope that it will provide new and richer insights, raise important debates and inspire further scholarship in the field.

Note

1. Flexibilisation of labour refers to the increasing trend in employment towards outsourcing, casualisation, piecework and home-based work that cuts the firm's formal labour establishment and expenses.

References

Blowfield, M. and J.G. Frynas. 2005. 'Setting New Agendas: Critical Perspectives on Corporate Social Responsibility in the Developing World'. *International Affairs* 81 (3): 499–513.

Fig, D. 2000. 'Towards a Research Agenda on Corporate Environmental Responsibility in South Africa: Moving Beyond Apartheid, Embracing Compliance and Building

Sustainable Systems'. Paper presented to the United Nations Research Institute on Social Development, Geneva, 23–25 October.

Forestry Stewardship Council (FSC). 2007. *FSC Certified Forests*. Bonn: FSC.

Fox, T. 2004. 'Corporate Social Responsibility and Development: In Quest of an Agenda'. *Development* 47 (3): 29–36.

———. 2005. *Small and Medium-Sized Enterprises (SMEs) and Corporate Social Responsibility: A Discussion Paper*. London: International Institute for Environment and Development.

Gramsci, A. 1998. *Selections from the Prison Notebooks of Antonio Gramsci*, edited by Q. Hoare and G. Nowell Smith. London: Lawrence and Wishart.

Hamann, R. 2006. 'Can Business Make Decisive Contributions to Development? Towards a Research Agenda on Corporate Citizenship and Beyond'. *Development Southern Africa* 23 (2): 175–95.

Jeppesen, S. and Lise G. 2002. 'Does Corporate Social Responsibility Matter to Small Medium and Micro-Enterprises?' Copenhagen: Department of Intercultural Communication and Management, Copenhagen Business School.

Karumbidza, J.B. 2005. *A Study of the Social and Economic Impacts of Industrial Tree Plantations in the KwaZulu-Natal Province of South Africa*. Montevideo: World Rainforest Movement.

Luetkenhorst, W. 2004. 'Corporate Social Responsibility and the Development Agenda: The Case for Actively Involving Small and Medium Enterprises'. *Intereconomics: the Journal of European Economic Policy* 39 (3): 157–66.

Prieto-Carrón, M, et al. 2006. 'Critical Perspectives on CSR: What We Know, What We Don't Know and What We Need to Know'. *International Affairs* 82 (5): 977–87.

Sharp, J. 2006. 'Corporate Social Responsibility: An Anthropological Perspective'. *Development Southern Africa* 23 (2): 213–22.

Truth and Reconciliation Commission (TRC). 2003. *Truth and Reconciliation Commission Report*. Vol. 6: 727.

Utting, P. 2003. 'Corporate Social Responsibility and Development: Is a New Agenda Needed?' In *Corporate Social Responsibility and Development: Towards a New Agenda: Summaries of the Presentations Made at UNRISD Conference, 17–18 November*. Geneva: UNRISD.

2

Political economy

Andries Bezuidenhout
David Fig
Ralph Hamann
Rahmat Omar

Introduction

Increasingly, the global economy is dominated by a few corporations. Indeed, the turnover of the top five multinational corporations is more than double the gross domestic products of the 100 poorest countries (United Nations Development Programme 1999: 32). Social movements which oppose neo-liberal economic policies, and which have become known as anti-globalisation movements, are challenging the role played by multinational corporations and the institutions of global governance. Some call for major reforms of international institutions such as the World Trade Organisation (WTO), the World Bank and the International Monetary Fund (IMF) in order to regulate the global economy and the activities of multinational corporations. Others call for the outright abolition of these institutions.

In this context, some business leaders argue that it is possible for corporations to do business responsibly, in a way that contributes to sustainable development. Some observers respond to these claims with scepticism, while others argue that corporate social and environmental responsibility (CSER) can contribute to a more humane society. It is very difficult to evaluate such vast claims without grounding one's analysis in actual experience. The local is relevant when one attempts to understand the global. The aim of this overview is to contribute to these debates by analysing the political economy of CSER in the South

African context. We look at these initiatives historically, as well as at more recent developments.

The overview attempts to contextualise CSER programmes by grounding discourse in a particular social context. The analysis is based on interviews with key role players in the field, as well as a review of existing data, literature and other documents relevant to the subject. Throughout the chapter, we refer to relevant case studies to illustrate some of the dynamics.

We begin our analysis by providing a cursory overview of the history of CSER programmes. We then attempt to understand the particular meanings attached to these concepts in the South African context. The nature and content given to these programmes were fundamentally shaped by the apartheid state. However, since the transition to democracy in the 1990s and South Africa's reintegration into a global economy, new dynamics have come to the fore – the local interacts with the global in a particular way.

In order to understand the form and content of CSER programmes better, we analyse a number of programmes, examining codes of conduct, certification initiatives, the use of cleaner technology, social and environmental reporting, fair trade schemes, multi-stakeholder partnerships, corporate social investment (CSI), philanthropy, black economic empowerment (BEE) and socially responsible investment (SRI). We identify the main sectors of the economy where these programmes are located, as well as some of the lead companies. An attempt is then made to understand why corporations get involved in social and environmental programmes, by assessing some of the drivers of these programmes.

We conclude with an analysis of the significance of CSER programmes given certain other social trends in the South African context.

History and context
Implications of the political economy of apartheid
South Africa dominates the economy not only of Southern Africa, but also of sub-Saharan Africa. It accounts for approximately 44 per cent of the total gross domestic product (GDP) and 52 per cent of the industrial output of sub-Saharan Africa (Saul and Leys 1999: 23). While South Africa's economic growth rate has been relatively modest in comparison with other countries in the Southern African region, the country still accounts for 74 per cent of the GDP and 85 per cent of

the manufacturing capacity of the Southern African Development Community (SADC) (Harvey 2000: 4, 7).

Historically, the industrial structure of Southern Africa was shaped by several forces, including processes of colonisation, various wars for liberation from colonial rule and the dominance of the subcontinent's mining industry. In more recent times, the relationship between South Africa and its neighbours was soured by the apartheid regime's attempts to destabilise and weaken states whose governments supported the African National Congress (ANC) in exile.

The industrial policies of the apartheid state contained three key elements. First, there was some degree of import-substitution industrialisation arising from the implementation of import tariffs to protect local industries from competition. However, the significance of these tariffs, and the extent to which they really protected local industries, are subject to debate (Macroeconomic Research Group 1993; Bell 1995; Fine and Rustomjee 1996). Second, the state played a significant role in setting up state-owned corporations to drive a programme of industrialisation. State monopolies were created to manage the transport infrastructure, iron and steel manufacturing, electricity provision and telecommunications. During the era of sanctions against apartheid, the state attempted to use these corporations to supply key resources: for instance, oil extracted from coal through SASOL; and arms for its war in Angola and other destabilisation operations in Southern Africa through the state-owned arms manufacturing enterprise, Armscor (Fine and Rustomjee 1996). Third, a dual labour market was created. White South Africans were incorporated into a limited welfare state and were accorded labour rights, while black South Africans were formally excluded through a repressive labour regime (Joffe, Maller and Webster 1995).

Apartheid's pattern of industrialisation and land use also had significant implications for the environment, and these impacts were primarily felt by the poor (Cock and Koch 1991; Ngobese and Cock 1997; Hamann, Booth and O'Riordan 2000). Millions of black people were penned inside ethnic homelands whose already marginal agricultural value was further eroded due to high population density.

The mining industry, based on migrant labour, became responsible for generating huge amounts of solid waste, with minimal rehabilitation and little obligation to workers or neighbouring communities for the health and pollution impacts. Power generation, based entirely on fossil fuels like coal and uranium, created significant pollution and contributed to some of the highest levels of respiratory diseases in Africa. As will be seen below, under apartheid corporate responsibility in relation to the environment was mostly confined to support for nature conservation initiatives.

In the context of apartheid, the role of the corporate sector in South Africa was always considered controversial. Indeed, the nature of the relationship between business and the apartheid state was central to one of the major South African debates, which became known as the race/class debate. Questions revolved around the extent to which industry benefited from the apartheid regime and even the extent to which it played an active role in the establishment and reproduction of the system.

From the 1970s onwards, so-called revisionists argued that major corporations had been central to the creation of the apartheid system. Mining corporations, long dominant in the economy, were specifically singled out for criticism, since they were responsible for introducing the migrant labour system long before the formal introduction of apartheid as a state ideology. In the apartheid years, cheap labour was supplied to mines by the bantustan-subsidised migrant labour system (Wolpe 1972). While these perspectives gained increased prominence, anti-apartheid social movements were challenging some of the basic foundations of the system. A spontaneous strike wave in 1973 and the Soweto uprisings in 1976 were examples of this.

In opposition to the revisionist approach, the liberal school of thought maintained that apartheid was an anomalous system that resulted from Afrikaner nationalism as an ideology. Apartheid regulations were seen as dysfunctional to the development of an industrial capitalist economy (O'Dowd 1966; Lipton 1986).

The emergence of corporate social responsibility

It was in the early 1970s that the notion of corporate social responsibility (CSR) was raised formally for the first time. Meyer Feldberg (1972), in his inaugural lecture as Professor of Business Administration at the University of Cape Town, argued that business was not responsible for the creation of the apartheid system, but, following an argument of enlightened self-interest, it was important for business in South Africa to take CSR seriously (see also Mann 1992; Alperson 1995).

However, it was only when the campaign for sanctions against apartheid gathered momentum that corporations responded by setting up voluntary initiatives. A prominent effort was the introduction of a statement of principles for US multinationals with affiliates in South Africa. This code of conduct became known as the Sullivan Principles (see Box 2.1). Signatories committed themselves to non-segregated facilities, the training and development of black staff, equal and fair employment practices, increasing the number of black staff in supervisory and managerial positions; and to contributing to the improvement of housing, transport, education, health and recreational amenities of staff members outside the immediate workplace (Mann 1992: 251; Mangaliso 1999).

Box 2.1
The Sullivan Principles

1. Non-segregation of the races in all eating, comfort and work facilities.
2. Equal and fair employment practices for all employees.
3. Equal pay for all employees doing equal or comparable work for the same period of time.
4. Initiation and development of training programs that will prepare, in substantial numbers, Blacks and other non-whites for supervisory, administrative, clerical and technical jobs.
5. Increasing the number of Blacks and other non-whites in management and supervisory positions.
6. Improving the quality of employees' lives outside the work environment in such areas as housing, transportation, schooling, recreation and health facilities.

We agree to further implement these principles. Where implementation requires a modification of existing South African working conditions, we will seek such modification through appropriate channels.

We believe that the implementation of the foregoing principles is consistent with respect for human dignity and will contribute greatly to the general economic welfare of all the people of the Republic of South Africa.

Source: Schmidt 1980: 16.

Only a minority of multinational corporations reluctantly embraced the Sullivan Principles, essentially to head off disinvestment pressure from abroad (Table 2.1) (Orkin 1989: 27). Yet the independent labour movement used the principles as a form of pressure on multinational employers to recognise and negotiate with the emerging black trade unions (Joffe 1989: 57). Alperson (1995: 5) argues that the Sullivan Principles can be seen as a turning point in the vocabulary of CSR in South Africa. Officially, adherence to them was voluntary, but anti-apartheid lobby groups kept a close watch on the degree to which companies complied.

Table 2.1: Companies engaged with the Sullivan Principles.

Category	Category Name	Firms typical of this category*
I	Making good progress	Avis, Caltex, Chase Manhattan, Citibank, Colgate-Palmolive, Control Data, Eli Lilley, Exxon, Ford, Hewlett-Packard, IBM, John Deere, Kodak, Merck, Mobil, 3M, NCR, Schering, Sperry, Union Carbide
II	Making acceptable progress	Abbott, American Express, Borden, Burroughs, Caterpillar, Del Monte, Firestone, GE, GM, Gillette, Goodyear, Honeywell, Hoover, Johnson & Johnson, Kellogg, Monsanto, Otis, Readers Digest, Singer, Smith-Kline, Sterling, Westinghouse, Xerox
III	Need to be active	Carnation, International Harvester, Tampax
IV	Inadequate reporting	Pan American Airways, Engelhard
V	Submitting first report	Bristol-Myers, Nashua
VI	Few or no employees	Bethlehem, DuPont, Nabisco, Oshkosh
VII	New signatories	Dow, Fluor, Gerber, Hyster
VIII	No report	ITT, Phelps Dodge, Revlon, Scholl
IX	Non-US-based	East Asiatic
X	Non-signatories	Allis Chalmers, Arthur Andersen, AP, BBDO, Bechtel, Boeing, CBS, Chesebrough-Ponds, Chrysler, Coca-Cola, General Tire, Kimberly-Clark, Newmont Mining, US Steel, Valvoline

* As at October 1979. For full list see Schmidt 1980: 96–106.

Hence, the pressure in the 1970s on companies to disinvest led to a voluntary code of conduct as a response. In 1976, following large-scale protest action in Soweto, corporations set up the Urban Foundation as a private-sector initiative to address critical urban development issues in volatile townships nationwide (Alperson 1995: 5). The initiative was led by Harry Oppenheimer of Anglo American Corporation and Anton Rupert of Rembrandt. From the 1970s to the mid-1980s more companies followed suit by setting up charitable trusts, partly to accommodate expanded community investment, but also for tax purposes. Tertiary education institutions were the main beneficiaries of these funds. Attempts were made to establish more formal networks between companies involved in social responsibility in the 1980s, but these did not succeed (Alperson 1995: 5–6).

While using the Sullivan Principles to put pressure on companies to recognise trade unions in the 1970s, the labour movement in apartheid South Africa was generally negative, and sometimes even hostile, toward CSI programmes (Alperson 1995: 17). In the 1980s, the two major trade union federations, the Congress of South African Trade Unions (COSATU) and the National Council of Trade Unions (NACTU), rejected the Sullivan Principles and dismissed the code as irrelevant (Joffe 1989: 57). Indeed, a survey of trade-union officials conducted in 1988 found that trade unionists were generally sceptical about CSER programmes. Such programmes were seen as 'something companies are forced to do because of anti-capitalist resistance and the disinvestment campaign', as 'propaganda for private enterprise' and as 'a smokescreen' for unsolved, deeper-lying problems (Webster 1988: 3). However, some unionists interviewed gave an indication that they would be willing to get involved in such programmes if they were negotiated, and if 'the promotion of private enterprise was underplayed' (Webster 1988: 6).

The transition

During the 1980s, the industrial policy of the apartheid government started to shift towards a position supportive of tariff reform and privatisation. The militant labour movement also successfully challenged the government's labour-repressive policies. However, decisive steps toward privatisation could not be taken because of the illegitimate nature of the government (Macroeconomic Research Group 1993: 214–5).

During the mid-1980s, resistance to apartheid grew substantially and the mass democratic movement that arose could not be appeased by any late attempts at reforming the system. The intransigent state at first attempted heavy repression, but this resulted in further international isolation, deeper sanctions and significant capital flight. To ward off further crisis, the regime began to take the lead from civil society and engaged in dialogue with the ANC in exile, as well as with the still-imprisoned Nelson Mandela. Following a stroke which afflicted President P.W. Botha in 1989, the ruling party appointed the more reformist F.W. de Klerk, who rapidly legalised the exiled opposition movements and entered into a negotiated settlement for a new constitutional democracy.

A process of transition followed. In this context, various social actors started to debate South Africa's future developmental path and the role played by the state to address the legacy of apartheid. Major corporations became involved in shaping the contours of the future state. One technique was to sponsor a series of exercises in scenario-building, involving the business sector as well as leaders of the internal and formerly exiled opposition in providing alternative development models. Inside the broad progressive movement there were competing perspectives on the mapping of South Africa's developmental path. One approach, influenced by the view that South Africa's economy was dominated by a minerals-energy complex that prevented a viable downstream manufacturing sector from developing, proposed a strong role for the state (Fine and Rustomjee 1996). A group of economists, the Macroeconomic Research Group (MERG), modelled a neo-Keynesian approach which proposed the building of infrastructure through public work programmes, massive investment in skills development and the introduction of a national minimum wage to boost domestic aggregate demand (Macroeconomic Research Group 1993). Resulting from this, as well as from initiatives taken by the ANC-aligned trade unions, the Reconstruction and Development Programme (RDP) was put forward by the ANC and its allies as a blueprint for post-apartheid develop-ment. The introduction of this programme implied a central role for the state in the reconstruction of society as well as restructuring the economy to strengthen the manufacturing sector by moving away from exporting raw materials.

In opposition to this, a group of developmental economists saw the stagnation of the economy resulting from the limits to the inward industrialisation path South Africa had taken. High import tariffs were seen as a reason for poor manufacturing performance. Their approach focused more on industrial policy instruments and supply-side measures, coupled with a process of trade liberalisation to integrate South Africa into the global economy (Joffe et al. 1995).

The corporate sector generally opposed state interventionist approaches, arguing for greater reliance on market forces. There was widespread uncertainty as to what direction the new government would take, and to what extent it would have to accommodate the liberation movement's potential economic radicalism. It is in this context that business adopted a number of strategies. One was aimed at co-opting elements of the potential new leadership; while another was an attempt to ameliorate any severe critique of the record of business under apartheid by embarking on a programme of expanded CSER and investment programmes (Reddy and Moodley 1991: 34). The pledging of R100 million by the Liberty Life Foundation towards educare initiatives and the setting up of the Joint Education Trust (JET) (see Box 2.2) by a number of companies, trade unions, political parties and other interest groups in 1992 marked the growing prominence of the trend (Alperson 1995: 6).

Box 2.2
The Joint Education Trust

The Joint Education Trust (JET) was established in 1992 as a multi-stakeholder partnership to administer a R500 million contribution to education development by a consortium of twenty leading South African companies. Community organisations, including the leading political parties, trade unions and education organisations, were also represented. JET supported over 400 NGOs working in the four focus areas of teacher development, early childhood development, adult basic education and youth development. It adopted a sectoral approach to grant making, characterised by the establishment of quality assurance mechanisms for grantees within each sector and periodic sector-wide evaluations. In addition to these grant-making activities, JET began to diversify its services following the election of South Africa's first democratic government in 1994. Thus, it offered project management services to donors, generally in partnership with the national and provincial departments of education.

The Trust originally managed some R400 million from a variety of local and offshore donors. Research and evaluation are integral to JET's work. JET has an annual operating budget of about R6.5 million and employs 21 full-time staff members and approximately 40 contract workers.

JET does not view itself as an organisation involved in corporate social responsibility (CSR), but rather as a development agency trying to provide assistance and support for social development. However, the corporate partners do see JET as part of their ongoing CSR work. Nevertheless, the initiative to establish JET in 1992 differed from traditional CSR activities. Motivated primarily by political considerations – as an attempt to overcome the polarisation between business and a range of political actors – it was established to create a forum for making contact through structured working relationships with organisations who would play a major role in constituting the first post-apartheid government in South Africa.

JET is unique in that it arose out of a major initiative supported by the main national actors in South Africa. This meant that JET was a major actor with high status, legitimacy and authority and could therefore make a serious impact. It could develop systems in certain areas and make a substantial difference, most notably in quality assurance in adult basic education and training.

Macroeconomic shifts: From RDP to GEAR

Following the elections in 1994, the new government embarked on a programme of legislative reform. Existing negotiating structures, bringing together government and representatives from organised business and labour, were formalised in the National Economic Development and Labour Council (NEDLAC). Changes to labour legislation were negotiated in this forum, and culminated in new Acts of Parliament governing labour relations, minimum employment standards, affirmative action, and education and training. The aim of this programme of legislative reform was to address the key legacies of the apartheid labour market. There was opposition from business to this programme of labour market reform and arguments that the labour market was becoming too rigid gained momentum in the 1990s. With regard to the labour market, business lobbies successfully shifted the 'language of rights' to a 'language of flexibility' (Kenny and Bezuidenhout 1999). While using the language of patriotism and commitment to the RDP to describe their responsibility programmes, on a broader level business aggressively started to lobby for an alternative developmental path. Their own programme was based on privatisation, fiscal discipline, the flexibilisation of the labour market, and monetary and trade liberalisation. This campaign culminated in a document, entitled *Growth for All*, released by the South Africa Foundation, a business-funded think tank (South Africa Foundation 1996).

In the context of a decline in employment levels, as well as a devaluating currency, the government adopted a new macroeconomic programme that resembled the one proposed by the South Africa Foundation and essentially abandoned the vision of development proposed by the RDP. By now, big business had established its hegemony in the realm of macroeconomic, industrial and labour market policy. By 1996 the RDP was sidelined in favour of a neo-liberal programme called Growth, Employment and Redistribution (GEAR), over which no public debate was entertained. Mokhethi Moshoeshoe, former director of the Southern African Grantmakers' Association (SAGA)[1], put it as follows: '[T]he clarity on government's GEAR policy put business in a clearer position . . . And furthermore, the companies are under less pressure now, since the ANC government has come to support a market economy' (Interview, Moshoeshoe, 21 September 2001).

These shifts in government policy have to be understood within a certain political context. Parliamentary democracy came to South Africa for the first time in April 1994. Under negotiated electoral arrangements a coalition was formed from the parties that had won 2 per cent or more of the vote. This included the majority-supported ANC (itself a broad cross-class alliance of centre and left interests), the Inkatha Freedom Party (representing conservative Zulu nationalist interests), and the National Party (a conservative white party which had been dominant during the 46 years of apartheid and co-author of the negotiated solution). This Government of National Unity (GNU) lasted for two years, during which time all three parties enjoyed Cabinet representation. With the finalisation of the 1996 Constitution, which included a Bill of Rights, the National Party felt affronted and left the coalition. Until 2001, the renamed New National Party (NNP) remained in opposition, in close combination with the Democratic Party (a centre-right liberal party close to big capital), together forming the Democratic Alliance (DA). However, tensions over regional politics caused a rift in the DA and the rump of the NNP returned to its coalition with the ANC, subsequently being absorbed into it and ceasing to exist. Since 1994, and more intensely since 1999, the ANC jettisoned most of its populist or progressive principles and consolidated a neo-liberal agenda, moving steadily to the centre. The ruling ANC faces a fragmented and diminished opposition, which has little chance of unseating it in the near future.

In the first few years of democracy there were more opportunities for the popular sectors of society (unions, civic organisations and progressive non-governmental organisations or NGOs) to influence government's position. Newly-appointed ministers, politicians and bureaucrats had their origins in these sectors, or were closely aligned with civil society aspirations. Once in office they faced the old guard, which in many cases was forced to adapt to the new circumstances but embodied a set of less progressive values. At first the new guard within government turned to civil society for some of its intellectual support. However, a number of influences were at work in moving the new guard much closer to the business sector. Some NGO leaders were drawn into the new bureaucracy, creating a gap in the watchdog capacity of civil society. Some of the new guard had completed internships at the World Bank or with conservative governments abroad. As elements of the new guard gradually consolidated their position, they found it more convenient to make alliances with the old guard than to fight for more radical policies. Many succumbed to the influences and the exigencies of a globalising world.

In terms of policy this had a number of effects. First, the pioneering and carefully crafted model of multi-stakeholder policy-making processes was abandoned in favour of more traditional top-down processes that proved to be less transparent and less participatory and clearly represented more narrowly-defined pro-corporate interests. Second, the government committed itself to implement more rigorously neo-liberal measures such as privatisation, deregulation and trade liberalisation, all of which had negative consequences for job creation, the maintenance of labour standards, provision of social welfare, and environmental protection. The state began to redefine service delivery as a non-core function and more earnestly outsourced and privatised these functions. It shed capacity, and in some areas lost its ability to regulate the private sector effectively. It began to encourage private-public partnerships instead of safeguarding the state's traditional exclusive role in the delivery of water, sanitation, energy, waste collection, health care and other essential services. Not only did this result in job losses and lower pay, but the services, when managed for profit, excluded the poorest sectors from access. Thus the state actively forfeited its role as an agent of redistribution in a country whose levels of wealth and poverty are extreme. Under GEAR, there was neither growth nor more employment nor a significant degree of redistribution. Third, as a consequence, government turned directly to business to help compensate for its diminishing capacity in numerous fields. This led to government appeals to business to help bankroll, for example, the fight against crime, inner-city development, tourism promotion, and its hosting of the World Summit on Sustainable Development (WSSD) in August–September 2002.

There were also consequences for corporate social spending. As the welfare safety net for the destitute and unemployed began to fray, the state put the onus on the private sector to invest more in education, health and food security projects. Realising that its regulatory functions would be weaker, the state also encouraged more voluntary initiatives in the private sector. It began to be seduced by notions of co-regulation, in which the private and public partners jointly take responsibility for regulatory actions. We shall see how this evolved more clearly in the environmental sector in particular.

Historical overview of corporate environmental responsibility

While CSER programmes were very much a product of the 1970s and the anti-apartheid campaign, corporate environmental responsibility largely remained tied to nature conservation and was devoid of social content. Only from the mid-1990s was the agenda extended to include environmental issues relating to community livelihoods, environmental education, recycling and greening projects.

The impact of the United Nations Conference on Environment and Development, held in Rio de Janeiro in June 1992, in stimulating corporate environmental responsibility initiatives in South Africa was very slight. At that time, South Africa's membership of the UN was still suspended because of apartheid and it could not participate in full in a formal sense. However, there was some civil society participation in the Global Forum and the government was permitted observer status. One notable business exception was the role of Raymond Ackerman, a supermarket mogul, in the World Business Council for Sustainable Development (WBCSD). Ackerman subsequently introduced a line of green products in his supermarket chain, Pick 'n Pay, and issued a set of educational brochures on the environment for shoppers. However, there was no attempt to change shoppers' habits or to cease selling environmentally-harmful products. Ackerman failed to develop a pro-environmental profile, and no longer serves on the WBCSD.

Corporate support for the environment in South Africa traditionally took the form of backing nature conservation initiatives. This arose from the prevailing paradigm under apartheid in which 'the dominant understanding of environmental issues was an authoritarian conservation perspective' (Cock 1991: 1). This tended to elevate the protection of charismatic animal and plant species or landscapes, blaming the poor majority of people for overpopulation and inappropriate resource use. The oldest environmental NGOs were organisations comprising concerned middle-class whites (Khan 1990: 37) and these enjoyed significant corporate support. The Southern African Nature Foundation (SANF), for instance, was established in 1968 by Anton Rupert, an entrepreneur whose wealth was based on wine, tobacco, luxury brands, medical clinics and manufacturing (Mansson 2000). In 1986, Rupert created the South African National Parks Trust charged with funding the acquisition of land for new national parks. He also established the Peace Parks Foundation in 1997, aimed at setting up transfrontier parks. During the 1990s, the SANF became known as the Worldwide Fund for Nature – South Africa (WWF-SA). It still relies significantly on corporate donors, as well as being able to lever millions of dollars from the Global Environmental Facility (GEF), a fund managed by the World Bank to implement the Rio treaties (Worldwide Fund for Nature-South Africa 2001: 23–30).

Corporations' strategy to compensate for their tarnished public images has been to provide grants to environmental projects, particularly in the sphere of conservation. Eskom, the state monopoly on energy generation, is perhaps the country's heaviest polluter, and supports projects with the Endangered Wildlife Trust, helping birds to avoid being damaged by electricity pylons. SAPPI, whose pulp mill at Ngodwana in Mpumalanga province is a large-scale polluter, sponsors a project which uses snout beetles to control alien plants in the river systems of KwaZulu-Natal province. Mazda, a vehicle manufacturer, supports a number of conservation projects with donations of utility vehicles and financial support. Certain companies provide awards for environmental role models, successful projects and research, and these include Nedbank's Green Trust Awards and Audi's Terra Nova Awards.

Oppositional environmentalism, on the other hand, took the form of issue-based campaigns, most of which were founded in the 1980s. One such initiative was Koeberg Alert, formed in opposition to the apartheid state's nuclear programme. Another campaign was set up to Save St Lucia, a wetland of international significance, from the threat of titanium mining. Organisations with broader aims, such as the Soweto-based National Environment Action Campaign and Earthlife Africa, were founded towards the end of this decade.

The authoritarian conservation paradigm began to be challenged in the early 1990s by a new wave of civil society organisations (CSOs). These included a number of newly-formed NGOs (such as the Group for Environmental Monitoring) that contested the corporate culture of conservation agencies at national and provincial levels, arguing for the inclusion of rural communities as beneficiaries of conservation and nature tourism. This new wave of NGOs was not confined to conservation interventions, but also challenged industrial environmental malpractices in significant ways. Earthlife Africa took on numerous campaigns, including opposition to the building of hazardous waste sites close to urban communities, the leakage of mercury waste into the environment at the Thor Chemicals factory in KwaZulu-Natal, and expansion of the nuclear industry. Other policy and advocacy groups took on environmental aspects of the mining, waste management, petrochemical, energy and genetic modification industries. The Environmental Justice Networking Forum, an umbrella organisation, emerged in 1992, with the participation of environmental NGOs, trade-union branches and community organisations. Affiliated NGOs tended not to accept state or corporate support as a matter of principle in an effort to maintain independence and the potential to retain a whistle-blowing role. Instead, the new wave of NGOs relied on donor finance from foreign NGOs, foundations and development agencies.

Corporate funding for environmental initiatives has itself undergone change. The concerns of the new wave have in some senses been mainstreamed. Traditional white-membership organisations such as the Wildlife Society (now known as the Wildlife and Environment Society) have taken up issues of sustainable development and community management of natural resources. Even WWF-SA has established lines of support for community-based conservation, eco-tourism, food security and sustainable agriculture projects. Although it is supporting over 150 projects, the preferred strategy of WWF-SA is to move towards support for larger schemes such as the Southern African Wildlife College, the Cape Action Plan for the Environment and the Table Mountain Fund. Corporates are thus more easily able to brand their support to specific environmental projects. Such support is often aired in the pages of *Earthyear*, a biannual publication purchased by the weekly *Mail & Guardian* (formerly owned largely by *The Guardian* of London), which has also published supplements on the corporate-funded Green Trust Awards and the WSSD.

South Africa's Constitution promotes decentralisation of government, creating subordinate tiers in the form of provinces and local authorities. Environmental management functions are shared between the various tiers. National government is charged with policy making and regulation, while the other tiers are responsible for operational and certain minor regulatory functions. Provinces have some responsibilities for waste management, environmental impact assessment and nature conservation. Local government retains responsibility for town and regional planning, and is required to establish integrated development plans (IDPs) incorporating local economic development (LED) projects. These are meant to embody principles of sustainable development, which are, however, seldom implemented.

The business sector is highly conscious of the state's limited ability to regulate. This has allowed corporate lobbyists to push for recognition by the state of less formal regulation and more co-regulation and voluntary initiatives (Hanks 2002a). For example, in the latter stages of the negotiation of new framework legislation in the form of the National

Environmental Management Act (NEMA) (107 of 1998) the government agreed to include a section on co-regulation, through Environmental Management Co-operative Agreements (EMCAs).[2]

The crafting of NEMA involved an intricate multi-stakeholder approach during the period 1994–97. During this initial phase of the new democracy, the business sector seemed uncertain of its bearings and unable to assert itself to the maximum. Given its origins in the liberation movement, and its strong ties with civil society, the new government seemed more responsive to civil society's interests, particularly those of the trade unions and community organisations, or civics. Government was also much more prepared to consult with progressive NGOs and think tanks, particularly in formulating policies in areas where it had little prior expertise. It was during this phase, while the private sector was not hegemonic, that broad interests were balanced. Generous donor resources were made available for think tanks as well as transparent and inclusive multi-sectoral policy-making processes (Fig 2000).

However, there is a discernible shift after 1996 with the introduction of GEAR, which marked a greater commitment to neo-liberalism and the private sector. This intensified after June 1999 when the ANC entered its second term of office under President Thabo Mbeki. In terms of environmental policy, the government revisited NEMA under pressure from the business sector, which regarded it as unworkable. Various revisions were subsequently planned behind closed doors. Supplementary legislation on biodiversity, protected areas and air quality was passed in 2004, but a multi-sectoral participatory approach has not been maintained. In the case of nuclear laws and biotechnology strategies, the state has turned to the private sector to do the drafting. NGOs, trade unions and civics have been weakened, and have not been able to maintain the thrust they enjoyed in the previous phase. This leaves the private sector in a strong position to influence policy.

Some of the business lobbies have taken advantage of the state's more amenable stance. While the Business Council on Sustainable Development (BCSD-SA, formerly the Industrial Environmental Forum) existed, it promoted more sustainable approaches among its members. Yet in representing their interests to government, it generally opted for the least stringent pathways and for legislation which was gradualist and avoided fundamental change. Its membership did not back strenuous anti-pollution standards partly because it comprised the very corporations which were the country's greatest offenders in terms of air pollution. In 2003 the BCSD-SA lost its autonomous existence and was absorbed into the more diluted activities of the National Business Initiative's Sustainable Futures Unit.

The Chamber of Mines is mindful of the fact that its industry produces around 80 per cent of South Africa's solid waste, and that many of the more contaminated slimes dams – storage ponds for liquid mining effluent – are too costly to remediate. The chemical industrial lobby, the Chemical and Allied Industries' Association (CAIA) that monitors the industry's Responsible Care programme, which will be discussed in more detail later in this chapter, has done little to get its members to resolve the problems faced by communities in key pollution hot spots such as South Durban, the Vaal Triangle, central Gauteng and the area around the Chevron refinery north of Cape Town.

The corporate focus on feel-good community and biodiversity enhancement projects often represents attempts to create more positive corporate images while diverting consumers away from the fundamental question of how to ensure that there is at least corporate environmental compliance with existing national norms and standards, especially on pollution and waste management. Until this can be resolved satisfactorily, corporate environmental responsibility will remain in the realm of public relations and greenwash, rendering private sector initiatives susceptible to accusations of business as usual, narrow self-interest, and an inability to redress the unjust environmental legacy of the apartheid past.

Emerging institutions

As argued earlier, before the 1990s very few institutions had been established to coordinate CSER programmes at national level. Since then, however, a number of broader initiatives have emerged. Among the most prominent are the following:

- The Joint Education Trust (JET) established in 1992 to support education. JET is a multi-stakeholder initiative spearheaded by the private sector. It allocates funds committed by its members, as well as funds provided by foreign donor agencies;
- The National Business Initiative (NBI) formed in 1995. The NBI built on the lessons of the Urban Foundation (established 1976) and the Consultative Business Movement (1989). It was a

business-supported organisation aimed at realising the sector's commitment to the new democracy. The NBI coordinates a number of projects related to CSI and policy formulation. One of its most prominent projects is the Business Trust. Founded in mid-1999, the Trust set itself the task of raising one billion rand over five years through the donation of 0.15 per cent of the profits of participating companies listed on the JSE Securities Exchange (the former Johannesburg Stock Exchange) and two per cent of a year's profits spread over five years from participating unlisted companies. The Trust's projects focus on job creation, capacity building, crime and malaria control, and are managed by the NBI (Laurence 2000). Another initiative of the NBI, the Big Business Working Group, meets monthly with President Thabo Mbeki and sees itself as a communication conduit with the government in terms of policy development. From 2003, the NBI's Sustainable Futures Unit has been active in promoting sustainable development in the business sector;

- The Business Council on Sustainable Development-South Africa (BCSD-SA), formerly the Industrial Environmental Forum (IEF) was established in 1992 to advise its members – mainly the larger corporations – on environmental best practice and on the development of a balance between wealth creation, social progress, and environmental protection. Its affiliation to the WBCSD became an increasingly important factor, prompting the name change. Initially the IEF was housed at and heavily subsidised by Eskom. It represented business and industry in the multi-stakeholder management team of the Consultative National Environmental Policy Process (1995–98). It was prominent at the WSSD, but subsequently its members lost interest and the organisation was closed down;

- In addition to these broad-based organisations, there are important sector-specific associations that contribute to CSER initiatives and information provision. Prominent examples include the Chamber of Mines and the CAIA. In addition to representing their members in government policy-making processes and to the media, they act as platforms for the sharing of information and best practice, as well as the implementation of voluntary initiatives (such as Responsible Care or the gold mining industry's Cyanide Code).

With respect to advisory, consulting or education services, a few institutions have been established with a specific focus on corporate responsibility. Established consulting firms have initiated new services promoting corporate responsibility, while some business schools are creating appropriate study programmes:

- SAGA and the Charities Aid Foundation (CAF) have played important roles in facilitating the CSER initiatives of South African companies as well as overseas donors. Interestingly, SAGA has ceased to exist after performing an important role in raising the profile of CSER.
- The African Institute of Corporate Citizenship (AICC), established in 2000, sees itself as being both an advocacy and consulting group with an emphasis on integrating CSER into core business management. It is producing a report on CSI for the BoE financial group, recently sold to Nedbank;
- The Accountability Institute, initially affiliated to the UK-based AccountAbility, works predominantly with government agencies, but is increasingly working with companies;
- The Centre for Development and Enterprise, a policy research institute which emerged in succession to the Urban Foundation, has also conducted research on CSER;
- Established management and accounting consultants are increasingly offering social, ethical or environmental accounting, certification or assurance services. KPMG, for instance, has recently combined its ethics and environment departments into a Global Sustainability Services programme;
- The Ethical Trade Initiative has initiated a project on the treatment of labour in the winelands of the Western Cape;
- A number of business schools are beginning to include sustainability issues in their course offerings. The University of Cape Town's Graduate School of Business, for instance, is currently establishing a short course on business and sustainability, modelled on the Prince of Wales' Cambridge Business Leadership Programme. The University of Pretoria offers an environmental MBA;
- Other academic centres have been active in relation to CSR. The University of South Africa (UNISA), a distance learning institution, is the only one to have created a Centre

for Corporate Citizenship linked to its Graduate School of Business Leadership. Together with the AICC, it organised the first Southern African Symposium on Corporate Citizenship in July 2005. The University of the Witwatersrand's Sociology of Work Unit (SWOP) has collaborated with the United Nations Research Institute on Social Development (UNRISD) on a project promoting the analysis of CSER in developing countries. The University of KwaZulu-Natal's Centre for Civil Society has embarked on a large research project on the state of giving in South Africa and has commissioned the Centre for Policy Studies, an independent think tank, to conduct the CSER aspects of this study. The Sustainability Institute, linked to the University of Stellenbosch, is incorporating CSER courses in a new MA degree on sustainable development, while the Graduate Business School of the University of Cape Town also includes CSER in various courses.

Several NGOs are also active in this realm. They can be divided essentially into three types. The first consists of NGOs that were founded on or mostly depend on corporate support – an example would be the WWF-SA. The second type comprises NGOs that are recipients of corporate assistance. These include projects like Food and Trees for Africa and EcoLink, whose activities are extensive in townships and rural communities. Such NGOs rely on corporate philanthropy to maintain their activities and therefore have not developed a critical stance on questions of poor environmental citizenship in the private sector. A third grouping involves NGO networks that see themselves linked to an agenda highly critical of corporate damage to the lives of the poor and their environment (see Fig 2005: 613 for a full list of this type of NGO). The Social Movements Indaba combines groups such as anti-debt Jubilee South Africa, and those campaigning against the privatisation of energy, water and waste services such as the Soweto Electricity Crisis Campaign, the Anti-Privatisation Forum and the Landless People's Movement. The tireless Treatment Action Campaign (TAC) has taken on both government and the private pharmaceutical companies by insisting on the provision of affordable anti-retroviral treatment for people with AIDS.

In the sphere of environment, groups calling for corporate accountability include the Environmental Justice Networking Forum,

the Trade Policy Network, and notable key affiliates like GroundWork
and Earthlife Africa. These organisations see themselves linked to an
agenda critical of corporate damage to the environment. They prefer,
therefore, to remain independent of any corporate financial support,
leaving them able to monitor and whistle-blow where necessary. At
times it has been deemed appropriate to draw on public-interest law
firms, such as the Legal Resources Centre, to advance litigation against
transgressor corporations. Such NGOs have also participated in multi-
stakeholder agreements such as the gold mining industry's Cyanide
Code. Of all the NGOs in this group, GroundWork and Transparency
International South Africa have gone the furthest in taking up the
question of corporate environmental accountability. Each has linked up
with counterpart international NGOs, and, in the run-up to the WSSD,
commissioned a number of studies and popular booklets on corporate
environmental behaviour. Together with the University of KwaZulu-
Natal's Centre for Civil Society, GroundWork has sponsored the Corpse
Awards for corporate abuse.

The final element in emerging institutions is that of organised
labour. Numerous deaths of workers in mining accidents, exposure to
harmful substances such as asbestos, mercury, uranium and cyanide,
and to industrial pollution, have galvanised the trade union movement
into taking action on health, safety and environmental matters (Lukey
1995). Key among these are the Food and Allied Workers' Union
(FAWU), the Chemicals, Energy, Paper, Printing, Wood and Allied
Workers' Union (CEPPWAWU) and the National Union of Mineworkers
(NUM), all affiliates of COSATU. NUM has created the Mineworkers'
Development Agency to combat retrenchments and to retrain migrant
miners who have returned to their rural base by setting up alternative
employment, using co-operatives and other models. Unions have
acted on numerous occasions in support of better corporate social and
environmental practices. To this end, they have participated in multi-
stakeholder agreements, and play a significant role in NEDLAC. Labour
representatives have taken part in a number of key policy processes
with respect to the environment.

Implications of social and environmental pressures
From the above we see that, in both the social and environment realms,
vibrant civil society organisations emerged to challenge existing

practices by the state and corporate sector. In the 1970s, the anti-apartheid movement forced both the state and corporations to respond to its calls for sanctions. Oppositional environmental movements steadily emerged from the early 1980s. With the advent of democracy, the labour movement succeeded in challenging one of the key features of apartheid – a racially segmented labour market – through a legislative programme. The environmental movement utilised broad processes of participation to reform environmental legislation, yet this space closed down when government policy shifted towards neo-liberalism in content and became more technocratic in process. Nevertheless, there are still numerous factors pressurising corporations to improve their record.

South Africa has long been part of the global market. Its primary agricultural products, its mineral wealth and its manufacturing have all tied it into circuits of global capitalism. During the apartheid years, significant pressures emerged for foreign direct investment to deracialise the workplace. Transnational corporations were increasingly under scrutiny in their home countries, and contending pressures were exerted on them to stay in South Africa and reform, or to sell up and leave. Many left. With democracy, a number of the departed corporations have returned, and others have felt free to set up shop. The transnational sector has experienced rising pressures – and sometimes legal obligations imposed in their home countries – to improve environmental management practices. Transnational corporations, being mindful of domestic pressures, have been expected to apply their corporate codes of conduct wherever they invest. This has not always worked to local benefit. For example, new cradle-to-grave packaging legislation in Germany obliged Daimler-Benz to return packing crates containing knocked-down auto kits from its plant in East London back to their point of origin in Germany. Previously, local workers had access to these crates, which had been a useful source of building materials. Along with its political transition, South Africa has undergone economic liberalisation. This has resulted in the state intervening less in the economy and has created new spaces for corporations to demonstrate their social responsibility. In a liberal economy there is less effective regulation and this has led to companies favouring different modes of self-regulation in order to implement voluntary initiatives.

Many of the country's corporations have become global players and in some cases they have decamped to the developed countries in order to enjoy easier access to finance, better interest rates and more stable operating environments. Others have remained loyal to their original base, but are attempting to reposition themselves globally. In both cases, they have to take global standards, codes and customer preferences into account.

South Africa's adherence to multilateral environmental agreements and the hosting of the Rio+10 Summit have added extra pressures to demonstrate greater conformity with international norms. Innovative industrial associations strongly argue the merits of the triple-bottom-line, adding social and environmental accounting to their usual balance sheets. Consumers and NGOs are increasingly exercising their watchdog roles, while investors increase their demands for more ethical and socially responsible corporate practices.

The South African media have in general played a fairly passive role in relation to investigations of instances of corporate irresponsibility. Before 1994, broadcasting was entirely a state monopoly and the printed media were largely owned by interests favourable to the state or to the large mining houses. While a certain degree of diversification has occurred in recent years, the independent media is still weak. The weekly *Mail & Guardian* is one of the few press voices consistently critical of corruption and corporate misdemeanours. Yet, for some years, it held ownership of the publication *Earthyear*, a showcase for corporate greenwash advertorial matter. Another independent publication which regularly investigates abuse is the monthly *Noseweek*, which often documents cases of corruption and other misdemeanours in the public and private sectors.

Corruption scandals, when aired in the conventional media, have tended to focus on the behaviour of individuals rather than corporations. It has been left to a handful of journalists to exploit the limited space available to expose malpractices. Investigative reporting slots on television, such as SABC3's *Special Assignment* and MNet's *Carte Blanche*, have occasionally applied their minds to in-depth exposures of mining pollution or the nuclear industry. The opportunities for naming and shaming are sometimes constrained, but when they do occur they have a disproportionate impact on the culprits.

All these factors will be shown to play a part in shifting corporate behaviour. Sponsorship of snout beetle projects are fine, but cannot be a substitute for the internalisation of better social and environmental management, which South Africa sorely needs to overcome the social and ecological damage of the blighted apartheid years.

Rhetoric and discourse
Corporate social investment as a South African concept
South Africa's peculiar history impacted on the way in which CSER came to be understood. Hence it has taken on a particular flavour, in terms of both terminology and content. Indeed, the term corporate social responsibility is frequently rejected by industry representatives, who interpret the word responsibility as an obligation imposed on companies with reference to past misdeeds. In this sense, they often argue, the responsibility of companies is to abide by laws and to pay taxes. Much preferred is the term corporate social investment (CSI), which has arisen out of the context of South African history. The history of apartheid has resulted in some companies embracing broader developmental objectives by means of social investment initiatives (Nel 1992: 26).

'Corporate social investment in South Africa takes more the form of philanthropy or charity,' argued Mokhethi Moshoeshoe, a former director of the Southern African Grantmakers' Association. He explained:

> Corporate social investment is a kind of South African term which actually means corporate social relations, and corporate community relations. The South Africans' understanding was that they were going beyond their responsibility of paying tax, saying that it is an investment in the community. But the problem was that there was no measure of what the social returns would be, because it was not an integral part of the business. While it was called an investment, in actual fact it was corporate philanthropy or charity. But it sounded better – in this sector there are always interesting phrases (Interview, Moshoeshoe, 21 September 2001).

The key incentive for these initiatives was to improve social conditions and diminish social conflict, in order to provide a safer and more conducive business environment in terms of higher skills levels and better human resources, and growth in national markets. Other incentives included international pressure, such as the Sullivan Principles which were discussed above. Available data indicates that in the early 1990s, 66 per cent of all CSI spending went to education, followed by environmental conservation and health at seven per cent each (Nel 1992: 28). The main recipients of CSI funds were NGOs or community initiatives, while the geographical scale of company CSI strategies was commonly national, although mining companies in particular also targeted areas surrounding their operations.

Strategic corporate social investment

Following the 1994 elections, CSI strategies changed to adapt to the new political imperatives. The new government's RDP strategy, in particular, played an important role in guiding corporate social funding decisions. CSER projects became known as RDP projects. This did not imply that the RDP, as a developmental programme, was supported universally by the business community. Indeed, as argued above, a number of business lobby groups actively argued against it. The implication was that the meaning of the RDP could be altered by focusing on business-led micro-initiatives.

Although community-based projects were still funded to some extent, business developed a new emphasis on alignment with new governmental initiatives. This included a general shift towards a more strategic kind of social investment regarded as seed funding for initiatives that would become self-sustaining once they were up and running. The aim was to decrease dependence on corporate funding among beneficiaries, including government projects. Another emerging trend has been for companies to focus their funding on fields related to their core business. So, for instance, pharmaceutical companies commonly specialise in CSI initiatives related to health. There has also been a greater emphasis on collective social investment initiatives, involving broad participation by numerous leading firms, as epitomised by the National Business Initiative (NBI).

Corporate social investment or corporate social responsibility? The tension between before-profit and after-profit responsibility

It is apparent that in the South African context CSI is akin to what is known in North America as strategic philanthropy, in which corporate giving is intended to benefit the benefactor in the long run (Pinney

2001). Even the traditional notion of CSER considered philanthropy as merely one of its four aspects, the others being legal compliance, economic performance and ethical conduct (Carroll 1999). The emerging international discourse surrounding CSER has been invigorated and informed by that of sustainable development, whereby companies are increasingly required to prove their net benefit to sustainable development by minimising negative social and environmental impacts and maximising positive effects. CSER calls for a company to respond not only to its shareholders, but also to other stakeholders, including employees, customers, affected communities and the general public, on issues such as human rights, employee welfare and climate change. Most significantly, whereas CSI or philanthropy concerns the way a certain proportion of profits is spent on worthy causes, CSER is primarily about how those profits are made in the first place.

The preference of South African business for the terminology of social investment, however, often diverts attention from the debate about whether business should take on any responsibility for methods of accumulation which included racial oppression during the eras of colonial and apartheid rule (Fig 2005).

The emphasis on add-on strategic philanthropy might constrain the ability of South African companies to respond to international demands for the incorporation of sustainability into core strategy. This constraint might be manifested in terms of managerial and employee attitudes and other forms of institutional inertia. On the other hand, the experience of South African companies with CSI might have benefited them in terms of a more sophisticated understanding of social development issues. For instance, while trailing international trends in the practice of environmental reporting, South African companies have led the way in terms of social reporting, drawing on their experience with social investment initiatives. This is particularly significant given the specific challenges related to doing business in South Africa, including the battle against HIV / AIDS and support for BEE. It is important that this understanding is communicated to international observers, analysts and investors who might otherwise tend to apply universal standards or Northern expectations.

The emergence of partnerships
In the international discourse surrounding CSER, partnerships between companies, government and communities are being touted as

a more intelligent and effective way to implement social investment programmes, and to minimise negative and maximise positive impacts of business activity (Hamann 2001). Partnership benefits are believed to include the more effective use of available resources, better knowledge management, the creation of better trust between stakeholders (and hence lower transaction costs), and general synergies arising from the coordination of complementary core competencies. South African companies and industries have already implemented such partnerships, for instance in the form of the JET. The notion of partnerships has also become prominent in the context of privatisation, with public-private partnerships marketed as the middle ground between state control and full privatisation.

However, there is the possibility that the discourse surrounding partnerships veils an underlying divergence of interests. By assuming that partnering will benefit all partners and by neglecting the effectiveness with which powerful actors can influence the discourse around partnerships, such arrangements may inordinately disadvantage certain groups or the environment. Although a balance of power may not be a prerequisite for partnering, the way in which power is exerted will be crucial – a fair and transparent appraisal of the costs and benefits of partnering is essential. It is also important that civil society participants entering into partnerships should have the capacity to participate fully. In South Africa this is not always the case and new models for enhancing the capacity to participate need to be investigated. For instance, some attention should be paid to the Canadian experience, which allows for empowerment of communities during environmental assessment processes. Hence, the evolving discourse surrounding partnerships, the establishment of methodologies for partnership creation, and existing experiences should be important subjects of investigation in the next few years.

The discourse of sustainable development
The concept of sustainable development entered United Nations discourse in 1987, when the World Commission on Environment and Development (WCED), also known as the Brundtland Commission, published its report entitled *Our Common Future* (World Commission on Environment and Development 1987). The WCED attempted to reconcile the concepts of environmental protection and economic

development. The context was one of Northern environmentalists arguing for minimisation of consumption to cut back on natural resource use. In the South, the developing countries argued that reducing consumption was not the answer, and that overcoming poverty meant extending people's ability to consume. The Brundtland Commission tried to reconcile environmental protection with the South's economic development. The concept of sustainable development was seen as a bridge, since it permitted the notion of consumption within certain limits. The definition provided in the Commission's report stated:

> sustainable development is development that meets the needs of the present generation without compromising the ability of future generations to meet their own needs. It contains within it two key concepts: the concept of 'needs', in particular, the essential needs of the world's poor, to which overriding priority should be given; and the idea of limitations imposed by the state of technology and social organisation on the environment's ability to meet present and future needs (World Commission on Environment and Development 1987: 43).

The definition certainly recognises inter-generational equity, while arguing for respect for environmental limits and promoting the South's need for economic development. The concept of sustainable development thus tended to satisfy most environmentalists as well as those concerned with economic development in the South.

Simultaneously, the concept began to enter the discourse of global governance. At the Conference on Environment and Development, which took place in Rio de Janeiro in June 1992, the United Nations established a Commission on Sustainable Development charged with meeting annually in New York to review the state of global environmental protection. The concept was adopted for use by numerous institutions, including the European Union (EU), the World Bank and the WBCSD, as well as numerous countries, corporations and local authorities. In South Africa the concept was given formal status within the 1996 Constitution.

However, it remains imprecise and problematic. In the early 1990s it was often used interchangeably with the notion of sustainable growth, particularly by those economists, politicians and entrepreneurs who remained untouched by the environmental world. Sustainable growth implies continuous expansion of a country's GDP, whereas sustainable development questions it as an adequate instrument for measuring development.

More recently the concept is being used as a synonym for poverty eradication. In the preparations for the WSSD in Johannesburg, some of the local organisers distanced themselves from an understanding that the summit should deal solely with the environment. The participation of environmental organisations was diluted in favour of the recognition of broader social formations. The local Civil Society Secretariat of the WSSD stigmatised environmentalists as being concerned only with green issues, despite the decade of work done within environmental circles to develop a post-colonial paradigm that demonstrates concern with people as much as with nature.

This shift in the discourse was endorsed by the local business sector, which helped to bankroll the event. In a recent report on CSI in South Africa, Anglo American Corporation clearly articulated this shift in a quote from Michael Spicer, then its executive vice-president for corporate affairs:

> Sustainable development may seem a rather nebulous concept that began with concerns over the environment – global warming and damage to the ozone layer, for example – but by the late 1980s and early 1990s it has spread to the idea of broader community involvement as a business imperative for large commercial endeavours. Particularly for companies operating in developing countries, environmental impact studies must now be accompanied by community involvement studies. It's as unacceptable for companies, when they move on, to leave great holes in the earth and polluted rivers as it is to leave disrupted or unenriched communities (Anglo American Corporation of South Africa [2000]: 3).

The new discourse on sustainable development in South Africa, especially in official and business circles, seems indistinguishable from classic modernisation narratives, with the added business imperative of good neighbourliness. As South Africa grapples to define its National Strategy for Sustainable Development, this more dilute understanding of the concept is likely to justify business as usual approaches to development.

Shifting meanings

From the discussion above, we see how the language of CSER is mobilised in the South African context. Local discourse often draws on global debates. However, the shifting meaning of concepts is also influenced by the way in which they are used: altruistic philanthropy becomes strategic and self-serving CSI; the language of the RDP is used on one level, but opposed on another; privatisation is often euphemistically packaged as an exercise in partnership; the concept of sustainable development is used interchangeably with the concept of sustainable growth (possibly an oxymoron); and business as usual is repackaged as CSER. In light of the shifting meanings attached to a number of discourses, it is important to disaggregate concepts and to ground them in everyday experience.

Initiatives

Voluntary initiatives for more responsible corporate behaviour play a number of roles. They may take the form of self-regulation by groups of firms, often sectorally based. Adherence might bring rewards, such as a licence to operate in a particular jurisdiction, or eligibility for contracts and markets. They may set standards and give firms incentives to apply best practice in relation to technologies or stakeholders. South Africa has had important recent experience of a number of voluntary initiatives enhancing CSER. This section will review and evaluate a range of such initiatives.

Codes of conduct

As described earlier, the Sullivan Principles provided a code of conduct that had a significant effect on business activity in South Africa; indeed, they still inform approaches to CSER in this country today. Just as the Sullivan Principles were an attempt to avert stricter enforcement of anti-apartheid sanctions, codes of conduct are seen as a way to pre-empt stricter government regulation. As Mokhethi Moshoeshoe (Interview, 21 September 2001) argues, 'Everybody is trying to avoid government intervention, and the codes of conduct are a basis for self-regulation'. Gillian Hattingh from the NBI adds another word of caution:

> I think codes of conduct are very important, but I'm not sure
> if companies actually implement them properly. Sometimes

companies can get away with doing less than they say they're
going to do, because we're not up to global standards at this
point – and the monitoring and evaluation systems are not in
place (Interview, Hattingh, 20 September 2001).

There is a variety of codes of conduct (Jenkins 2001), with varying degrees
of importance or effectiveness. Company-level codes, for instance, if
supported by accompanying policies and management systems, can
have important benefits for social and environmental performance. Yet,
Bill Lacey from the South African Federation of Chambers of Commerce
(SAFCOC) argues that codes of conduct are more appropriate for large
corporations, who see them as 'an important adjunct to their image. But
for small business, I'd say it's pretty much peripheral' (Interview, Lacey,
29 October 2001). South Africa has not yet seen the advent of huge global
brand-name sweatshops, but the American Growth and Opportunities
Act has made similar conditions possible in neighbouring Lesotho. The
free trade agreement between the Southern African Customs Union
(South Africa, Namibia, Botswana, Lesotho and Swaziland) and the
United States may increase such investments, which would require
monitoring existing corporate codes of conduct.

   At a sector level, one of the most prominent codes is the chemical
industry's Responsible Care programme. This code, introduced in
the wake of the 1984 Bhopal disaster in India, was an attempt by the
industry to improve environmental performance through its own
internal monitoring rather than being compulsorily subjected to further
regulation. In South Africa, strong peer pressure is exerted by the
CAIA and its leading members in order to get the industry as a whole
to comply with Responsible Care provisions. They want to improve
the industry's image and minimise the high community health and
environmental risks associated with it. While CAIA has admitted
that some of its members have been less responsive in implementing
Responsible Care than others, at least better environmental management
has been incentivised by the industry acting voluntarily. Some
chemical corporations have not yet reached the standards necessary for
conformity with regulations, but there is also a perception of weak state
regulatory capacity. By enrolling in the Responsible Care programme,
CAIA claims it can monitor progress towards compliance (Interview,
Lötter, 11 October 2000).

However, the traditional concerns related to the drivers behind voluntary initiatives are well illustrated by this case. A key limitation of the programme is that monitoring is not independent of the chemical industry. Affected stakeholders accuse companies of trying to dilute regulation by means of this and other codes. Chemical companies are also accused of attempting to sideline NGOs and affected communities in the preparation of a national industry-specific code of conduct (see also Chapter 3 in this book).

During its ten-year existence (1992–2003), the WBCSD's local affiliate strove to promote its own national industry association code, the WBCSD (formerly IEF) Charter. However, this was never considered effective despite efforts to relaunch it during 2001. Its contents were seen as vague and not many companies took it seriously. Similarly, most informants considered the United Nations Global Compact – proposed by UN Secretary General Kofi Annan in the run-up to the WSSD – to have limited significance in South Africa. Only ten South African companies have adopted the Global Compact (Table 2.2). These include power utility Eskom, chemical corporation SASOL, the PG Group (motor glass and building materials) and Bell Products (heavy construction and mining vehicles and machinery). These firms are either large exporters or have extensive interests abroad.

Table 2.2: South African-listed members of the Global Compact at 1 June 2007.

Sector	Company/Organisation
Aerospace and Aviation	Starlite Aviation
Business Association	Services Sector Education and Training Authority
Chemical	Bell Products, SASOL
Cities	City of Tshwane (formerly Pretoria)
Commercial Services and Supplies	Adeco Recruitment Services
Finance and Insurance	First Rand, Health Management Institute, Nedbank
Foundations	Global Alliance for Improved Nutrition
Industrial Conglomerate	Barloworld, PG Group
Information Technology, Consulting and Software	Waymark Infotech
Labour	Congress of South African Trade Unions

Manufacturing	Southern Trident
Media, Communications, Entertainment	Mail & Guardian
Minerals and Mining	Anglogold Ashanti, BHP Billiton, De Beers, Exxaro Resources, Gold Fields Ltd
Personal Care and Household Products	Tru-Lite
Pharmaceutical and Biotechnology	Merck SA
Professional, Scientific, Technical Services	Accenture SA, Deloitte and Touche SA
Utilities	Eskom, Rand Water
Other	Bonnie Delta

Source: UN Global Compact site: www.globalcompact.org (accessed 1 June 2007).

Significantly, Jenkins' (2001) argument that codes of conduct are more effective when they are agreed to by other stakeholders is borne out by the South African experience, with the important caveat that they be local stakeholders. This applies, for instance, to the attempts of mining companies to establish policies on HIV/AIDS. An example of a successful multi-stakeholder code is that developed by the mining industry together with government, NGOs and other groups for the regulation of cyanide in the gold mining industry.

Finally, an important recent development has been the second edition of the King Report on Corporate Governance for South Africa, generally known as King 2 (King Committee on Corporate Governance 2002). King was approached by the Institute of Directors to develop guidelines for good corporate governance, and the first report (King Committee on Corporate Governance 1994) was well received by business and its principles applied in many boardrooms. The first report stressed making management structures more logical, more transparent and more accountable to stakeholders. The second report specifically mentions CSER, particularly in connection with the reporting, accounting and auditing of non-financial matters (discussed in greater detail below). It includes appendices on the UN Global Compact, the Global Sullivan Principles, the AA 1000 Standard, and the recommendations of the Global Reporting Initiative (King Committee on Corporate Governance 2002: 226–74). The King reports are non-statutory and voluntary in character, but are extremely influential in shaping boardroom practice. The enforceability of these guidelines is limited to their inclusion as listing requirements for the JSE Securities Exchange. We are therefore likely to see, as a direct result of its influence, a rise in the mainstreaming of CSER among a broader range of South African corporations in the medium term.

Certification

The most prevalent certification scheme in South Africa is probably ISO 14000, the international environmental management standard. By 2004, 393 certifications had occurred (Table 2.3). According to Mike McDonald (Interview, 5 November 2001) from the Steel and Engineering Industries' Federation of South Africa (SEIFSA), a federation for employers' organisations, incentives to acquire this certificate relate primarily to whether corporations are involved in the export market, their size and the type of products they produce.

Table 2.3:   ISO 14000 certification granted to South African plants, 1998–2005.

	1998	1999	2000	2001	2002	2003	2004	2005
Number in South Africa	30	82	126	169	264	378	393	540
% Africa	n/a	64	56	55.6	65.2	62.4	50	46.9
% World	n/a	0.58	0.55	0.46	0.53	0.57	0.43	0.49

Source: International Standards Organisation, www.iso.org (accessed 1 June 2007).

In this regard, Zoë Budnik-Lees, executive director of the BCSD-SA, argues that certification is mostly limited to the manufacturing sectors, since

> they are the ones who experience the trade issues. From a trade perspective it is important to take certification seriously, but it is also important from a reputation perspective, as well as a standardisation perspective. However, because you can choose the pace at which you can go, it doesn't necessarily mean very much. But what it does is to sensitise management to the commitment that they take when they draw up an environmental policy or a social policy. And I think it forces them to take leadership on those things, because they are quite

publicly committing themselves to certain things, and to keep the certification current (Interview, Budnik-Lees, 27 September 2001).

Common criticisms of this standard relate to the absence of any external reporting requirements and to its failure to measure actual performance. Instead, it requires continual improvement, which itself is vaguely defined and interpreted.

Social certification schemes, such as SA 8000, have not found broad acceptance among South African companies. The incentive to acquire such standards seems to be fairly weak, particularly in the context of a fairly progressive framework of labour relations legislation, and the need to implement some of the requirements of the legislation on employment equity plans. However, in industries with poor reputations in the area of labour practice, such as the wine industry, trade pressures have forced compliance with a social code drafted by the Ethical Trade Initiative in the United Kingdom (see Box 2.3 and section below on fair trade).

Box 2.3

Triple-bottom-line management on a wine estate

There is great interest in what is being attempted by the Spier group of companies at the Spier wine estate in Stellenbosch, Western Cape province. Activities range from the wine business to green technology companies. Former co-directors Mark Swilling and Eve Annecke, now running the Sustainability Institute, were then enthusiastic promoters of the concept, but they are also candid about the mistakes they have made. Swilling describes how, faced with severe financial problems and declining income, the owners and managers of the estate decided three years ago to embark on a programme of renewal based on sustainability principles, and how this emphasis on the triple-bottom-line has allowed them to become more profitable, attract more guests and build a superior reputation. They have learned important lessons in the process.

Spier's vision was redrafted to reflect the prime role of establishing a sustainable ecology in the winelands and of supporting a community lifestyle. Significantly, development was to be integrated into the core business according to the maxim, 'The business of business is development, and the business of development is business'. Hence, the companies' workers now own 25 per cent of the business and there are substantial efforts to promote gender and race equity, training, and a work-life balance. The surrounding community is assisted by work for local business, affirmative procurement policies, the application of social and environmental criteria to contracts, participation by means of representation on the executive board, encouragement of voluntary work among company employees, and support for local schools. In terms of environmental issues, the Spier estate has managed, among other things, to reduce the amount of waste sent to the municipal dump by 95 per cent.

The Lynedoch community project, in particular, is seen as a vital experiment in the creation of localised, self-reliant, low-waste, communal living environments in the winelands. Spier's contribution to this community has included town planning and architectural design, partnerships with government in the establishment of a school, environmental projects related to waste recycling, and the establishment of local businesses. These efforts have also resulted in the creation of green technology companies, one of which provides biological sewage waste treatment facilities, while another offers an innovative plastic moulding technology for the purpose of plastic recycling.

Spier's experience shows that social and environmental issues must be considered jointly by the same people if the difficult trade-offs surrounding CSER are to be managed. In terms of the key challenges, Swilling and Annecke acknowledge that the large number of issues being considered in Spier's sustainability efforts may have led to a loss of focus. Furthermore, although the various people involved may be using the same concepts – such as sustainability and triple-bottom-line – there are still many divergent visions and meanings, and this makes the attainment of commitment and common agendas difficult. Finally, the triple-bottom-line approach requires a great deal of experimentation. Such learning entails mistakes and failures which cost money, so it is a perpetual effort to convince the board of the value of this path. In total, however, the Spier experiment shows that genuine triple-bottom-line management can have significant business benefits, even in the short term.

In addition, there are sector-specific certification schemes such as that of the Forest Stewardship Council (FSC). The FSC scheme is implemented by the major South African forestry companies, primarily for the purpose of export. Indeed, South Africa is considered a world leader in the certification of timber plantations, with over 55 per cent of plantation areas being certified.[3] Although this seems high, it should be remembered that three companies (Safcol, Mondi and SAPPI) dominate the sector and operate massive pine and eucalyptus plantations that have been given blanket certification. Liberal certification criteria have been criticised by Timberwatch Coalition, claiming that the FSC is quick to certify despite poor working conditions, low wages and unsustainable impacts of timber monoculture on the environment.

The Kimberley Process is an attempt initiated by De Beers and other stakeholders in the diamond industry to identify and avoid the trade in conflict diamonds. The process uses a form of certification to guarantee the legitimacy of diamonds produced outside areas of conflict, such as Sierra Leone, Liberia and the Democratic Republic of Congo, protecting them through the chain of custody.

Cleaner technology

There are a number of severely polluting industries in South Africa, including coal mining and power generation, SASOL's synthetic fuel production, petroleum refining, paper and cellulose production, mining, and high-input commercial agriculture. Significantly, the state has yet to implement its National Waste Management Strategy, which was designed in 1998 to establish a coordinated regulatory approach to waste management and pollution control. Further, while there are some incentives for the introduction of cleaner technologies, there is still no holistic push by government. For instance, the government has been slow to provide guidance regarding the heavily-polluted South Durban basin and is trying to rely more and more on voluntary initiatives by business. Violations of laws are not often challenged, least of all in court, and in fact those with a genuine grievance prefer to sue polluters in other jurisdictions.[4]

Other problems related to government policy on pollution include an increasingly behind closed doors approach to policy making (for instance, in reviewing the National Environmental Management Act), a focused effort on banning plastic bags (instead of focusing on the main pollution sources and implementing better waste-collection services), the failure to improve the public transport system, and – perhaps most important – a problematic energy policy which, *inter alia*, heavily subsidises the cost of electricity for bulk users and exporters.

Are industries cleaning up?

Although there has been no fundamental change, industries are being forced or encouraged to institute environmental management systems within their plants. Some firms are trying to set targets for the introduction of cleaner technologies. SASOL has moved away from coal to natural gas as a synthetic fuel feedstock, and this will result in a cleaner process. BP and Shell are both exploring the renewable energy market and instituting projects that may need to be followed up, while the University of Johannesburg is collaborating with German leaders in the field of solar energy to provide financially viable energy to poor and middle-income households.

The flexible mechanisms arising from the Kyoto Protocol, aimed at reducing greenhouse gas emissions globally, apply to South Africa. One of our respondents, John Kilani, environmental advisor to the Chamber of Mines at the time of our interviews, is on the executive board of the Clean Development Mechanism (CDM). The CDM attempts to transfer capital and technology to the South for the purpose of reducing greenhouse gas emissions, which will be credited to those countries with Kyoto obligations. This mechanism is extremely controversial and was criticised in the Durban Declaration (Bond and Dada 2005).

Recent strengthening of air quality legislation and the creation of a new environmental inspectorate (nicknamed the Green Scorpions) may result in better regulation and enforcement in the future. Meanwhile, pressures for industry to clean up mostly arise from residents of over-polluted areas in heavy industrial complexes and around oil refineries and pulp and paper plants. The numerous community pollution monitoring groups, linked to GroundWork, are likely to monitor the implementation of the Act very closely.

According to Mike McDonald from SEIFSA (Interview, 5 November 2001), their members involved in the steel and ferro-alloy industries 'are taking [the use of cleaner technology] very seriously', but 'others less so'. Since many corporations have ignored this issue for so long, he argues, it is going to cost 'millions, if not billions, to fix those problems'. Zoë Budnik-Lees points out:

> new technologies are very expensive, require infrastructural change and a large capital outlay. This often requires new staff,

and perhaps the application of completely new standards to the business. By and large, we deal with the large corporations, continuously helping them to investigate the financial viability of cleaner technologies. So the driving force to be a cleaner company may not necessarily override the cost of that technology (Interview, Budnik-Lees, 27 September 2001).

This attitude seems surprising, since it runs counter to the win-win argument that cleaner technologies increase profits. However, the limitation on South African industry may be its restricted capacity to innovate and develop cleaner technologies on a sufficiently large scale to make it worthwhile. Given the post-1994 scarcity of foreign direct investment in manufacturing, access to new capital for the introduction of cleaner technologies is likely to be limited to the few projects that qualify for assistance under the CDM.

Reporting

South African companies are increasingly becoming involved with public reporting, either in terms of disclosure in annual reports or by means of separate social or environmental reports. The companies listed in Table 2.4 claim that they use the Global Reporting Initiative (GRI) guidelines in the presentation of their annual reports. The AICC in Johannesburg has been appointed as a local agency for the promotion of adherence to these reporting guidelines.

Table 2.4: South African companies adopting GRI guidelines in reporting.

Sector	Company
Chemical	AECI, SASOL
Commercial Services	Deloitte and Touche
Consumer Durables	Proctor and Gamble
Construction	Concor, Pretoria Portland Cement
Finance, Insurance	ABSA, African Bank, Bidvest, First Rand, Investec, Nedbank, Old Mutual, Standard Bank
Fishing	Oceana
Forestry and Paper Products	Mondi Paper, SAPPI

Industrial Conglomerate	Barloworld
Minerals and Mining	Anglo Coal, Anglo Platinum, Anglogold Ashanti, BHP Billiton, Chamber of Mines of South Africa, Gold Fields, Harmony Gold, Hillside Aluminium, Impala Platinum, Kumba Resources, Northam Platinum
Motor Vehicle	Toyota SA
Petroleum and Gas	Engen Petroleum
Retail	Foschini, Pick 'n Pay, Woolworths
Technology and Telecommunications	Bytes Technology, MTN
Tobacco	British American Tobacco – South Africa
Tourism and Leisure	Spier Holdings
Utilities	Eskom, Telkom, Umgeni Water

Source: Global Reporting Initiative, www.corporateregister.com/gri (accessed 1 June 2007).

At an award ceremony held in Johannesburg for the best sustainability reports, hosted by KPMG, an AngloGold representative noted that public reporting has become crucial due to increased stakeholder expectations in the wake of their listing in London, as well as increased peer pressure. Significantly, the preparation of a public report entailed a number of unintended benefits, such as integrating the management systems of the corporation and its divisions, accelerating corporate change and raising the performance levels of group companies to a minimum level. However, it is only a small number of companies in South Africa that actually prepare reports, primarily those exposed to reporting requirements of foreign stock markets or those with a high public profile. Even fewer prepare reports that conform to standards such as those of the GRI, including a commitment to measurable targets. Hence, the overall significance of public reporting is quite low – although it is increasing, especially in terms of disclosure in annual reports.

External verification is widely considered to be important in order to increase stakeholder confidence in the reports and to improve corporate governance (KPMG 2001). Yet few companies allow for such external audits, and even when they do the verification procedure is often narrowly defined – focusing on the use of data rather than its source – and closely controlled by the company. As a result, there is still a high degree of scepticism among NGOs and affected communities towards company reports. Another criticism, also shared by some company representatives, is that companies sometimes emphasise the reporting process and devote extensive resources to the production of glossy reports at the expense of improved social and environmental performance on the ground.

The winner of the KPMG 2002 reporting award was British American Tobacco (BAT) of South Africa. While BAT has made strides in accepting a tough regulatory environment and stakeholder consultation, it could be argued that its core business is fundamentally at odds with social responsibility.

Fair trade

The concept of fair trade is aimed at ensuring that small-scale producers in developing countries receive a reasonable share of the market price of the commodities or products they sell in developed countries or to visitors from developed countries. The notion of fair trade also encompasses the concept of fair labour practice, including the absence of child labour. In South Africa, the application of the concept has been limited, although there is increasing involvement of local communities in tourism and related projects. Some active fair trade projects have been established. For example, the World Conservation Union (IUCN) country office in South Africa is supporting a Fair Trade in Tourism programme that promotes small-scale tourism initiatives. The programme offers its trademark to partners who abide by its principles of 'fair shares, democracy, respect, reliability, transparency and sustainability'. Other initiatives also link to tourism-related projects, including accommodation, guiding and sales of arts and crafts. For example, Global Exchange sponsors the Power Station Project in Grahamstown in Eastern Cape province, which provides outlets for community craft projects. Similarly, the Just Exchange organisation in Cape Town is linked to the International Federation for Alternative Trade, and the Liberty Life Foundation is sponsoring South African craft groups that market their wares through the Internet.

Aside from local initiatives, several external organisations have promoted fair trade. In November 2001 the UK-based Body Shop plc began to establish a chain of outlets in South Africa through local franchisees New Clicks. Anita Roddick, founder of the firm, visited South Africa and connected with ethical trading groups. Body Shop operates 1 800 stores in 50 countries. Products worth about £5 million a year are bought from community traders throughout the world. Body Shop claims its goods are not tested on animals and that it does not exploit workers in Third World countries, although this has occasionally been contested. Roddick is said to be the only senior executive to have been tear-gassed along with the other anti-globalisation activists during the demonstrations in Seattle (Shevel 2001). The Ethical Trade Initiative (ETI), also based in the United Kingdom, is a consortium of trade unions, NGOs and corporations which has developed a code of conduct whereby corporations undertake to work with their suppliers to implement internationally-accepted workplace labour standards. During the late 1990s, the ETI conducted a pilot study on three cases, which included the South African wine industry. The industry had been notorious under apartheid for low wages, employer paternalism including tied housing, and part-payment of wages in the form of alcohol. The pilot studies aimed to provide strategies for implementing the ETI Base Code. One outcome of the pilot study was the formation of the Ethical Trade Forum, an alliance of local producers, trade unions, academics and NGOs which aimed to establish its own programme and capacity in ethical trade in agriculture in Western Cape province (Ethical Trade Initiative 2000). However, some independent researchers have warned that traditional patterns of gendered inequality underlying the poorest labour conditions in the wine industry are unlikely to be altered by codes of conduct alone (Barrientos, McClenaghan and Orton 2000: 156).

Corporate social investment and philanthropy

Because of the peculiar history of CSER programmes in South Africa, major figures in the field historically preferred to refer to a broad range of voluntary initiatives as CSI. A variety of different programmes are subsumed under this term.

Research on actual spending is sketchy, since many firms prefer not to make figures available. However, sporadic surveys conducted by different agencies give an indication of the level of spending, as well as spending priorities. A survey conducted in the early 1990s (Nel 1992) shows that the vast majority of CSI spending was directed at education programmes (Table 2.5).

Table 2.5: Average social investment contributions according to type of programme, 1990–91.

Programme	Millions of rand	% contribution
Education	554	66
Environmental conservation	59	7
Health	57	7
Welfare	51	6
General community projects	42	5
Small business development and job creation	30	4
Arts and culture	27	3
Housing	13	1
Other	8	1
Total	841	100

Source: Nel 1992: 28.

In 1998 the Centre for Development and Enterprise (CDE) conducted two surveys to ascertain levels of corporate social spending (Schlemmer et al. 1998). The first survey of large and prominent corporations achieved a response rate of 34 per cent (75 corporations). A second survey was conducted which randomly drew on 545 corporations of all sizes. The survey of large corporations found that about R580 million was spent on CSR programmes annually. An average of R7.7 million was spent by these large corporations in the 1997 financial year. Table 2.6 provides a proportional breakdown of spending priority.

Table 2.6: Percentage breakdown of CSI spending of selected companies, 1997–98.

Education and related	44
Small business development	15
Arts, music, drama	13
Welfare and benevolence	13
Sports development*	6
Policy/research grants to NGOs	5
Environment	4
Total	100

* Sports development is the social portion of a much larger amount spent on all forms of sports sponsorship. The development label indicates funds devoted to reversing racism in sport and ensuring that national teams become more representative of the population as a whole. This is effected through intensive sports training programmes for black youth (*Source*: Schlemmer et al. 1998).

The CDE researchers estimate that, when the large corporations which did not respond to their survey are included, the overall spending on CSI by these firms could be about R725 million per annum. The survey of smaller firms did not isolate sport sponsorships from CSI initiatives and tended to be less reliable. However, the researchers found that smaller firms spend proportionally more on local welfare and benevolent agencies than on the other categories listed in Table 2.6. Based on a very rough generalisation that includes sport sponsorships, the CDE researchers estimate the annual contribution of the corporate sector to CSI programmes at R4–5 billion annually. This accounts for roughly 0.26 per cent of turnover of large corporations, and 0.15 per cent of turnover of small and medium enterprises.

Education still seems to be the main beneficiary of social spending. Mokheti Moshoeshoe (Interview, 21 September 2001) argues that much of this spending goes to the tertiary education sector, since this qualifies for a tax rebate. There are indications that spending priorities are changing, being redirected specifically towards the areas of HIV / AIDS and crime (Interview, McDonald, 5 November 2001).

Some interviewees expressed the opinion that most of the philanthropic activities of the big foundations boiled down to public relations exercises (Interview, Angus, 5 November 2001; Interview,

McDonald, 5 November 2001). Colleen du Toit, director of SAGA, pointed out that her organisation believed that there should be a shift from philanthropy to a developmental focus:

> We're not about welfare or about handouts. So in the CSI arena we would always be working to ensure that the investments from corporates are used in a developmental way (Interview, Du Toit, 19 November 2001).

Multi-stakeholder partnerships

Partnerships across sectors can sometimes broaden the horizons of business, government and civil society decision makers and create new insights. For this to occur effectively, power should be diffused relatively evenly between the partners, and the factors of transparency and trust are crucial.

Mokhethi Moshoeshoe (Interview, 21 September 2001) argues that it is difficult to build multi-stakeholder partnerships in a country 'where sectors are completely divided'. According to him, there is a lack of commitment and trust. Colleen du Toit pointed out:

> I think all the players are realising that partnerships in theory present a very exciting opportunity. In practice they're quite difficult, as you have a whole set of conflicting interests. Those partners aren't just coming to the table because they're feeling philanthropic or developmental. And the partnerships also put a lot of strain on the recipients, because they have to be more accountable, and sometimes they do not have the resources or the skills to do that (Interview, Du Toit, 19 November 2001).

The transition to democracy in South Africa brought with it a new paradigm in environmental policy and decision making that emphasised inclusive and meaningful participation of stakeholders. The Consultative National Environmental Policy Process (CONNEPP) during the mid-1990s set a precedent in terms of participatory decision making, and has become a benchmark for subsequent environmental policy processes, including those covering coastal zone management, biodiversity, and integrated waste management and pollution control. CONNEPP laid the groundwork for representation within policy processes by sector. These created space for national and provincial government, labour, business and industry, environmental NGOs and community organisations. Missing from this list were local government and the research and consultancy communities, each of whom are important stakeholders.

Beyond the stakeholder forum model there has also been increasing emphasis on multi-stakeholder partnerships in resolving local environmental problems. An early example of this type of partnership is the sulphur dioxide committee in South Durban. The purpose of the committee is to manage a sulphur dioxide monitoring network within the heavily-polluted South Durban basin. The committee comprises the eight largest sulphur dioxide polluters as well as representatives from government and NGOs. The partnership is constituted as a section 21 non-profit company, and funding is based on the polluter-pays principle, whereby companies make financial contributions in proportion to site emissions. This is an example of a long-standing partnership that has resulted in the establishment of the only ongoing monitoring system within the industrial basin. However, the partnership is in the process of transition as the result of broader regional institutional changes and conflict within the committee regarding the expansion of its mandate to include the monitoring of other pollutants. The future role of the partnership is therefore uncertain.

However, the existing monitoring network is likely to be incorporated within a new multi-point air quality management plan for South Durban. This is a recent example of a multi-stakeholder partnership between government, industry and civil society to address the problem of air pollution in South Durban. The process is being driven by a steering committee consisting of representatives from local, provincial and national government, industry, labour, and the community. The plan centres on the key issues of air quality management, dirty fuels, health risk assessment, epidemiological research and vehicle emissions. The process has been hampered by lack of leadership and resources from government. However, with some commitment of donor funding from the Norwegian government the process appears to be gaining momentum.

Apart from environmentally-related multi-stakeholder partnerships and processes, it should be noted that there are similar initiatives focused on social and developmental issues. It is clear that these types of institutional arrangements are playing an increasing role in environmental governance in South Africa. However, a number of critical issues emerge. The key concern is the long-term sustainability of the initiatives. It appears that initial enthusiasm and commitment tends to dwindle over time, or gives way to conflicts and divergent agendas. Thus there appears to be a lack of clearly-defined time scales, roles and responsibilities of parties, and, importantly, mechanisms to deal with change and conflict resolution. These are of course procedural issues that, with appropriate attention, could – in theory – be resolved.

In his work at Lund University, Hanks (2002b) analysed a number of voluntary multi-stakeholder agreements that had emerged in Colombia, Mexico, Costa Rica, South Africa (referring to provisions in NEMA for co-operative agreements) and South East Asia. He argued that as command-and-control regulation becomes more difficult in a globalised world in which the state is relatively less powerful, voluntary co-operative arrangements would lead to co-regulation between the private sector and the state, which in developing countries would be increasingly more feasible in terms of cost and skills (Hanks 2002a). South Africa's experience with co-operative agreements has, however, shown that this proposal is premature, that there is an absence of trust, and that civil society sees the need for more strenuous state regulation and business compliance before there is voluntary co-operation. The implementation of the new air quality legislation will provide a test of this.

Socially responsible investment

Here we distinguish between the idea of CSI, a broad term which South African business often substitutes for CSER, and SRI which looks directly at financial investment mechanisms and attempts to order these more ethically.

The idea for SRI funds arose from the trade union movement during the 1980s. The emergent unions linked to COSATU established a Community Growth Fund, brainchild of the Labour Research Service in Cape Town. The Fund drew investor attention to those companies that recognised unions, paid living wages and engaged in socially responsible practices. Ironically, when the unions matured and developed their own investment arms, their investments did not always conform to those firms that had been selected as responsible by the Community Growth Fund. In general, investor response lagged behind the good intentions of the Fund.

Perhaps the biggest initiative aimed at drawing on SRI has been that of the JSE Securities Exchange. In an attempt to redirect investment toward what it called more sustainable areas of the economy, the JSE linked up with FTSE to create a Social Responsibility Index modelled on the UK's FTSE4Good Index, which it adapted to South African circumstances. Candidate listed firms joined the index on a voluntary basis and have been subjected to annual assessments by independent consultants employed by the JSE. The first assessment occurred in 2004, but eligibility and reporting criteria were tightened in 2005, with only a small amount of attrition. The JSE offers awards for the outstanding performers in three categories based on different levels of intensity of resource use.

Two financial firms, FutureGrowth and Sasfin Frankel Pollak Securities, have launched socially-responsible funds linked to the JSE's Social Responsibility Index (*Business Report*, 19 October 2005). FutureGrowth's fund had been set up some years earlier, but it decided to base itself on the JSE's criteria after the index became operational.

In 2002, the AICC issued a report that examined SRI in South Africa. The report is aimed at raising awareness around SRI, especially in the light of the potential role it can play in taking forward the country's transformation agenda. Their preliminary findings indicated a number of issues. First, SRI is confined to extending BEE and enhancing government infrastructure, the latter mainly in the form of bonds and the former in a variety of investments. Second, many people interviewed for AICC's study were cautious about investing in traditional South African SRI funds, largely because of poor returns. Many investors were adversely affected by the crash of BEE companies in the late 1990s. Third, while internationally SRI is driven by consumer demands for investment opportunities that conform to ethical requirements and provide financial returns, in South Africa SRI is driven from the top down, in the sense that the main incentives and guiding parameters are provided by government policies and advisory institutions, such as the King Committee. Lastly, SRI is a diffuse and undefined asset class, and for it to mature it requires definition and collaboration from all involved.

A key development would be the incorporation of social and environmental criteria in pension fund investments. Brian Angus from SEIFSA's steel industry pension fund pointed out that there were social criteria that had to be considered when pension investment decisions were made: 'Any project which comes forward, we will look at . . . provided that it doesn't involve us in an excessive risk or unacceptably low returns' (Interview, Angus, 5 November 2001).

Generally, however, SRI is still not very significant in South Africa, although the potential exists for it to become so. Gillian Hattingh from the NBI argued:

> I think that if we could make socially responsible investment more effective, it could be very powerful, because companies are getting something out. But I'm not sure if it's being demonstrated how effective it could be. So, if it could be shown how effective it could be and there were more opportunities for it, then I would think it could become very important – because there's a return. The FutureGrowth Fund has performed well. But again, people don't know about it. It's not well communicated (Interview, Hattingh, 20 September 2001).

Black economic empowerment

BEE is a crucial element of the changing South African business environment. In its broadest sense it entails the economic upliftment of the previously disadvantaged black population in both rural and urban environments. The Black Economic Empowerment Commission (BEE Com), established by government, considers key aspects or indicators of BEE to include improved access to land, increased levels of black equity participation on the JSE Securities Exchange, targeted public and private sector procurement, small business development, tertiary education, and public sector restructuring. The Commission recommended to government that targeted government intervention, including legislation and institutional support, was necessary (Black Economic Empowerment Commission 2001). Government is at present considering the promulgation of such legislation, which would compel companies to explain what they are doing to support BEE, while banks will have to disclose their lending and financing levels in black communities. The recommendations of the report were supported by one of the main black business associations, the National Federation of Chambers of Commerce (NAFCOC), but opposed by the (mainly white) South African Chambers of Business (SACOB)[5] (*Business Day* 28 November 2001).

Rather than being regarded as a broad programme of poverty alleviation, BEE has come to be seen primarily as the targeted support of black people taking on positions of management and ownership in the formal economy. In the context of CSER, BEE creates a significant tension. On the one hand, the social responsibility of companies requires them to support and implement BEE in the interests of nation building and addressing the injustices of the past. On the other hand, there is a widespread fear that BEE, as currently implemented, leads to the enrichment of a few at the expense of the poor majority and environmental quality. Unions, for instance, have frequently opposed specific BEE deals on the grounds that they would lead to downsizing, worse working conditions and a slackening of environmental controls. Suggested reasons for this include the use of BEE as an excuse to downsize operations or as a means to bypass government enforcement (as government is seen to be more lenient with BEE companies), as well as the often insecure financial position of emerging BEE companies. Indeed, CSER has become an important issue of debate within the emerging black business sector, as illustrated by the theme of a recent Black Management Forum conference: 'Can capitalism be socially responsible?' The evolving significance of BEE with respect to CSER deserves careful scrutiny (for further analysis of this issue, see Chapter 6 in this book).

Corporate responses to the HIV and AIDS pandemic
South Africa suffers from one of the highest rates of HIV infection on the continent, estimated at over 11.4 per cent of the population two years and older. Until very recently, the state health services were unwilling to provide comprehensive and affordable anti-retroviral (ARV) treatment to people with AIDS. Part of the blame for this lies in the political will of senior politicians such as the President and his Minister of Health, whose arguments on causality of AIDS, poverty, diet and the toxicity of ARVs were only overturned late in 2003. The efficacy of the TAC in pressing relentlessly in the courts and streets for cheap ARVs through the public health service have finally succeeded, and the provincial systems are developing plans for the release of these drugs.

The response of business has been 'slow, partial and erratic' and there is considerable denial of the problem (Innes, Dickinson and Henwood

2003: 3). A September 2002 study of 500 companies, undertaken by insurance giant SANLAM, indicated that 75 per cent of businesses had never undertaken an assessment of risks within their own workforce, and 60 per cent had not implemented a responsive strategy to manage the disease in the workplace; while 46 per cent of the respondents had no AIDS policy at all (Rusconi 2002). A key problem was the continuation of the system of migrant labour, in which workers live away from families in overcrowded single-sex hostels at the workplace. Sexual activity relies on prostitution and multiple partners are normal. Sexually transmitted diseases (STDs), including HIV, are passed on to rural partners on return from a labour contract. Therefore, the rapid spread of HIV in the region has been exacerbated by the migrant labour system. Fearful of a fall in productivity as infected workers become sicker, some businesses have calculated that HIV could contribute to a fall in profits of up to twenty per cent, as well as diminishing the skills base. With government failure to address the issue, business has had to act more vigorously. It has established the South African Business Coalition on HIV/AIDS (SABCOA) in an attempt to co-ordinate a response to the problem. Within NEDLAC, the statutory tripartite negotiating forum, a Code of Good Practice on Key Aspects of HIV/ AIDS and Employment was negotiated during 2000.

Big business has also recognised that the impact of HIV on productivity over time is likely to be devastating without the prolongation of life through ARVs. Failure to treat the virus would result in the loss of hundreds of thousands of experienced workers. This is nowhere more stark than in the mining industry, where infection rates have been high. In some cases, notably AngloGold, De Beers and Kumba Resources, the firms' AIDS policies have ensured that ARVs have been made available in-house to sero-positive workers. This is an acknowledgement that business has to take the lead on such an important social issue in view of government failure to do so. With the impact on the bottom line increasing, more companies are likely to follow suit. However, the migrant labour system, a central contributing factor to the spread of the disease, is not about to be abolished.

Main sectors and companies involved in corporate social and environmental responsibility

There are three main measurements with which to assess the significance of certain sectors or companies with respect to CSER. The first is the size or strategic importance of the sector or company in the national economy. Second, one must evaluate the risks involved in terms of health, safety and environment: for example, mining or chemical industries face inherent environmental risk challenges. Third, it is necessary to examine the profile of the sector or company's involvement in CSER initiatives. This may be discernible from the extent of certification in the sector, company involvement in voluntary initiatives, prizes won in reporting awards (such as KPMG's sustainability reporting awards), rankings in third party assessments (such as the *Financial Mail* list of top 100 companies) or perceptions among key stakeholders.

In an attempt to categorise the main players in CSR in South Africa, we have formulated a matrix that lists companies, according to sector, with respect to three criteria:

- Criterion A: whether they are members of the erstwhile BCSD, the NBI and SAGA in terms of social initiatives;
- Criterion B: those companies granted awards in KPMG's survey on sustainability reporting in South Africa; and
- Criterion C: the subjective perceptions of our interviewees when asked directly who they felt were the lead companies in CSR activities in South Africa.

We have further coded the matrix with respect to criteria drawn from the analysis of Philip Armstrong, a member of the King Committee on Corporate Governance. When asked how South African companies would respond to the revised King Report, he listed four categories:

- Category 1: publicly-owned companies such as Eskom and Telkom, which face particular circumstances as state enterprises since the profit incentive does not override social and environmental motivations as may be the case in private-sector companies. This category is shaded darkest in Table 2.7.
- Category 2: multinational corporations (MNCs) – particularly those South African companies that have recently listed on the London or New York stock exchanges, such as Anglo American plc,[6] SA Breweries and, most recently, Investec – face stringent reporting requirements and stakeholder demands, which have in many instances significantly impacted on their policies and management systems. This category is shaded second darkest in Table 2.7.

- Category 3: the top 40 companies on the JSE Securities Exchange do not face the same pressures as the MNCs, but they are beginning to be exposed to them by way of supply-chain relationships, export or government pressure. This category is shaded third darkest in Table 2.7.
- Category 4: the remaining companies have generally yet to consider issues related to CSER in a formal manner. This category is shaded lightest in Table 2.7.

It should be noted, however, that this categorisation is not always entirely precise, depending on the availability of specific information and the criteria used. One puzzle, for example, was deciding on the proportion of share ownership that might re-categorise a subsidiary of a multinational corporation as an MNC itself.

These categories undoubtedly contain a bias towards large sectors (for example, mining) and large companies (for example, Anglo American plc). In this respect, it is important to withstand the temptation to make generalisations about which companies are more responsible than others. Indeed, the picture of CSER in South Africa is characterised by diversity and contingency. So, for instance, while big international companies might experience a unique set of drivers for CSER and have certain management systems and funds available, a smaller company might have established a better relationship with its surrounding communities due to its manager's predisposition. A further complication results from multiple tiers of company management. For instance, perceptions of Anglo American plc's performance need to be disentangled in terms of corporate level, operational divisions and specific mines.

Table 2.7: List of companies in South Africa with a high corporate social and environmental responsibility profile.

Sector	Energy and chemical	Food, beverage and tobacco	Forestry and paper	Insurance and financial services	Manufacturing and automotive	Mining	Other
CRITERION A: Membership of business associations	Eskom Sasol; Dow-Sentrachem; Shell Engen	Coca-Cola; SABMiller;[a] Pioneer Foods; Tongaat-Hulett; SA Sugar Association	Mondi; Sappi		Daimler Chrysler; Nissan; Barloworld; Johnson Matthey	Anglo Platinum; Anglo American plc; Samancor;[b] Ingwe Coal[c] Iscor; Impala Platinum	Telkom PPC;[d] MTN; Pick 'n Pay Umgeni Water
CRITERION B: Recipients of awards in KPMG reporting survey	Eskom Sasol; AECI	SABMiller;[f] BAT-SA	Mondi; Kraft; Sappi	First Rand; Investec; ABSA; Old Mutual; African Bank; Standard Bank; Nedbank	Barloworld; Bell	Anglo American; Anglogold Ashanti; Anglo Platinum; De Beers;[g] BHP Billiton; Kumba Goldfields; Impala Platinum; Mittal Steel; Palabora[h]	CSIR;[e] Umgeni Water GlaxoSmithKline; PPC
CRITERION C: Perceptions of interviewees	Eskom	SABMiller	Sappi; Mondi	Old Mutual Liberty	BMW	Anglo American plc; De Beers; BHP Billiton; Richards Bay Minerals[i] Palabora	

a SABMiller was formerly South African Breweries, now also quoted on the London Stock Exchange.

b Samancor is 60 per cent owned by BHP Billiton and 40 per cent by Anglo American plc.

c Ingwe Coal is owned by BHP Billiton.

d Pretoria Portland Cement forms part of the Barloworld group.

e CSIR, now known by its acronym, is the commercialised successor of the parastatal Council for Scientific and Industrial Research.

f Although not originally South African, it assumed all the mining assets of Gencor Limited, a company which had been created in the 1950s to provide Afrikaners with a stake in the mining sector.

g De Beers is privately owned following recent restructuring, but is listed in this category because of its size and institutional affiliation to Anglo American plc.

h Palabora is 49 per cent owned by Rio Tinto.

i Richards Bay Minerals is jointly owned by Rio Tinto and BHP Billiton.

Sources: BCSD-SA, NBI and company webpages; South African Grantmakers' Association 2000; KPMG 2001; various interviews.

Factors impelling corporate accountability

What forces are being exerted on business to behave – or to make claims to be behaving – in a more socially responsible fashion? What is motivating the switch to triple-bottom-line accounting? The motivational forces are diverse and interlocking. For South Africa they have been rooted in a number of key historical processes, including responding to the peculiar conditions of the apartheid, transitional and democratic phases. Responses can broadly be ascribed to some of the following conditions in which business:

- compensated for state inaction in addressing social problems that impacted on business during and since apartheid
- feared sanctions, delistings, litigation and other potential impediments to its activities
- felt the need to conform to international norms or to local initiatives attempting to emulate global norms
- sought to establish, maintain or enhance its brand and marketing positions.

Below we examine some of the so-called drivers specific to South Africa.

Globalisation

As the South African economy continues to liberalise, globalisation affects certain strata, particularly exporting companies, companies with external investments, companies that have relocated offshore (the depatriation phenomenon), and companies whose supply chains extend beyond national borders. Companies in the last category tend to be sizeable, leading corporations. In most interviews respondents rated this factor as very significant.

There is an increase in the number of larger South African firms trying to position themselves as global players. This has played a role in their gradual shift from cosmetic, public-relations-type CSER towards making real changes in the integration of environmental and social issues into their core activities.

The depatriation of firms such as SABMiller, Anglo American, BHP Billiton, Dimension Data, Old Mutual and Liberty Life has created further pressures on them to increase their commitment to a triple-bottom-line approach. A significant influence here has been the desire of such firms to seek listings on the London or New York Stock Exchanges. Both the listings procedures and the exigencies of asset managers and other potential large-scale investors have required extensive preconditions based on fulfilment of CSER criteria.

A further external influence on the larger players has been increasing pressure to comply with codes of conduct. Some of these have been drafted elsewhere, but global pressures have also had a hand in the development of dedicated domestic codes and guidelines. Chief of these has been the King Committee, a local attempt sponsored by the Institute of Directors to meet global standards of corporate governance. As discussed above, the first King Report, issued in the mid-1990s, had a substantial impact, particularly on making management structures accountable to stakeholders. The second report, launched in March 2002, laid specific stress on triple-bottom-line accounting and reporting. Local applications of the ISO 14000 series, the Global Reporting Initiative guidelines, Global Compact, Responsible Care practices in the chemical industry, and various forms of international certification have all expanded in recent years.

Investment has played an important role in reintegrating South Africa into the world economy. Democratisation saw a re-entry of US, European, Japanese, Indian, Saudi Arabian and Malaysian capital. However, foreign investment has been slow to expand significantly since then, despite the attention given to Africa by the G8 countries and the initiatives of the Blair government in the United Kingdom. As a regional economy, South Africa has been able to expand its capital to the rest of the continent and further afield. In the domestic market, formerly protected industries – clothing and textiles, for example – now face intensive competition in a newly-liberalised environment. Re-integration and liberalisation measures inevitably mean that global influences have played an increasing role in local practices.

International organisations and treaties
Given South Africa's relative isolation during the apartheid years, the restoration of normal international relations and a sanctions-free trading and investment environment has made a large difference to corporate practice. Until 1994, South Africa was excluded from the UN system and hence played little role in shaping multilateral agreements. Since then, although some questions could be raised about the coherence of the country's post-apartheid foreign policy, South Africa has begun to play a much more significant international role.

For example, it is the key economy in the Southern African sub-region, and therefore has an influential place in sub-regional and regional organisations such as the Southern African Development Community (SADC) and the African Union (AU), successor to the Organisation of African Unity (OAU). President Mbeki has been a staunch advocate of an African renaissance and, together with other continental leaders, has crafted a New Partnership for Africa's Development (NEPAD). At a global level, South Africa has played an important leadership role in the United Nations Conference on Trade and Development; and has enjoyed a certain prominence in shaping nuclear non-proliferation, abolition of landmines and bio-safety regimes. It has also become a strong advocate of a controversial new post-Uruguay negotiations round within the World Trade Organisation (WTO). In negotiations of the Doha round within the WTO, it has sided with a group of middle-income, developing countries (the G20+) to challenge US, EU and Japanese agricultural subsidies.

While South Africa adheres to many of the International Labour Organisation (ILO) conventions endorsed by local trade unions, these have not generally been influential in guiding business practice. Similarly, the aid agencies and international financial institutions have not been able to place their stamp on local business. As a result, respondents have not generally ranked this driver as a significant factor.

However, there are some niche areas in which local industry has been taking multilateral environmental agreements quite seriously. South African agricultural and sugar lobbies regularly participate in WTO ministerial meetings. Eskom, the CAIA and the Chamber of Mines (representing key coal mining interests) have participated in the National Committee on Climate Change as well as in the national delegations to the Conferences of the Parties of the United Nations Framework Convention on Climate Change. These sectors have calculated the potential harm to their activities of global warming, especially the potential of the global climate-change regime to limit South African emissions in the long run. Currently South Africa is regarded as a non-Annex I country, which does not need to take action under the Kyoto Protocol to reduce its emissions. However, because of its coal endowments, South African industry is a major emitter, and it is likely that modifications of the climate-change regimes after 2012 will make more extensive demands for emission cuts. Meanwhile, South

Africa is engaging in reduction activities in conjunction with Annex I countries, and gaining capital and some technology in the process, as part of the Clean Development Mechanism agreed at Marrakesh in November 2001, although this process is not without its critics (Bond and Dada 2005).

Up to now, South Africa has privileged its small but increasingly important biotechnology industry, and is Africa's longest standing signatory of the UPOV 1991 Convention, which favours plant breeding corporations over recognition of community rights to biodiversity. This stance flies in the face of the spirit of the United Nations Convention on Biological Diversity as well as OAU model legislation on farmers' and communities' rights of access and benefit sharing (Ekpere 2000). As South Africa's biological resources become more commodified, the state's unrepentant bias in favour of biotechnology multinationals is likely to be challenged more rigorously by NGOs and community-based organisations who argue that livelihoods could be placed under stress by insensitive policy interventions.

The impact of the World Summit on Sustainable Development
The participation of the business sector in the WSSD, held in Johannesburg in August-September 2002, took a number of forms. First, local business in South Africa was included in the sponsorship of the Summit – Eskom, South Africa's largest polluter, was one of six major sponsors. Second, it was estimated that over 700 firms and over 50 company CEOs took part in the summit. Business associations, including the WBCSD, sponsored numerous side events. In addition to those dealing with the five key themes of the summit, such as water, business also addressed the issues of CSR and partnerships. One key meeting which highlighted CSR was the high-level *Lekgotla* (a SeSotho word for consultation) sponsored by the Johannesburg-based newspaper *Business Day*.

The United Nations looked to business to utilise the opportunities presented by the WSSD to forge new partnerships, seen as type II outcomes of the summit involving voluntary arrangements rather than the product of regulation. Over 200 such partnerships were made public by the UN in Johannesburg.

The final summit document, the Johannesburg Plan of Implementation (United Nations 2002), contained a number of important clauses on CSER:

III.18. Enhance corporate environmental and social responsibility and accountability. This would include actions at all levels to: (a) encourage industry to improve social and environmental performance through voluntary initiatives, including environmental management systems, codes of conduct, certification and public reporting on environmental and social issues, taking into account such initiatives as the International Organisation for Standardisation standards and Global Reporting Initiative guidelines on sustainability reporting, bearing in mind principle 11 of the Rio Declaration on Environment and Development; (b) encourage dialogue between enterprises and the communities in which they operate and other stakeholders; (c) encourage financial institutions to incorporate sustainable development considerations into their decision-making process; (d) develop workplace-based partnerships and programmes, including training and education programmes.

V. 49. Actively promote corporate responsibility and account-ability including, through the full development and effective implementation of intergovernmental agreements and measures, international initiatives and public-private partnerships and appropriate national regulations, and support continuous improvement in corporate practices in all countries.

XI. 140 (f). Promote corporate responsibility and account-ability and the exchange of best practice in the context of sustainable development, including, as appropriate, through multi-stakeholder dialogue, such as through the Commission on Sustainable Development, and other initiatives.

At first glance, it seems that these three clauses contain very different suggestions for the promotion of CSER. All include the concept of accountability, but none mention liability. Hamann, Acutt and Kapelus (2003: 32) log the debate over V. 49, indicating the contest over meaning. Those promoting a strong interpretation of accountability managed to modify the clause to take into account possible mandatory measures in the future. The other clauses continue to stress a path of voluntary initiatives and dialogue.

The accountability lobby was able to mobilise widely for a Corporate Accountability Week, which preceded the WSSD. The event presented the cases of a number of victims of corporate malpractice, including the Ogoni in Nigeria (Shell), the victims of asbestos mining (Cape plc), small farmers being squeezed by biotechnology companies (Monsanto), and the aftermath of Bhopal (Dow-Union Carbide). Hosted by a number of NGOs including South Africa's GroundWork, Corpwatch and Friends of the Earth International, the meeting called for the establishment of an International Convention on Corporate Accountability. Various corporations were selected for greenwash awards. Friends of the Earth teamed up with artists in Soweto to manufacture a forest of papier-mâché figures that were placed outside the Sandton Convention Centre to remind delegates of those who had suffered at the hands of global corporations.

Despite the rhetorical emphasis on dialogue, the interests of CSR practitioners and the accountability lobby at the WSSD were so much at odds with one another that there was scarcely space for any dialogue. The lobby continued to criticise the way in which business had assumed control of many aspects of the summit. Since the WSSD, the lobby's calls for an international convention have been more muted, but campaigns against specific corporations continue. The United Nations continues to sign up members to the Global Compact, but the pious sentiments of the Johannesburg Plan of Implementation have not really been etched in the global mind. Critics of the new UN turn towards business have accused the organisation of bluewash, or endorsing corporations' declaratory positions without acknowledging their record of environmental malpractice (corporate environmental public relations is referred to as greenwash and the term bluewash is derived from the blue colour of the UN flag).

For a number of South African corporations, the summit was a chance to see the global business lobbies and the UN system at close quarters. However, local companies were not experienced enough to contribute strongly to the workings of the summit. On the one hand, they were able to draw from the confidence of international business in relation to CSER and the United Nations, but on the other their own CSER association, BCSD-SA, failed to outlive the summit by more than a few months.

Peer pressure

Many respondents agreed that this was a very significant driver. The behaviour of lead companies is often very visible, with a high public profile, and the setting of standards has a demonstration effect on emergent companies in similar sectors. However, respondents were quick to point out the congruence between leaders and the larger corporations. Many of the smaller players do not generate the turnover or profit to be able to emulate the CSER budgets of the larger firms. Nevertheless, there are a number of ways in which the smaller operators are obliged to follow the leaders. Some parts of the larger firms' supply chains of products and services have increasingly been outsourced to smaller service providers. The outsourcing agreements often play a part in insisting that the providers adhere to specified social and environmental standards. Both SAGA and the NBI referred to the demonstration effect of innovators in CSER on rival firms in their sectors.

There were mixed responses to the role of industrial associations. Respondents from such associations saw their organisations as catalysts rather than drivers. The BCSD-SA, when it was still in existence, identified its role as one of circulating information about CSER activities and best practice, and this role has since been subsumed to some extent by the NBI. The Chamber of Mines felt that it could only facilitate the activities of members and not dictate policy to them. SAFCOC plays no part in shaping CSER practice among its 40 000 members. Within the chemical sector, CAIA is more interventionist, promoting the Responsible Care approach as widely as possible. In the tourism sector, the Tourism Business Council prides itself on being one voice for the industry, setting norms for CSER. Yet despite these diverse approaches, the industrial associations play a pivotal role in raising collective responses to certain social and environmental issues, whether for advocacy purposes or in shaping conditions for improved practices amongst their membership.

Civil society pressures

In some cases, respondents had reservations about the ability of civil society to influence CSER behaviour in firms. Such respondents viewed churches, NGOs, trade unions and community groups as being too weakly organised to constitute any strong lobby in this regard. SEIFSA felt that civil society had played a significant role during the apartheid period, but that this was no longer the case. However, those respondents who had prior experience of multi-stakeholder processes tended to stress the importance or potential importance of this driver. The IEF and the Chamber of Mines felt civil society had an important watchdog role. SAFCOC commented favourably on a steadily successful series of public interventions, citing the cases of St Lucia (keeping mining out of a wetland area) and Merriespruit (gaining compensation for a burst slimes dam that destroyed a local community). The test of success for multi-stakeholder co-regulation processes will be the extent to which civil society groups take an influential position.

Notwithstanding the above opinion, organisations like GroundWork have taken a significant lead in holding worst-offender polluting corporations to account. GroundWork's interventions include working with community-based organisations to challenge past and current business practice. Its research, networking and advocacy support includes working with:

- the South Durban Community Environmental Alliance – due to apartheid planning, the Merebank and Wentworth communities are surrounded by a group of refineries, pulp and paper mills, paint factories and other polluting industries, cumulatively causing health problems for the community; and
- communities that are close to petrochemical plants and oil refineries at places like Zamdela (a township outside Sasolburg), Embalenhle (close to Secunda, also a SASOL plant) and Table View (close to a Chevron oil refinery).

GroundWork's success to date includes pressurising a succession of environmental ministers to commit their efforts to resolving the crisis in South Durban and to emphasise community demands in introducing new air quality legislation.

In relation to the mining industry, NGOs like the Environmental Monitoring Group, based in Cape Town, have helped to set up a project in Witbank, Mpumalanga province, to monitor the impact of coal mining in the area – communities have suffered from land degradation and the consequences of long-standing underground coal fires which the authorities cannot stop. The Johannesburg-based Group for Environmental Monitoring (GEM) has worked with communities in the

Witwatersrand gold mining area. Such communities have their homes invaded by tailings dust from the mines, which settles in their lungs and creates respiratory problems. Working with the Legal Resources Centre, GEM and affected communities have effected some changes, including redress for victims, adoption by mining companies of new waste management regimes, and an increase in provincial regulatory and conflict management capacity. There is still much to be done and sometimes the struggle is to get mining companies to conform to their statutory commitments rather than voluntarily expand their social responsibility behaviour.

One of the most successful NGO initiatives has come from the TAC, which advocates free state provision of anti-retroviral medication for people with AIDS. In a country with over four million HIV-positive citizens, this is a lifeline. Until very recently, the government has failed to oblige, citing cost and inefficacy of ARVs as problems. The TAC has fought the pharmaceutical corporations in an effort to gain compulsory licensing of generic versions of ARVs. The pharmaceutical companies have responded by reducing prices significantly. The delivery systems for comprehensive ARV treatment are currently being explored in each province with a view to rolling out the treatment. This was a great victory for the TAC, and it retains its monitoring role.

Organised labour – although in the past critical of the Sullivan Principles because they allowed continued investment in apartheid – now recognises the reality of CSR programmes, but seeks to shape them. 'Unions have a choice to influence these programmes or leave them entirely in the hands of employers. What is needed is a national framework to guide specific initiatives at different levels', said Tony Ehrenreich, COSATU's Western Cape secretary (Interview, 2 May 2002). Labour has constantly stressed the need to go beyond piecemeal approaches, and has vigorously entered into NEDLAC negotiations and a series of sectoral summits with employers and government.

The labour movement entered the democratic era in alliance with the ruling ANC. It was granted a number of seats on the ANC parliamentary lists, and hence participated directly in legislative politics. In the first few years, the fruits of this were visible advantages: more balanced labour legislation, recognition of rights in the workplace, a drive toward employment equity, and the implementation of systematic vocational skills training. However, the terms of the alliance prevented the labour movement from expressing its increasing disquiet over creeping liberalisation and privatisation initiatives, with attendant casualisation and job losses. Union membership fell dramatically in the 1990s, causing an economic crisis in a movement which had prided itself on its self-financing ability. This has placed organised labour in a defensive posture, dedicated to survival and pared down to providing workers with essential services. The vision of broad social transformation which once imbued the movement has become less visible. Past transformative efforts have included setting up an infrastructure for unemployed mineworkers, advocating a basic income grant for all to offset poverty and unemployment, helping to build the co-operative movement, and backing greater support for micro-enterprises.

Unions had also lent their names to investment corporations, originally in an attempt to take advantage of BEE opportunities. These investment companies were set up in such a way that their boards excluded national office bearers, who could not be seen to be involved in any conflict of interest. Although this was an opportunity to direct investment to corporations with good employment, health, safety and environment records, these criteria were seldom used in making investment decisions. Unions gradually lost any executive control over these companies, and today there is little transparency or influence over their policies. Some of these companies have placed investments in privatised firms, going against the spirit of the position of their unions on these questions. 'When you have a union investment company buying into privatisation in its own sector, we have a problem', stated Neva Makgetla, a prominent economist in the Office of the President and formerly with COSATU (Interview, 15 April 2002).

Hence the shaping by labour of the CSER agenda has not been particularly successful. Labour has participated in co-operative efforts within NEDLAC and the EMCAs in the petrochemical industry, but without great results for workers or communities. There is still residual suspicion of voluntary initiatives. According to Pelelo Magane, safety, health and environmental (SHE) officer for chemical union CEPPWAWU:

> Some managers are seeing it piecemeal. They just take what they want. As a result those things give a very bad impression, and workers think that the scheme was just set in place in order

to trick them into working in a different manner, and actually reducing jobs (Interview, Magane, 27 April 2002).

Comprehensive debate on CSER has yet to happen within the labour movement. The perception remains that CSER is not socially transformative, is partly cosmetic and partly plugs gaps in the state's ability to deliver. For the union movement, the first prize is to get the state to take on more of the responsibility for social development. Ravi Naidoo, director of COSATU's economic think tank, the National Labour and Economic Development Institute (NALEDI), feels the role of unions is to push the state into a more serious regulatory role, with better worker and consumer protection. In his view CSER should not be about firms using up their spare change, but seeing actual investment in jobs and keeping money in the country (Interview, Naidoo, 26 April 2002).

Consumers, shareholders and investors

While consumer groups are not well organised in South Africa, their counterparts in the developed countries exercise considerable influence on CSER behaviour of local firms. This was particularly important during the early transition phase from apartheid, when firms needed to demonstrate a clear distance from the apartheid legacy. It applied in particular to firms with foreign partnerships, clients, employees or shareholders. This survey has also shown, in the section on free trade, the influence of ethical investment, particularly over employment practices in the wine and fruit growing areas of South Africa. The listing of South African firms on external bourses has also required high standards of CSER, and it has been important to convince the more significant asset managers of good faith in this regard.

Consumer groups allied with organic farmers, halal inspectors and environmental activists have succeeded in pressurising certain food chains (such as Woolworths, the South African equivalent of Marks & Spencer) to agree not to stock genetically modified (GM) foods. Such coalitions have also threatened to challenge the legality and constitutionality of South Africa's Genetically Modified Organisms Act. This may impact on the activities of Monsanto and other GM corporations in persuading groups of peasants to grow GM cotton and maize.

Government pressures

Business has played an increasingly important part in shaping state economic, social and environmental policy. This occurs in a number of ways. One key institution is the tripartite NEDLAC in which government, labour and industry debate certain bills that have come before Parliament in an effort to gain consensus and buy-in from each party in advance of the legislation. Discrete policy processes have moved from a multi-stakeholder model to one in which the state determines selective participation, usually privileging the business sector.

In general, social responsibility initiatives remain voluntary. However, in recent years there have been statutory initiatives on questions of employment equity (attempting to redress apartheid-era job reservation) and on corporate ownership (the Mining Charter and the Charter on Financial Services that attempt to address the question of entry of black capital into these sectors). Environmental responsibilities are often legislated, as the voluntary route is seldom effective. The study indicated that the most recent framework environmental legislation, the National Environmental Management Act (NEMA) (1998), is already undergoing substantial revision. Whereas the drafting of the original Act enjoyed wide public participation and transparency, further elaboration of environmental legislation has taken place behind closed doors with access limited to the business sector and with public consultation a post hoc, minimal affair.

In terms of water, forestry and mining legislation, the state is responding to popular pressures. The National Water Act (36 of 1998) cancels the historical rights to water of owners of riparian land and vests the allocation of water rights in newly formed catchment management authorities. This created some uneasiness among commercial farmers whose properties were formerly valued in terms of riparian access to water. The Act privileges allocations to the environment and to communities. Despite the shifts, the government entered into a partnership with Shell which agreed to publicise the provisions of the Act through every petrol station.

The restructuring of the forestry sector was also met with some misgivings on the part of the business sector because of rights accorded to community forestry. In terms of mining, proposed new legislation vests mineral rights in the state and that too has created unease within the larger mining corporations.

In relation to manufacturing industry, there has been one minor case in which the state has clashed with industry and unions. This is over the question of plastic bags, in the past provided free to shoppers by most supermarkets. While extremely useful for transporting goods, discarded bags created a litter problem around the country. The Environment Minister, Valli Moosa, persuaded the Cabinet to ban such bags, and to replace them with much sturdier but more expensive polymer bags. This decision caused an uproar among certain plastics firms and supermarket chains, who claimed that 17 000 jobs would be lost and substantial costs added to the shoppers' account due to the price of imported polymers. The matter went before NEDLAC and a voluntary agreement was made setting uniform prices for the new bags that would be charged to customers. The high price was an incentive to encourage reuse and part of the cost was intended to be diverted into a bag recycling project. However, supermarket companies began to lower the price soon after introduction and not all retailers held to the agreement.

Despite fairly comprehensive environmental legislation, the law is seldom implemented effectively due to weak regulatory capacity on the part of the state (Hanks 2002a). Some respondents claimed that environmental assessment procedures are slow and inhibit investments and developments from taking place efficiently. NGOs linked to community advocacy have often complained about the nature of environmental assessment in the mining industry, which is reviewed by the same department that promotes mining activities. The Chamber of Mines felt that rehabilitation trust funds swallowed a good deal of mining capital but that this was both an obligation and a responsibility. Communities affected by asbestos and mercury poisoning have recently sued the responsible companies, both British, through the courts of England and Wales (Ward 2001). Many in the business sector feel that, owing to regulatory weaknesses in the state sector, self-regulation by business would be preferable. The NBI felt that government was in a position to insist on better corporate practices by means of the state tendering system.

New biodiversity, marine and coastal management and air quality legislation requires the active regulatory involvement of an environmental inspectorate, nicknamed the Green Scorpions. Training of inspectors is going ahead and several hundred South African National

Parks officials have also been given credentials as inspectors. In 2003, the country's first environmental court, dedicated to the prosecution of marine poachers, was established at Hermanus in Western Cape province.

Market conditions and incentives

Liberalisation of markets has meant less state intervention and therefore fewer incentives. Sometimes membership of the WTO prevents incentives if these are in the form of subsidies or if they are seen to create non-tariff trade barriers. Export incentive schemes have steadily been abolished. However, a number of respondents felt that certain CSER activities should be tax deductible, in line with US practice. The IEF, SAGA and NBI advocated such tax incentives, while SEIFSA argued for the state to provide incentives for the introduction of cleaner technologies.

The Oppenheimer family, owners of large amounts of De Beers and Anglo American plc stock, recently launched a proposal that any corporate moves to increase black ownership of the economy should be encouraged through tax deductions. This proposal, named the Brenthurst Initiative after the family mansion in Johannesburg, was canvassed widely within the business sector.

The limitations of the domestic market impact on the economies of scale of certain environmentally-friendly activities. These include recycling, renewable energy and other pollution-reduction activities. It is likely that incentives for these activities may come from external agencies, such as the GEF (which has already sponsored the spread of micro-fluorescent light bulbs), the Clean Development Mechanism and other climate-change-related emission-reduction plans.

South African coal-fired electricity is the world's cheapest. The price is low partly because it does not take into account health and environmental costs. These are externalised and borne instead by other state sectors or by workers and communities. If South African electricity were properly costed, this would immediately raise consumer prices, affecting the poorest members of the community most harshly. It would also put an end to certain industries and local economies – for example, the beneficiation of imported bauxite, which happens on a large scale at Richard's Bay, a coal terminal and export harbour in northern KwaZulu-Natal. Hence there are built-in disincentives to charging the full costs of coal.

Privatisation of services has raised costs for South Africa's poor and unemployed. This has created considerable social tensions in communities where services have become less affordable. While the provision of services has expanded considerably since 1994, cut offs due to payment difficulties have eroded the claims about delivery. Water cut offs have seen an increase in the spread of cholera in rural KwaZulu-Natal and Limpopo provinces (Bond 2002). Tensions resulting from such privatisation have affected relations between COSATU and its allies in government. In communities a new social movement, led by the Anti-Privatisation Forum, has arisen to demand that basic services remain within the public domain and not be left to market forces.

Evaluating corporate social and environmental responsibility in South Africa

Evaluating the significance of CSER is an extremely difficult task. Often such an assessment is approached from an ideological position. Both conservative and radical approaches reject it outright. A conservative position, such as that of Milton Friedman, argues that corporations already provide employment and pay taxes. Any additional spending is tantamount to theft from shareholders. A radical position argues that such programmes merely serve to legitimise the position of corporations in society. The argument for CSER often draws on notions of enlightened self-interest, for example, in seeking to ensure a firm's social licence to operate.

Another important theme in the debate is whether corporations actually change their approach to business, or merely spend a certain amount of profit on responsibility programmes. Our research showed that despite good declaratory intentions by some CEOs or senior officials, firms are complex and hierarchical. Corporate culture may be at odds with implementing more visionary approaches. Often we found that CSER managers did not possess sufficient seniority to challenge other parts of their enterprise into shifting their practice. This means that CSER implementation is often patchy, partial and fragmented within firms.

One way of approaching such an evaluation would be to quantify the impact of CSER. This would imply a national exercise of triple-bottom-line accounting. However, to carry out such an exercise one would need access to data that is not available. Existing attempts to quantify this are useful, but rest on wild speculation (Schlemmer et al. 1998). A recent study on the state of social philanthropy, commissioned by the Centre for Civil Society at the University of KwaZulu-Natal, has abandoned any attempt to quantify CSER in South Africa (Everatt and Solanki 2005).

Our approach has been to give as broad as possible an overview of such programmes by contextualising them in political economy terms. We have argued that the industrial structure of apartheid had three significant characteristics. First, it contained some elements of import substitution industrialisation. This has significantly changed, with the average import tariffs on manufactured goods reduced from 14 per cent in 1994 to 5.6 per cent in 1998 (Hayter, Reinecke and Torres 1999: 76). The government's macroeconomic programme also implied a strict adherence to principles of fiscal discipline, as well as monetary liberalisation. The government's stance on industrial policy supports an export-oriented approach, and some manufacturing and beneficiation sectors succeeded in building up relatively successful export drives – notably the automobile manufacturing industry and the steel industry. The economy remains one that is essentially based on coal, with the mining industry still accounting for roughly 80 per cent of all waste. Economic liberalisation has not led to an inflow of foreign direct investment. Indeed, for some years (1996, 1998 and 1999) there was actually a net outflow of direct investment (Hirsch 2005, quoting from SA Reserve Bank *Quarterly Bulletin* figures).

Second, the state played a significant role in the economy by setting up major corporations – mostly in what became known as the minerals-energy complex. Most of these corporations have now been privatised (such as ISCOR – recently sold to Mittal Steel – and SASOL), and Eskom has been placed on a more commercial footing. Hence, there has been a retreat by the state in terms of ownership patterns, although this might have reached its limits for the present. Another significant change is the depatriation of major South African corporations, who have moved their primary listings out of the country, mostly to the London and New York stock exchanges.

Third, the apartheid labour market was segmented according to race, with different rules applying for white and black workers. These rules have now been reformed, but both the official and expanded unemployment rates have increased steadily since the early 1990s. Apart from this, the labour market has been re-segmented by the increase in various forms of precarious contracts of employment (Kenny and Webster 1999).

Apart from the these changes to the industrial structure, the impact of the AIDS pandemic is devastating, leading to a significant decrease in life expectancy. The poor are most affected by AIDS and other diseases. Less than twenty per cent of ultra-poor and poor households have access to electricity, flush toilets or piped water. The contours of disadvantage remain racially defined, with 60.7 per cent of Africans classified as poor in 1998, while only one per cent of whites were so classified (South Africa, Department of Social Development, National Population Unit 2000: 30, 43).

While South Africa has succeeded in dismantling the formal legislative framework of apartheid, many of its legacies remain. In this context, the relationship between business and the state, and between companies and communities, will continue to be strained. Several of our interviewees expressed concern that the state is not delivering on social and physical infrastructure. The NBI was set up as a response to this. Ironically, one of the NBI's key programmes facilitates the privatisation of municipal services as public-private partnerships. Business is also increasingly concerned about the cost of operating in South Africa – the South Africa Foundation is conducting a formal study on the impact of new legislation on business profitability.

Historically speaking, the involvement of the corporate sector did play a role in the political transition and the demise of apartheid, motivated primarily by enlightened self-interest. This is a complex issue involving the relationship between state and capital, and there are a variety of perspectives on the role of the private sector in political transition. Importantly, however, this history has played a significant role in informing the way South African companies engage with CSER issues. For instance, it is often argued that the experience of business in providing social investments during apartheid, and the general incentive to establish a more stable operating environment, imposes upon South African companies a more socially sensitive attitude than, say, in Europe, and a greater awareness of the need to contribute to poverty alleviation. However, it is apparent that such general statements are problematic. For instance, while some companies may have contributed to the political transition or to urban development, other companies, or even those same companies in different instances, may have contributed to the mistreatment of labour or the environment.

Our research found that there are, indeed, increased expectations of business in South Africa. Interestingly, these emerge as the result of a complex interplay between local South African dynamics – alluded to above – and the international discourse. There are also important pressures coming from government, especially related to BEE. Often, corporate voluntary initiatives are designed to pre-empt government regulations. Bill Lacey pointed out, 'I think business, and certainly SACOB, has always taken a self-regulatory approach, if there is such a thing. But we would like to think that there is such a thing as self-regulation being preferable to government regulation' (Interview, Lacey, 29 October 2001).

However, there are significant questions about whether these expectations and business initiatives result in actual improvements in performance. Our research has indicated the large gap between declarations and practice of large-scale corporations with regard to ecologically sustainable development. Despite limited philanthropy and strategic investment in community-based projects, most corporations still lack a full-scale commitment to the internalisation of environmental costs, significant waste reduction, remediation of past environmental damage and the substitution of clean for dirty technologies. There is an increasing tendency to move to a stronger defence of ecological modernisation[7] in the name of job creation and poverty reduction. There has been a marked shift from a discourse of commitment to the environment to one of commitment to broadly-defined sustainable development. This shift is subtly creating space for loosening compliance with environmental regulations and deferring the mainstreaming of environmental management within corporate line functions, and has led to a lukewarm attitude towards the implementation of voluntary commitments. The discourse often takes the form of refuge in a reactionary version of Third-Worldism, in which it is argued that the highest environmental standards are inapplicable in a developing country like South Africa on the grounds of affordability and lack of regulatory expertise.

The phenomenon of subcontracting to smaller firms proceeds apace, with fewer pressures on the smaller firms to conform to best international practice. Our study of mining showed how subcontracting to certain BEE firms diluted wages and led to unacceptable working conditions. This hiving off of responsibility is likely to weaken CSR efforts significantly, unless all parties recognise the need for standards to be maintained across the value chain.

But to go beyond the question of performance in production and distribution standards, to what extent are firms being held responsible for addressing the fundamental social issues that beset their stakeholders? For example, it has been noted in our study of the food and drink sector that little responsibility is taken by the industry to ensure food security within South Africa. This would entail taking an interest in supporting land restitution, small-scale agriculture, adequate extension for small farmers, low input and organic farming practices, affordable food prices, and the like. Apart from some limited forays into short-term hunger relief, the food and drink industry remains aloof from taking on such broader responsibilities.

Restoration of human rights and redress for past impoverishment are imperative, although there is much criticism of narrow BEE practices for simply creating a new elite and continuing to give it further ownership of the economy. The state has aligned with business in resisting the efforts of groups like Jubilee 2000 and Khulumani to litigate against big firms on behalf of victims of apartheid. It is also argued that the anodyne use of the term CSI, as opposed to CSER, indicates the repudiation by business of any historical responsibility for redress (Fig 2005).

The challenge, therefore, is to move beyond traditional definitions of CSI in South Africa towards an approach where the actual business of doing business is changed (Hamann and Kapelus 2001). As Colleen du Toit argues:

> A young woman who talked at this Black Management Forum conference said corporates get involved in CSI to improve their public image; and indeed, I'm sure some do, quite a lot. But I think . . . the more progressive corporations know that corporate citizenship, if you want to use the label, is not something that's going to be optional for much longer. Corporations want to stay around. The international moves towards socially accountable business practice – that wind is definitely blowing through South Africa (Interview, Du Toit, 19 November 2001).

At times we have touched on the concern that the increasing phenomena of deregulation, subcontracting and flexibilisation of labour markets in South Africa undercut labour standards and social and environmental performance. These trends have attained a significance that counters progress towards corporate responsibility. Can CSR deliver in South Africa? Can the private sector itself voluntarily redress some of the worst social inequality on the planet, even if only to secure a more amenable operating environment?

Our research has reviewed some of the steps being taken and some of the imperatives motivating such steps. Our view is that in a transforming society like that of South Africa, CSER is still too fragmented and partial to be effective on its own as a tool for transformation. Social and environmental transformation in South Africa cannot be delivered voluntarily in the marketplace. In the context of a developing country with such a high degree of social exclusion, it is still necessary to build compliance through enhancing the state's capacities in fiscal, regulatory and enforcement arenas.

While we encourage initiatives that business is taking to become more accountable, ethical and environmentally and socially responsive, the fundamentals of product stewardship need careful monitoring, particularly in the mining, energy and chemical sectors. There is still an enormous gap in compliance with legislation, as well as legislation which is too lenient – to polluters, for example. These conclusions fly in the face of verdicts by some commentators who report 'significant strides towards maturity in corporate citizenship practice' (Visser 2005). The distinction must be made between incremental progress on a narrow agenda and the requirement for a fundamental commitment to a sustainable and just society.

Social movements and civil society in general have a role to play in acting in the public interest by monitoring corporate malpractice. In South Africa there has been a small renaissance in civil society's capacity to act as watchdog and whistleblower. CSER measures need to become more meaningful and rigorous, less cosmetic and ideological, more dedicated to fundamental transformation, before South Africans can trust private-sector collaboration in the business of effecting greater social and environmental justice.

Notes

1. SAGA was founded as a membership organisation of philanthropic foundations and development agencies. Its stated mission is to 'provide professional development and technical assistance to independent, voluntary, and nonprofit organizations and individuals involved in funding the development of Southern Africa' (www. wingsweb.org/network/participants/SAGA.html).

2. For more details on voluntary initiatives in the chemicals sector, see chapter 4 in this book.

3. It should be noted, however, that South Africa represents a special case with respect to FSC certification in that the harvesting of natural-growth, indigenous trees is not permitted. This is one of the main issues covered by the FSC standard.

4. The cases of Thor Chemicals (mercury poisoning) and Cape plc (asbestos residues causing leukaemia, asbestosis and mesothelioma) are being pursued in Britain after the House of Lords ruled that litigants were eligible to do so. Unfortunately, the slowness of the asbestos case is such that many of the victims will die before seeing any positive outcome and before receiving any compensation.

5. Interestingly, NAFCOC and SACOB and other business organisations, after a conflict-ridden merger process, agreed in 2003 to form the Chamber of Commerce of South Africa (CHAMSA).

6. Anglo American plc is the former Anglo American Corporation of South Africa Ltd, now headquartered in London. It is the parent company of Anglogold Ashanti, Anglo Platinum and FirstRand, and has a strong relationship with De Beers.

7. Ecological modernisation theory argues that advanced industrial countries and enterprises have an interest in preventing environmental damage, mainly through market mechanisms.

References

Alperson, M. 1995. *Foundations for a New Democracy: Corporate Social Investment in South Africa*. Johannesburg: Ravan.

Anglo American Corporation of South Africa Ltd (AAC). [2000]. *Anglo American's Corporate Social Investment in South Africa*. Johannesburg: AAC.

Barrientos, S., S. McClenaghan and L. Orton. 2000. 'Ethical Trade and South African Deciduous Fruit Exports: Addressing Gender Sensitivity'. *European Journal of Development Research* 12 (1): 140–58.

Bell, T. 1995. 'Improving Manufacturing Performance in South Africa: A Contrary View'. *Transformation* 28: 1–34.

Black Economic Empowerment Commission. 2001. *BEECom Report*. Johannesburg: Skotaville.

Bond, P. 2002. *Unsustainable South Africa*. Pietermaritzburg: University of Natal Press.

Bond, P. and R. Dada (eds.). 2005. *Trouble in the Air: Global Warming and the Privatised Atmosphere*. Durban: Centre for Civil Society, University of KwaZulu-Natal.

Carroll, A.B. 1999. 'Corporate Social Responsibility: Evolution of a Definitional Construct'. *Business & Society* 38 (3): 268–95.

Cock, J. 1991. 'Going Green at the Grassroots: The Environment as a Political Issue'. In *Going Green: People, Politics and the Environment in South Africa,* edited by J. Cock and E. Koch. Cape Town: OUP.

Cock, J. and E. Koch (eds). 1991. *Going Green: People, Politics and the Environment in South Africa.* Cape Town: OUP.

De Beers Consolidated. 2000. *Safety, Health, and Environment Review 2000.* Kimberley: De Beers Consolidated.

Ekpere, J. (ed.). 2000. *African Model Law for the Protection of the Rights of Local Communities, Farmers and Breeders, and for the Regulation of Access to Biological Resources.* Lagos: OAU Science and Technology Office.

Ethical Trade Initiative (ETI). 2000. *Annual Report 1999/2000.* London: ETI.

Everatt, D. and G. Solanki. 2005. *A Nation of Givers: The State of Social Giving in South Africa.* Durban: Centre for Civil Society, University of KwaZulu-Natal.

Feldberg, M. 1972. 'Business Profits and Social Responsibility'. Cape Town: University of Cape Town (Inaugural Lecture as Professor of Business Administration, 15 June).

Fig, D. 2000. 'The Environment Cannot Toyitoyi: South Africa's Environmental Challenges'. *Oxford International Review* 10 (1): 2–12.

———. 2005. 'Manufacturing Amnesia: Corporate Social Responsibility in South Africa'. *International Affairs* 81 (3): 615–33.

Fine, B. and Z. Rustomjee. 1996. *The Political Economy of South Africa: From Minerals-Energy Complex to Industrialisation.* London: Hurst.

Hamann, R. 2001. 'Mining Companies' Role in Sustainable Development: The "Why" and "How" of Corporate Responsibility'. Paper presented at the Chamber of Mines Conference, Johannesburg, 25–28 September.

Hamann, R., N. Acutt and P. Kapelus. 2003. 'Responsibility vs. Accountability? Interpreting the World Summit on Sustainable Development for a Synthesis Model of Corporate Citizenship'. *Journal of Corporate Citizenship* 9: 20–36.

Hamann, R., L. Booth and T. O'Riordan. 2000. 'South African Environmental Policy on the Move'. *South African Geographical Journal* 82 (2):11–22.

Hamann, R. and P. Kapelus. 2001. 'The Business of Business is Changing'. *Mail & Guardian,* 26 October.

Hanks, J. 2002a. 'Promoting Corporate Environmental Responsibility: What Role for "Self-regulatory" and "Co-regulatory" Policy Instruments in South Africa?' In *The Greening of Business in Developing Countries: Rhetoric, Reality and Prospects,* edited by P. Utting. London: Zed Books.

———. 2002b. 'A Role for Negotiated Environmental Agreements in Developing Countries?' In *Voluntary Environmental Agreements: Process, Practice and Future Use,* edited by P. Ten Brink. Sheffield: Greenleaf.

Harvey, C. 2000. *Macroeconomic Policy and Trade Integration in Southern Africa.* Cape Town: Development Policy Research Unit, University of Cape Town.

Hayter, S., G. Reinecke and R. Torres. 1999. *Studies on the Social Dimensions of Globalisation: South Africa.* Geneva: International Labour Organisation.

Hirsch, A. 2005. *Season of Hope: Economic Reform under Mandela and Mbeki.* Pietermaritzburg: University of KwaZulu-Natal Press.

Innes, D., D. Dickinson and L. Henwood. 2003. 'Report of Business Responses to HIV/AIDS in South Africa's Top 25 Companies'. Unpublished report commissioned by UNAIDS and UNRISD.

Jenkins, R. 2001. *Corporate Codes of Conduct: Self-Regulation in a Global Economy.* Geneva: UNRISD (Technology, Business and Society Programme Paper, 2).

Joffe, A. et al. 1995. *Improving Manufacturing Performance in South Africa: Report of the Industrial Strategy Project.* Cape Town: University of Cape Town Press.

Joffe, A., J. Maller and E. Webster. 1995. 'South Africa's Industrialization: The Challenge facing Labour'. In *Industrialization and Labour Relations: Contemporary Research in Seven Countries,* edited by S. Frenkel and J. Harrod. Ithaca, New York: ILR.

Joffe, H. 1989. 'The Policy of South African Trade Unions towards Sanctions and Disinvestment'. In *Sanctions Against Apartheid,* edited by M. Orkin. Cape Town: David Philip.

Kenny, B. and A. Bezuidenhout. 1999. 'The Language of Flexibility and the Flexibility of Language: Post-Apartheid South African Labour Market Debates'. Paper presented at the Annual Congress of the Industrial Relations Association of South Africa, 4–5 October, Cape Town.

Kenny, B. and E. Webster. 1999. 'Eroding the Core: Flexibility and the Re-segmentation of the South African Labour Market'. *Critical Sociology* 24 (3): 216–43.

Khan, F. 1990. 'Involvement of the Masses in Environmental Politics'. *Veld and Flora* 76 (2): 36–8.

King Committee on Corporate Governance. 1994. *King Report on Corporate Governance for South Africa, 1994 (King I Report).* Johannesburg: Institute of Directors.

———. 2002. *King Report on Corporate Governance for South Africa, 2002 (King II Report).* Johannesburg: Institute of Directors.

KPMG. 2001. *KPMG Survey of Sustainability Reporting in South Africa, 2001.* Johannesburg: KPMG.

Laurence, P. 2000. 'Auditing Business's Contribution to the Poor'. *Financial Mail,* 22 September.

Lipton. M. 1986. *Capitalism and Apartheid: South Africa, 1910–1986.* Cape Town: David Philip.

Lukey, P. 1995. *Health before Profits: An Access Guide to Trade Unions and Environmental Justice in South Africa.* Scottsville: Environmental Justice Networking Forum.

Macroeconomic Research Group (MERG). 1993. *Making Democracy Work: A Framework for Macroeconomic Policy in South Africa.* Bellville: Centre for Development Studies.

Mangaliso, M.P. 1999. 'Disinvestment by Multinational Corporations'. In *How Sanctions Work: Lessons from South Africa,* edited by N.C. Crawford and A. Klotz. London: Macmillan.

Mann, M. 1992. 'The Rise of Corporate Social Responsibility in South Africa'. In *Profit and Power: Politics, Labour and Business in South Africa,* edited by D. Innes, M. Kentridge and H. Perold. Cape Town: OUP.

Mansson, P.-H. 2000. 'Anton Rupert: King of Luxury'. *Wine Spectator,* 29 February.

Nel, B. 1992. 'Social Investment: Recent Trends'. *People Dynamics* 10 (10): 26–8.

Ngobese, P. and J. Cock. 1997. 'Development and the Environment'. In *Managing Sustainable Development in South Africa,* edited by P. Fitzgerald, A. McLennan and B. Munslow. Cape Town: OUP.

O'Dowd, M. 1966. *The O'Dowd Thesis and the Triumph of Democratic Liberalism*. Sandton: Free Market Foundation.

Orkin, M. (ed.). 1989. *Sanctions against Apartheid*. Cape Town: David Philip.

Pinney, C. 2001. 'More Than Charity: Towards a New Agenda for Canadian Corporate Citizenship'. Paper presented at the 4th Annual Warwick Corporate Citizenship Unit Conference, 9–10 July, Coventry.

Reddy, P.S. and S. Moodley. 1991. 'Corporate Social Responsibilities and Housing in South Africa: The Role of the Employer'. *South African Journal of Labour Relations* 15 (2): 34–41.

Rusconi, R. 2002. *SANLAM Retirement Funds Survey (Poll of 500 South African Corporations)*. Johannesburg: SANLAM.

Saul, J. and C. Leys. 1999. 'Sub-Saharan Africa in Global Capitalism'. *Monthly Review* 51 (3): 13–30.

Schlemmer, L. et al. 1998. 'Corporate Business in a Wider Role: Brief Results of Two CDE Surveys on Resource Flows from Business to Society in South Africa'. Johannesburg: Centre for Development and Enterprise.

Schmidt, E. 1980. *Decoding Corporate Camouflage: US Business Support for Apartheid*. Washington DC: Institute for Policy Studies.

Shevel, A. 2001. 'Business Rebel [Anita Roddick] Deals Body-blow to Selfish Corporates'. *Sunday Times* (Johannesburg), 25 November.

South Africa, Department of Social Development (DSD), National Population Unit. 2000. *State of South Africa Population Report 2000*. Pretoria: DSD.

Southern Africa Foundation. 1996. *Growth for All: An Economic Strategy for South Africa*. Johannesburg: South Africa Foundation.

South African Grant-makers' Association (SAGA). 2000. *Annual Report*. Johannesburg: SAGA.

United Nations (UN). 2002. *Plan of Implementation of the World Summit on Sustainable Development*. New York: United Nations (Document A/CONF.199/20).

United Nations Development Programme (UNDP). 1999. *Globalisation with a Human Face: Human Development Report*. Geneva: UNDP.

Visser, W. 2005. 'Corporate Citizenship in South Africa: A Review of Progress since Democracy'. *Journal of Corporate Citizenship* 18: 29–33.

Ward, H. 2001. 'Towards a New Convention on Corporate Accountability? Some Lessons from the Thor Chemicals and Cape plc Cases'. *Yearbook of International Environmental Law* 12: 105–43.

Webster, E. 1988. 'Corporate Social Responsibility: A Sociological Perspective'. Paper presented to Conference on Corporate Social Responsibility: Perspectives and Practice, 2–3 March, Johannesburg,

Wolpe, H. 1972. 'Capitalism and Cheap Labour-power in South Africa: From Segregation to Apartheid'. *Economy & Society* 1 (4): 425–56.

World Commission on Environment and Development (WCED). 1987. *Our Common Future: Report of the Brundtland Commission*. Oxford: OUP.

Worldwide Fund for Nature-South Africa (WWF-SA). 2001. *Annual Review 2000*. Stellenbosch: WWF-SA.

Interviews

Ackerman, Wendy. Director, Ackerman Foundation and Pick 'n Pay, Cape Town, 5 May 2003. Interviewed by David Fig.

Angus, Brian. Executive Director, SEIFSA, Johannesburg, 5 November 2001. Interviewed by Andries Bezuidenhout and Fiona Keartland.

Baxter, Roger. Chief Economist, Chamber of Mines, Johannesburg, 12 March 2003. Interviewed by Ralph Hamann.

Biesenbach, Werda. Manager, Corporate Communications, Parmalat, Stellenbosch, 29 April 2003. Interviewed by David Fig and Rahmat Omar.

Budnik-Lees, Zoë. Executive Director, BCSD-SA, Johannesburg, 27 September 2001. Interviewed by David Fig.

Crow, David. Managing Director, BAT-SA, Stellenbosch, 29 April 2003. Interviewed by David Fig and Rahmat Omar.

De Cleene, Sean. Director, AICC, Johannesburg, 9 November 2001. Interviewed by Ralph Hamann.

De Hoop, Henk. Analyst, Barnard Jacobs Mellet, Johannesburg, 11 April 2003. Interviewed by Ralph Hamann.

Drotskie, Peggie. Director, Policy Department, SACOB, Johannesburg, 24 June 2003. Interviewed by David Fig.

Du Toit, Colleen. Executive Director, SAGA, Johannesburg, 19 November 2001. Interviewed by Andries Bezuidenhout.

Ehrenreich, Tony. Western Cape Regional Secretary, COSATU, Cape Town, 2 May 2002. Interviewed by Rahmat Omar and David Fig.

Gcili-Tshana, Eric. Secretary, Health and Safety, NUM, 29 October 2001. Interviewed by Ralph Hamann.

Groome, John. Sustainability Director, Anglo American plc, 7 January 2002. Interviewed telephonically by Ralph Hamann.

Hall, Ed. Corporate Affairs Director, Unilever, Durban, 9 May 2003. Interviewed by David Fig.

Hanks, Jonathan. Common Ground Consulting, Cape Town, 20 August 2001. Interviewed by Ralph Hamann and Andries Bezuidenhout.

Hattingh, Gillian. Director of Membership and Communication, NBI, Johannesburg, 20 September 2001. Interviewed by Andries Bezuidenhout.

Ireton, Karin. Sustainability Manager, Anglo American plc, Johannesburg, 21 September 2001 and 27 November 2002. Interviewed by Ralph Hamann.

Johnson, Clyde. Executive Director, Mining, Mvelaphanda Resources, Johannesburg, 24 October 2001. Interviewed by Ralph Hamann.

Joseph, Michael. Manager, Community Affairs, Anglo Platinum, Johannesburg, 21 September 2001. Interviewed by Ralph Hamann.

Keeton, Margie. Executive Director, Tshikululu Social Investments, which manages the CSI initiatives of a number of companies in the Anglo Group, Johannesburg, 7 November 2001. Interviewed by David Fig and Ralph Hamann.

Kilani, John. Environmental Adviser, Chamber of Mines, Johannesburg, 14 November 2001. Interviewed by David Fig and Ralph Hamann.

Lacey, Bill. Economics and Taxation Consultant, SAFCOC, Johannesburg, 29 October 2001. Interviewed by Andries Bezuidenhout and Fiona Keartland.

Linnell, Richard. BHP Billiton, Johannesburg, 19 October 2001. Interviewed by Ralph Hamann.

Lötter, Lorraine. Executive Director, CAIA, Johannesburg, 11 October 2000. Interviewed by David Fig.

Magane, Pelelo. Environment Officer, CEPPWAWU, Johannesburg, 27 April 2002. Interviewed by David Fig.

Main, Tom. Former Chief Executive, Chamber of Mines, member of the South African Council of the International Chamber of Commerce, and chair of the Working Group on Cross-Cutting Issues of the WSSD, 1 November 2001. Interviewed by David Fig and Fiona Keartland.

Makgetla, Neva. Head, Economic Policy, COSATU, Johannesburg, 15 April 2002. Interviewed by Andries Bezuidenhout.

Masemola, Katishi. Deputy Secretary General, FAWU, Johannesburg, 12 May 2003. Interviewed by David Fig.

McDonald, Michael. Head, Economic and Commercial Services, SEIFSA, 5 November 2001. Interviewed by Andries Bezuidenhout and Fiona Keartland.

Mills-Hackman, Joy. Development Manager, South African Sugar Association, Durban, 9 May 2003. Interviewed by David Fig.

Millson, Simon. Director, Corporate and Regulatory Affairs, BAT-SA, Stellenbosch, 29 April 2003. Interviewed by David Fig and Rahmat Omar.

Moshoeshoe, Mokhethi. Executive Director, AICC and former Director, SAGA, 21 September 2001. Interviewed by Andries Bezuidenhout.

Mpufane, Glen. Secretary, Environment Department, NUM, Johannesburg, 29 October 2001. Interviewed by Ralph Hamann.

Naidoo, Ravi. Director, NALEDI, 26 April 2002. Interviewed by Andries Bezuidenhout.

Newton-King, Nicky. Deputy CEO, JSE Securities Exchange, Johannesburg, 30 October 2002. Interviewed by Andries Bezuidenhout, David Fig, Ralph Hamann and Rahmat Omar.

Pressend, Michelle and Doctor Mthethwa, GEM, 9 November 2001. Interviewed by Ralph Hamann.

Reichardt, Markus. Manager, Environment, AngloGold, Johannesburg, 30 October 2001. Interviewed by Ralph Hamann.

Robinson, Heather. Manager, Corporate Affairs, Nestlé, Johannesburg, 27 June 2003. Interviewed by David Fig.

Rocha, Jacinto. Director, Mineral Rights, Department of Minerals and Energy, Pretoria, 22 October 2001. Interviewed by Ralph Hamann.

Steyn, Faiza. Manager, Corporate Affairs, Pioneer Foods, Paarl, 30 April 2003. Interviewed by David Fig and Rahmat Omar.

Taylor, Nick. Chief Executive, JET, 15 November 2001. Interviewed by Rahmat Omar.

Tselentis, Nick. Legal and Regulatory Manager, Consumer Goods Council of South Africa, Johannesburg, 26 August 2003. Interviewed by David Fig.

Van Rensburg, André. CEO, Premier Foods, Johannesburg, 18 July 2003. Interviewed by David Fig.

Vukuza-Linda, Nolitha. Corporate Relations Manager, SAB, Johannesburg, 23 April 2003. Interviewed by David Fig.

Watkinson, Eric. Food Industry Researcher, NALEDI, Johannesburg, 3 April 2003. Interviewed by David Fig.

3

The mining industry[1]

Ralph Hamann
Andries Bezuidenhout

Introduction

Concerns regarding the social impacts of corporate activity are especially
salient in the mining industry (Mining, Minerals and Sustainable
Development 2002). They pertain to macroeconomic effects (Auty and
Mikesell 1998), environmental issues (Warhurst and Noronha 2000) and
impacts on affected communities (Ali and Behrendt 2001; Banerjee 2001).
Mining is a special case because of its transitory nature and the social
and environmental impacts of mine closure (Warhurst and Noronha
2000). In South Africa, such concerns are aggravated by the implication
of mining companies in South Africa's tortuous history (Crush, Jeeves
and Yudelman 1991; Mining, Minerals and Sustainable Development in
Southern Africa 2002; Truth and Reconciliation Commission 2003), as
well as the industry's socio-economic significance (Segal 2000).

Indeed, an assessment of the role and impact of the mining
industry in South Africa is a complex exercise. On the one hand, the
mining industry has long been a crucial provider of employment and
revenue, and it has been an important base for the country's industrial
development. On the other hand, the industry's historical structure and
practices – especially the migrant labour system – are often blamed for
many of the country's social problems. Mining's environmental impact
has also had dire consequences for many communities.

In this context, it is interesting to note the prominent role of the
mining sector in the corporate social and environmental responsibility
(CSER) discourse – that is, the various narratives and practices related to

enhancing the role of business in society and sustainable development. This prominent role is played by the mining sector internationally, but particularly so in South Africa. This is because of the industry's dual role as both a significant contributor to socio-economic development and as the cause of direct and very visible social and environmental problems. This has led, among other things, to government attention. Hence, special measures are expected of mining companies. Furthermore, the particular character of mining may contribute to a special emphasis on CSER: 'Mines are location specific and it is a long-term game; you have to look at things with a much longer view than many other businesses do in South Africa' (Interview, Baxter, 12 March 2003).

The aim of this chapter is to assess the emergence and implications of this increasingly prominent CSER discourse in the South African mining industry. It encompasses a range of concepts, rhetoric and practices related to the social role of mining companies even where the label CSER itself is not mentioned. Special attention is given to the historical and socio-economic conditions that have given rise to prevalent interpretations of CSER, how these interpretations have been manifested in corporate policies and practices, and how their significance and impact is perceived by different groups.

Central to our understanding of CSER is the importance of considering who carries the cost of doing business. To illustrate, the migrant labour system developed for and by the South African mining industry led to significant social disruption and hardship in the rural areas from which the migrant workers were recruited. The subsistence economies of rural communities subsidised mining operations by supplementing the incomes of mineworkers (Wolpe 1972; Crush, Jeeves and Yudelman 1991). In other words, the social costs of mining were externalised by mining companies to rural communities in Southern Africa. Also, when mining areas are not rehabilitated, the environmental cost of doing business is externalised to the state, and, when the state does not take responsibility, to the communities who live in those areas.

A political economy approach views the processes that lead to the externalisation of the costs of doing business as the outcome of a dynamic process of interest bargaining between the industry, the state and representatives of other organised interests, such as trade unions and community organisations. Hence, this chapter is based primarily on interviews with representatives from mining companies, government departments, unions, non-governmental organisations (NGOs), investment companies and other relevant institutions. Further data were generated during numerous meetings and workshops, in a year-long media review (up to mid-2003), and from a variety of published and unpublished documents.

Historical and structural context

The mining sector has been a crucial force in South Africa's industrialisation and modernisation process, including state development (Yudelman 1984; Crush, Jeeves and Yudelman 1991; Fine and Rustomjee 1996). This predominant role was premised on South Africa's endowment with the world's largest reserves of a number of minerals, including high-value commodities such as gold, platinum and titanium.

Although mining contributed only about twelve per cent of South Africa's Gross Domestic Product (GDP) between 1950 and 1990 (Mining, Minerals and Sustainable Development in Southern Africa 2002: 16), the economy's dependence on the sector has been significant because of the role of large, diversified mining houses, the large workforce occupied on the mines, and the sector's important contribution to the country's exports. The mining houses emerged in the wake of the discovery of diamonds in the 1860s and of gold in the 1880s. Rather than just operators of mines, they were, broadly speaking, facilitators of mining, bringing together the acquisition of mining rights, operation and management, and, most crucially, the international finance required for the capital-intensive mining of the low-grade, deep gold deposits buried beneath the Witwatersrand.

In the early 1990s, the six mining houses that dominated the mining scene, and indeed much of the South African economy, were Anglo American (which included significant interests in De Beers), Anglovaal, Gencor (which was formed by the merger of General Mining and Union Corporation), Gold Fields, Johannesburg Consolidated Investments, and Rand Mines (Flynn 1992: 312; Segal 2000). The predominant position of Anglo American, in particular, deserves mention (Pallister, Stewart and Lepper 1987; Anglo American Corporation 1998: 3).

Pallister, Stewart and Lepper (1987: 7) note that 'The most striking aspect of the South African economy is the degree to which it is dominated by just a few large companies, with the state and the private sector jointly controlling strategic areas such as transport, freight, engineering and shipbuilding'. Yet the interaction between mining companies and the state was obviously not a simply harmonious one. From the early beginnings of the Witwatersrand gold fields, for instance, the emerging mining houses and their financiers, the so-called Randlords, had a strained relationship with Kruger's Transvaal government, with some historians crediting their role as a crucial catalyst of the Anglo-Boer war in 1899 (Lang 1986).

This difficult relationship continued into the apartheid era, with the primarily English-speaking mining magnates being a common target of National Party vitriol (Hocking 1973; Pallister, Stewart and Lepper 1987). Lipton (1985) concludes that, though mining companies played an important role in the apartheid system as employers of migrant labour, 'The interests of the economically dominant mining and urban capitalists were often overridden when they were in conflict with those of white labour or the bureaucracy or of economically weaker agricultural capital' (Lipton 1985: 370). In the context of what has become known as the race-class debate, Lipton's approach can be characterised as one that sees apartheid as essentially contradictory to the developmental impulses of capitalism. In contrast, the class position saw apartheid as functional to capitalism – hence the claim that apartheid was 'colonialism of a special type' (Wolpe 1972; Mamdani 1996). Similarly, Yudelman (1984) insists that the relationship between the early South African state and mining capital was deeply symbiotic, even though the official rhetoric was often one of conflict, and he argues that this symbiosis has been cemented ever since.

Indeed, most commentators agree that the mining houses' activities were inextricably linked with and in some instances heralded the colonial and subsequent apartheid policies of the state. A key aspect of this interrelationship was migrant labour, which was an important feature of the mining industry from the start, due to the need for cheap, unskilled labour for the mining of deep, low-grade ores.

> The grade of South African gold ore is poor. What makes mine controllers and investors rich is the huge quantity of ore deep beneath the thin South African soil, so that colossal capital investment brings forth the dividends as long as costs can be kept down . . . [hence] labour was divided racially between well-remunerated white supervisory workers and management and exceedingly low-paid, compounded, and indentured migrant black miners (Moodie with Ndatshe 1994: 44).

In order to ensure a sufficient supply of low-income workers, mining companies spearheaded core elements of the South African state's racist policies and these included the taxation of rural blacks for the purpose of forcing them into wage labour (Jones 1995: 16–17). By the 1920s, the mining companies had developed a rigorous system of recruitment of migrant mine workers from rural areas throughout Southern Africa, coupled with a military-inspired compound system to house workers on the mines (Turrell 1987; Crush, Jeeves and Yudelman 1991; Moodie with Ndatshe 1994).

In conjunction with state legislation, these practices established a 'system with structural features that remained largely intact for the next fifty years' (Mining, Minerals and Sustainable Development in Southern Africa 2002: 8). It provided cheap labour to the mines – no real increase in wages took place between 1897 and 1969 – and contributed to the steady impoverishment of rural areas (Crush, Jeeves and Yudelman 1991). The connection between the mining industry, migrant labour and worker exploitation was overt and widely acknowledged even before the formalisation of the apartheid system. Hence the Truth and Reconciliation Commission (TRC) concluded in its final report, 'The blueprint for "grand apartheid" was provided by the mines and was not an Afrikaner state innovation' (Truth and Reconciliation Commission 2003: 150). It found that mining companies 'benefited from the provision of a relatively cheap migratory labour force, which was brought into being by land expropriation, forced removals, apartheid pass laws and influx controls' (Truth and Reconciliation Commission 2003: 140). The TRC's findings gave much impetus to litigation against companies accused of having supported the apartheid system (see Box 3.1).

Box 3.1

Litigation against mining company operations in South Africa

The Truth and Reconciliation Commission's final report (2003) recommended that big business should pay reparations to apartheid victims. This was received with great concern by business, the business media and investment analysts. On the other hand, the TRC's findings provided substantial impetus to litigation in which many companies, including multinational companies based in countries other than South Africa, stood accused of having knowingly gained from or supported unjust apartheid policies, primarily as they related to labour laws. The Apartheid Claims Taskforce (ACT) and Jubilee 2000 South Africa initiated separate legal proceedings in the United States, arguing that the accused firms 'knowingly propped up the apartheid state and made huge profits by doing so' (a representative of the claimants, quoted in *Business Day* 13 November 2002: 2). However, most of these claims have since been denied by the courts.

The best-known litigation against the operations of mining companies in South Africa is the case in which about 7 500 South Africans with asbestos-related diseases sued UK-based company Cape plc before British courts. This set a vital precedent because the House of Lords decided against the applicability of the *forum non conveniens* rule, on the basis that 'in South Africa in all probability the claimants would not be able to obtain the professional representation and the expert evidence that would be essential to justice in the case' (Ward 2002: 8). In addition, British laws allowed the claimants substantially higher compensation rewards. The Cape plc claimants won a large out-of-court settlement in early 2002 (*The Times* 15 January 2002: 5), but the company failed to honour the settlement and pay its first instalment in mid-2002 due to the threat of insolvency.

Parallel to the Cape plc litigation, asbestosis sufferers sued Gencor in South Africa. Gencor had controlled a number of asbestos mines at one stage (Jones 1995). One implication of this case was that Gencor was prohibited from unbundling its 46 per cent share in Impala Platinum (which comprised Gencor's main worth) prior to the case being settled. Furthermore, Gencor was added as a co-defendant in the Cape plc case, partly because of Cape plc's apparent inability to honour its settlement. Eventually, an out-of-court agreement was reached in mid-2003, in which both Cape plc and Gencor were to pay a one-off contribution to a trust fund that would support the critically ill (*Business Day* 2 July 2003: 3; Spoor 2003).

While the mining houses dominated the industry with remarkable continuity for most of the twentieth century, significant restructuring took place in the sector from about the 1970s onwards (Segal 2000; Fedderke and Pirouz 2002). This included a shift from the hierarchical, military model of production on the mines towards a more managerial style. This shift was motivated by the rise of black unionism in the 1980s (the National Union of Mineworkers [NUM] embarked on its first legal strike in 1984), a rise in real wages, political and legislative changes, and the twenty-year slump in gold prices, which fundamentally threatened the viability of many gold mines and led to large-scale retrenchments with severe social consequences.

The second dimension of structural change was at the corporate level, targeting increased productivity and efficiency and motivated by the reintegration of South Africa into global capital markets in the early 1990s. The mining houses unbundled their various non-mining activities, such as banking, and established themselves as holding companies with direct ownership of subsidiary operating companies. Furthermore, there has been a trend towards a share listing on one of the primary global capital markets, most commonly London or New York. An important implication of these developments has been that an estimated 70 per cent of the equity of the top five South African mining companies is currently owned by foreign investors (Interview, Baxter, 12 March 2003), with the bulk of this administered by the London Stock Exchange.

The historical emergence of corporate social responsibility
With the increasing formalisation of racist policies following the Second World War, some prominent mining leaders were actively involved in opposing the most oppressive aspects of the apartheid state. For instance, as a Member of Parliament in the 1940s and 1950s, Ernest Oppenheimer (founding chairman of the Anglo American Corporation) was an early and important advocate of family accommodation for black workers, as opposed to single-sex compounds (Pallister, Stewart and Lepper 1987: 42). His son and successor, Harry, argued as United Party Member of Parliament during the 1950s and 1960s that blacks should be given residential rights in urban areas and that constitutional reform should lead to voting rights for those blacks who were 'sufficiently educated and sophisticated' (Pallister, Stewart and Lepper. 1987: 51; see also Hocking 1973).

This political engagement by some leaders in the mining industry can be seen as an expression of the desire to resist and ameliorate the most oppressive characteristics of the apartheid regime in order to guard against social and political unrest among the disenfranchised black majority, and hence ensure the maintenance of capitalist production, including the reliable supply of cheap labour on which the mines had come to rely. Harry Oppenheimer 'was demonstrating the dilemma that all South African businessmen face: the repression which has offered today's riches is also the force which is jeopardising its profit-making abilities and ultimately its survival in private hands' (Pallister, Stewart and Lepper 1987: 52–3).

Such concerns in the mining sector grew in connection with the realisation that the state was doing little to alleviate social underdevelopment, particularly in black townships, and that this entailed significant risk of social upheaval. Thus, following the Soweto uprising in 1976, mining companies were prominent participants in the Urban Foundation, which is described in more detail in Chapter 2. Towards the end of the apartheid regime, there was an increase in philanthropic initiatives by individual companies, by which grants and managerial structures were set up to facilitate development projects, primarily in education (Alperson 1995). These philanthropic initiatives became known as corporate social investment (CSI) and are still a prominent interpretation of CSER.

Corporate social and environmental responsibility as corporate social investment

For many mining company managers in South Africa, CSER is still interpreted as CSI or philanthropic initiative, with an emphasis on education and health projects either national or in communities surrounding mine sites. Indeed, mining companies have often been considered the most generous and professional in their CSI programmes compared to other sectors (Rockey 2001). The largest CSI spender in South Africa has consistently been Anglo American, although the profile of its CSI initiatives has changed with the political situation in South Africa:

> There's been something of a shift from our old position of 'doing good by stealth'. Such an approach was probably necessary during apartheid. Now we are definitely looking to integrate what we do into the name and persona of the company. We need to be widely understood as a responsible corporate citizen, participating in society in a manner over and above the bedrock of wealth creation. This is undoubtedly part of the process of

validating our licence to operate (Michael Spicer, Executive Vice-President of Corporate Affairs, quoted in Anglo American 2002a: 22).

The CSI budgets of Anglo American and its affiliates are managed by a dedicated non-profit company, whose director emphasises the historical and social context:

> I think apartheid South Africa was . . . a unique case that probably precipitated a unique response . . . Companies like Anglo American, particularly under the leadership of someone like Harry Oppenheimer, saw some of this possibility in a more imaginative and creative way. It was very much under his direction that the Chairman's Fund was moved from being something that sat in the secretary's office with the cheque book in the bottom drawer and once a month you make donations to welfare causes . . . into something that was actually seeking to develop relationships (Interview, Keeton, 7 November 2001).

Similarly, the director of BHP Billiton's CSI trust, Richard Linnell, argued, 'We are not just giving money or writing out cheques but we are part of the process [of development.' He also mentioned some of the incentive for such CSI efforts:

> We work on community involvement to have a conducive environment for business growth. Unless you have people who are living in a good environment and stable communities, surely your performance as a business will not improve because you will have people who are sick; you will have communities that might not be responsive to your growth needs, because you don't have kids going to school; you don't have people who will come to work for you (Interview, Linnell, 19 October 2001).

In this more recent conception of CSI, the broad development ambit of historical initiatives, premised on a concern for social stability on a national scale or in areas of particular need, has been augmented by a more targeted approach focusing on communities surrounding the mines. The key incentive in this respect is contributing to the 'social licence to operate', which refers most directly to a company's efforts at establishing legitimacy, with local communities being seen as important stakeholders who could disrupt the smooth functioning of the business.

For some, the emphasis on CSI entails an explicit reluctance to deal with the social impacts of core business, as argued by one mining company employee:

> By CSER, people think of philanthropy, of giving money to causes. It's not about how you make that money in the first place, how you get to that triple-bottom-line, or whatever you want to call it. CSER means you dish out stuff on the side, from the profits you've (hopefully) made at the end of the day . . . The mining industry, and I would argue business in general, makes that fundamental difference. They view this social investment, the giving part, as a means of achieving their social licence to operate. They do not accept, at least not in South Africa, that part of their social responsibility is to make that money in a good, responsible way (Interview, Reichardt, 30 October 2001).

One indication of this separation between CSI and corporate strategy is seen in the relative isolation of CSI managers from core decision making in the businesses: 'The vast majority of CSI departments are isolated from the power and resource bases of corporations' (Du Toit 2001: 7). Another mining company employee said:

> The view that CSER is primarily CSI is a result of how things were structured, in the sense that businesses thought that they needed to pay what some people referred to as 'blood money', but it never needed to be part of the business processes. So in order to operate they needed to do some charity work or CSI, but it has never been key to their own business strategy (Interview, Joseph, 21 September 2001).

Corporate social and environmental responsibility as corporate citizenship and sustainable development

A broader conception of CSER has been emerging in the South African discourse under a variety of terms. One of the most prominent ones has been corporate citizenship:

Corporate citizenship ... advocates that a company that behaves ethically and contributes and builds relationships with all stakeholders will improve its long-term growth prospects ... Corporate citizenship is more than just CSI. It includes a number of other elements, such as business ethics and good corporate governance, workplace health and safety, labour practices and environmental standards. CSI is a key part of a corporate citizenship programme, but it remains only one of the legs on which corporate citizenship stands (Rockey 2001: 109–10).

One of the first South African organisations to use and perpetuate the term has been the African Institute of Corporate Citizenship (AICC), which was established in 2001. One of the institute's founding directors highlighted the enlightened self-interest and context-specific dimensions implicit in the term corporate citizenship, with particular reference to South Africa:

Behaving as a good corporate citizen is not a new concept; it is the phrase 'corporate citizenship' that has recently gained popular usage. Like humans, business enterprises are viewed as members and an integral part of the societies within which they exist and operate ... They can only secure their licence to continue operating if they live up to the social expectations ... and South Africa has a unique set of citizenship customs that are not even properly established yet. Instead, they continue to evolve as our young democracy goes through its growing pains (Rockey 2001: 110–11).

The African Institute of Corporate Citizenship (2002: 34) argues that 'Corporate citizenship requires the wholesale integration of social and environmental performance imperatives throughout all aspects of an organisation's activities'. The need to internalise the costs of business has thus become a prominent element of the CSER discourse.

In mining, the primary moment for internalising costs of doing business has been in terms of safety, health and environment (SHE). The Minerals Act (50 of 1991) determined that licensing new mines would require the provision of an Environmental Management Programme

Report (EMPR) that detailed the measures to be taken to minimise environmental impacts, as recommended by an environmental impact assessment. Health and safety, being a crucial concern to the unions and to the new government after 1994, was subject to a prominent commission of inquiry (Commission of Inquiry into Safety and Health in the Mining Industry 1995) and significant requirements were legislated through the Mine Health and Safety Act (29 of 1996).

It is thus apparent that the primary driver for SHE-related issues was regulation. However, market-based motives also became much more prominent in the 1990s, and these will be discussed in more detail later. It is these market-based forces in particular that have led to differences between companies in the way in which CSER is represented and manifested in their policies and reporting and management structures. Hence, it is the largest companies in particular and those with significant exposure to international markets that led in terms of formalised SHE policies and reporting processes. This is especially apparent in the case of the large South African companies that moved their primary listings to London in the late 1990s. The move to one of the primary stock exchanges is widely seen to have created a strong impetus to establish CSER policies and enhance public reporting because of the more comprehensive corporate governance and risk management requirements of those stock exchanges and greater stakeholder expectations and activism in Northern countries. As argued by one SHE manager, 'Our move to London was critical. We became subject to the Turnbull corporate governance requirements,[2] which is why we do these comprehensive risk reports. They essentially require that there be a formal and transparent system of internal controls to identify management risks' (Interview, Anonymous).[3]

With respect to the role of UK-based investors, another company representative commented as follows:

> Once we were listed in London, the whole world was watching . . . the rules changed. It's mainly because of London City analysts: they are very intimidating and have an enormous amount of power . . . Good CSER gives the impression that you are a more secure investment in a risky environment – there are so many risks involved that if you can mitigate any of the fringe risks, or give the impression that you are mitigating fringe risks,

then you'll get a higher PE [price earnings ratio], and your price will go up (Interview, Anonymous).

Investor confidence, risk management and reputation assurance, and the attendant need to maintain good relationships with key stakeholders – including government – are thus commonly identified as important drivers of CSER. Whereas consumer pressure seems to be an important incentive for CSER in sectors such as oil (Boele, Fabig and Wheeler 2001) this seems less so in the mining sector, where it is difficult to establish a clear link between the mined product and the final consumable. Rather, the reliance of mines on large, long-term and place-bound investments makes amenable relationships with local communities particularly important. Furthermore, mining companies require licences from the state to mine and the significance of this will be considered in greater detail in connection with South Africa's new mining law.

The formalisation of SHE as a coherent set of issues to be managed, measured and reported on was first apparent in the two largest South African mining corporations, Anglo American and BHP Billiton, which moved their headquarters overseas in the late 1990s. These two companies were also the first in South Africa to publish separate public reports on SHE issues. It is apparent from such reports that SHE-related issues have been established with greater rigour and internal accountability than the traditional CSI measures. As noted by an Anglo American SHE manager in 2001, 'The formalised SHE system is very much in development, and has been in the last two years, with a focus on target setting, objective setting and reporting' (Interview, Stacey, 11 September 2001).

The emphasis on environmental issues with regard to internalising the externalities of mining operations evolved into the increasing use of sustainable development as the dominant term of reference pertaining to CSER. Though it had been given formal status in the 1996 Constitution (Act 108 of 1996), the concept of sustainable development became particularly prominent in the lead up to the World Summit on Sustainable Development (WSSD), which was held in Johannesburg in August and September 2002. Sustainable development, of course, is commonly characterised as encompassing economic, social and environmental dimensions, and through terms such as triple-bottom-line (Elkington 1997) it has become a framework for conceptualising CSER for South African companies.

Hence, for instance, Anglo American employed a Group Manager: Sustainable Development in mid-2001. Though some argued that this post was primarily a public relations exercise in the run-up to the WSSD, the incumbent, Karin Ireton (Interview, 27 November 2002), is adamant that she has been given a mandate for real change in the organisation: 'The fact that, in a time when jobs are being shed, the company has created a new post with significant resources and an ability to access the executives is remarkable'. Ireton characterised her role as follows: 'I am a catalyst, facilitator, to help people understand that many different pieces form the jigsaw puzzle called sustainable development'.

While SHE is commonly seen as 'the foundation stone' (Interview, Ireton, 27 November 2002) for a company's sustainable development efforts, a more recent emphasis has been on the social aspects of sustainable development. As argued by Michael Spicer:

> Particularly for companies operating in developing countries, environmental impact studies must now be accompanied by community involvement studies. It's as unacceptable for companies, when they move on, to leave great holes in the earth and polluted rivers as it is to leave disrupted or unenriched communities (quoted in Anglo American 2002b: 3).

This emphasis on social issues in relation to sustainable development represents a crucial expansion of the traditional CSI agenda. Community participation in decision making and the prevention or mitigation of negative social impacts feature much more prominently in the sustainable development discourse than in the CSI discourse. Again, it was the largest mining companies that were the first to include issues such as community involvement and human rights in their narratives. Hence the BHP Billiton *2000 Health, Safety, Environment and Communities* report is the first to make explicit the company's intention to 'employ local people as far as possible and to provide further training to enhance skills' (BHP Billiton 2000: 24). Anglo American's SHE policy includes the ambition to 'promote good relationships with, and enhance capacities of, the local communities of which we are a part' (Anglo American 2000a). During 2002, Anglo American adopted community engagement guidelines with the expectation that 'by the end of 2003, over 90% of our significant managed operations will have Community Engagement plans in place' (Anglo American 2002b: 35). By 2004, however, this goal had not been reached.

With respect to community engagement, mining companies argue that the key challenge remains to find suitable indicators for the management and reporting of social performance. Indeed, the intrinsic difficulties and complexities related to company-community relations are an important reason why these issues have lagged behind the environmental ones in effective implementation: 'Tailings and environmental issues are probably well managed, because that's good engineering practice – they are much easier than the social, soft issues' (Interview, Linnell, 19 October 2001).

The sustainable development discourse is leading to an increasing consensus on the issues that companies need to address in terms of their social responsibilities. A content analysis of the so-called sustainability reports of JSE-listed mining companies illustrates the convergence, over the last five years, of a set of issues under the banner of sustainable development, motivated in particular by increasing adoption of the Global Reporting Initiative (GRI) guidelines (see Chapter 2):

- corporate governance, including company policy on sustainable development, board composition, management standards and reporting systems;
- economic issues, emphasising distribution of added value, also including in some reports aspects of black economic empowerment (BEE), such as transfer of assets and affirmative procurement;
- environmental issues, including environmental management systems and performance indicators; and
- social issues, comprising safety, occupational health, employment equity, community health, HIV/AIDS, CSI and product responsibility.

Though company reports are increasingly influenced by international discourse and practice, particularly the GRI guidelines, some issues are informed primarily by the South African context. These include the emphasis on HIV/AIDS (see Box 3.2) and issues related to BEE such as employment equity, affirmative procurement and equity transfer to previously disadvantaged South Africans. BEE will be discussed in more detail below.

Box 3.2
Mining company responses to HIV/AIDS

HIV/AIDS poses a severe threat to society and economy in South Africa. This threat is particularly acute in the mining sector, which is estimated to be the most affected component of the South African economy, with 27% of mine workers predicted to die of AIDS by 2005 (Mining, Minerals and Sustainable Development in Southern Africa 2001: 38, quoting *Business Day*. Mining companies feel the need to take comprehensive action to counteract the increase of HIV/AIDS prevalence and to mitigate its negative impact, in order to maintain a viable workforce and a conducive social and economic operating environment. At the same time, mining companies have been called upon to accept responsibility for having contributed to the creation of conditions that led to the intense spread of HIV/AIDS among mine workers.

The response of mining companies generally contains the twin strategies of prevention and treatment. The latter issue, however, is characterised by controversy, especially in connection with the supply of anti-retroviral drugs (ARVs). In 2004, Anglo American was praised for its commitment to investigate the feasibility of providing such drugs to workers and their families, particularly because of government inaction in this regard. However, the company has been more cautious recently, citing the extremely high costs of such treatment and the existence of many outstanding questions, such as whether or how far such treatment should extend beyond the workforce to other family members. However, treatment is not confined to ARVs. Many companies' policies include targeted wellness programmes to improve the living conditions and survival chances of HIV-infected workers and family members. Special emphasis is also placed on the prevention and effective treatment of other sexually transmitted diseases, as this radically diminishes the risk of HIV transmission.

Thus, prevention is the less controversial and more commonly emphasised component of mining companies' responses to the epidemic. Companies' prevention policies may include awareness-raising campaigns; socio-economic development support, including the provision of more family-friendly housing for workers; partnerships with community groups, NGOs and government; support for community health care; and scientific research (Anglo American 2000b; De Beers Corporation 2000). Most companies' policies do encompass many of the demands made by unions, including issues such as voluntary testing, improved nutrition, physical training, and peer education. However, the effectiveness of these broad policy statements at an operational level is still a matter of some debate.

In a study conducted for Save the Children, the AICC identified three primary challenges for mining companies in their battle against HIV/AIDS: (a) the provision of a comprehensive database and needs assessment with respect to HIV/AIDS in terms of its impact on the broader environment in which the company operates and in particular the company's labour force; (b) internal knowledge management within the company and coordination of the various activities that have a bearing on HIV/AIDS; and (c) an examination by companies of the broader nature of their business in terms of HIV/AIDS including a consideration of labour practices and migration, supply-chain management and support for small and medium enterprises in their policies on HIV/AIDS, and the establishment of a sector-wide, co-ordinated effort to combat the disease.

Indeed, many people identify the establishment of an industry-wide, co-ordinated programme as an important step forward. Early in 2002, after initial discussions between the National Union of Mineworkers and the Chamber of Mines, a tri-sector forum comprising representatives from industry, unions and government was convened by the Department of Minerals and Energy to facilitate the establishment of a co-ordinated strategy against HIV/AIDS.

It would seem that the HIV/AIDS problem represents an area of common interest among various stakeholders. However, such a convergence seems elusive. Several points pertaining to mining companies need to be considered in this respect. First, mining companies' responses to the epidemic are motivated by business interests – to protect their workforce and counteract the negative effect of HIV/AIDS as a barrier to investment. These incentives do not necessarily lead to conflict with other stakeholders, but they may bring about different priorities. Second, mining companies have yet to fully appreciate the significance of sensitive stakeholder engagement and communication with respect to HIV/AIDS. An illustrative example is provided by a firm in Swaziland, which publicised the prevalence of HIV among its workforce. Due to the stigma attached to the disease, the workforce was ostracised by its community and went on strike to force the company to retract its figures. The company eventually collapsed.

Close engagement of all stakeholders on the HIV/AIDS issue remains a crucial challenge for mining companies. According to Tracey Peterson of De Beers, mining companies are increasingly acknowledging the importance of involving the unions in policy making and implementation.

It is important to note, however, that some of the reasons for the lack of coordination between all stakeholders in the fight against the epidemic may lie in the conflicts generated between trade unions and the mining companies. Mining companies feel that the unions have used the HIV/AIDS issue as a platform to criticise business, without acknowledging the efforts made by companies. They perceive the unions' antagonism towards business as myopic, preventing constructive relationship building. Unions, on the other hand, are suspicious of the slow pace and lack of comprehensiveness of the mining companies' responses.

See also Chapter 7 in this book.

In recent years, this increasing consensus on CSER expectations has been furthered significantly by two important market-based initiatives, both of which have taken inspiration from international developments and sought to adapt and apply them to the South African context. The first is the publication in mid-2002 of the second *King Report on Corporate Governance for South Africa*, colloquially known as King II. It explicitly defines and motivates for concepts such as corporate citizenship and triple-bottom-line accounting, and it requires that 'every company should report at least annually on the nature and extent of its social, transformation [including black economic empowerment], ethical, safety, health, and environmental management policies and practices' (King Committee on Corporate Governance 2002: 35). Its direct endorsement of the GRI guidelines has contributed significantly to the prominence of the convergence of South African corporate sustainability reports, as noted above. The second development relates to the role of investors in pushing the CSER agenda. Whereas so-called socially responsible investment (SRI) is significant in North America and Europe, it is 'on the fringe of the mainstream investment market' in South Africa (African Institute of Corporate Citizenship 2002: 25). To provide more impetus to the South African SRI market, the JSE Securities Exchange developed a sustainability index at the end of 2003, based on the FTSE4Good, a similar index based at the London bourse adapted to South African circumstances (JSE Securities Exchange 2003). Mining companies have been among the most prominent members of the index.

Figure 3.1 illustrates the evolution of market-based drivers for a broader conception of CSER in South Africa in the decade following the transition to democracy. The important role of state policy will be considered in more detail below.

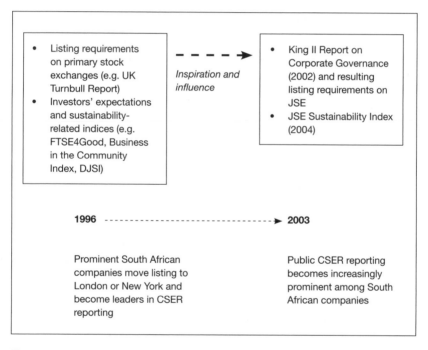

Figure 3.1:   **The evolution of market-based incentives for CSER and company responses in terms of CSER policies and reporting.**

The implementation gap: Managerial and critical perspectives
Notwithstanding the policies and reporting efforts considered above, many interviewees have insisted that there is still a significant gap between policy and practice. Mining company representatives noted that sustainable development policies have been a recent development for companies, and that they are experiencing a steep learning curve (Interview, Ireton, 27 November 2002). Hence company representatives commonly emphasise the technical and managerial elements of the implementation gap.

A key managerial challenge, in this view, is the link between corporate policies at the global level and the local operating environment:

> The challenge is to generate the necessary buy-in from all pertinent employees ... There is always the danger that corporate group-level directives are not translated to the operational level and that people on the ground just consider them as a pain, an add-on and an extra report that they have to produce (Interview, Hollesen, 27 March 2003).

A related problem identified by managers is the challenge of creating management systems that effectively co-ordinate the diverse and interrelated elements of sustainable development. 'Integration and co-ordination remain the biggest challenge, given that implementing the various sustainable development policies is too big for any one individual' (Interview, Ireton, 27 November 2002). The implementation of policy objectives is also hampered by turf wars between departments, insufficient co-ordination, multiple and overlapping reporting and performance management systems, and limited capacity – and the resulting reliance on external consultants.

Finally, company employees emphasise the inherent complexities and contradictions contained within the concept of sustainable development, which make the implementation of CSER policies difficult: 'For example, we have a mine ... that cannot pay for environmental standards but provides 6 000 jobs – what do you do, close it down? (Interview, Anonymous, 12 September 2001).

While the business perspective of the gap between corporate policies and operational practice relates primarily to managerial, technical issues which can and will be circumvented by more integrated policy making and better management systems within the company, a more critical approach sees the implementation gap in terms of underlying business motivations. First, it is pointed out that only a few companies actually publish corporate policies and reports though there has been a significant increase in public CSER reporting in the last two years. Second, the concern is that corporate reports are mainly public relations material, with little bearing on operational performance and without credible verification procedures. This greenwash perspective is also held by mining company employees:

> What are we talking about: intellectual discourse and nice little glossies, or are we talking reality on the ground? The discourse, the glossies, the statements, the public speeches – great! – You'll see South African business being among the more progressive, definitely among the developing countries, if not the world. But the reality isn't there . . . [Companies] develop a clear and I would argue conscious – in the case of many companies – split between what you do and what you say (Interview, Reichardt, 30 October 2001).

Similarly, activists refer to company sustainability reports as mainly tokenism. They argue that companies pay little heed to the environmental and social rights of local communities, particularly if they are poor, black and out of the public's attention. They also emphasise the crucial role of state regulation in forcing companies to comply with minimum social and environmental standards (Interview, Pressend and Mthethwa, 9 November 2001).

The role of the state and black economic empowerment

The preceding analysis emphasised business interpretations of CSER in terms of voluntary efforts conducted in response to market-based or contract-based incentives such as stock exchange listing requirements, reputation and the social licence to operate. This corresponds to definitions of CSER that explicitly exclude legislative requirements (McWilliams and Siegel 2001; Moon 2002; Waddock 2003). However, an alternative conception argues that voluntary initiatives cannot be relied upon; and that there is a need for measures that support corporate accountability, with particular emphasis on state regulation.

There are various reasons why the role of state policy and legislation is crucial in any consideration of CSER, particularly in South Africa. First, there is a significant gap between state policy and its implementation or enforcement (Acutt 2003) and much of this has to do with government capacity and resources. Hence, while there are a number of important pieces of legislation that pertain broadly to CSER in the mining sector, as summarised in Table 3.1, the extent to which companies actually adhere to these requirements is often seen in terms of voluntary initiatives as much as state enforcement and sanction. 'Companies could be cutting corners due to government capacity constraints, but they're not – so it is an issue of both obligation and responsibility' (Interview, Kilani, 14 November 2001).

Table 3.1:   Selected national legislation of pertinence to CSER in the mining sector.

Legislation	Overview and pertinence to CSER
Mineral and Petroleum Resources Development Act (28 of 2002)	Vests all mining rights in the state and requires mining companies to re-apply for mining permits, with preference given to BEE companies. Companies need to demonstrate due diligence in social and environmental matters, and directors may be held liable for environmental damage.
Promotion of Access to Information Act (2 of 2000)	Promulgated to enforce the constitutional right of access to information that is pertinent to the Bill of Rights. It allows access to (almost) all information held by the state, as well as significant types of information held by private persons.
National Environmental Management Act (107 of 1998)	Promotes development that is socially, environmentally and economically sustainable, seeks environmental justice and equitable access to environmental resources, promotes public participation in environmental decision making, and provides for duty of care and remediation responsibilities.
National Water Act (36 of 1998)	Designates water as a national resource and requires water users to apply for licences from the state. There is a basic water right allocation and a natural reserve with stringent water pollution regulations, a key concern in mining.

Employment Equity Act (55 of 1998)	Seeks to eliminate unfair discrimination in the workplace and to implement affirmative action for designated groups: black people, women and people with disabilities.
Constitution of the Republic of South Africa Act (108 of 1996)	Contains the Bill of Rights, including the rights to equality, a clean and healthy environment, access to information, administrative justice, and others.
Mine Health and Safety Act (29 of 1996)	The first element of the government's efforts to transform the mining industry, it focuses on the need to reduce the number of fatalities and injuries in the industry. It provides for tripartite (labour, business, government) structures at all levels of the industry for the purpose of implementing and monitoring health and safety management systems.
Labour Relations Act (66 of 1995)	Promotes collective bargaining at workplace and sector level and employee participation in company decision making through workplace forums.
Minerals Act (50 of 1991)	Requires the creation and implementation of an EMPR prior to licensing. Also requires the establishment of an environmental rehabilitation trust fund.
Companies Act (61 of 1973) and Closed Corporations Act (69 of 1984)	Contain various provisions regarding company registration and conduct, including the potential for lifting the corporate veil and adjudicating personal liability for directors (particularly section 424 of the Companies Act) though this has been criticised as being difficult to implement.

Furthermore, even if there were a threat of litigation in terms of South African legislation the penalties are often small. In the case of asbestosis sufferers suing Cape plc, for instance, South African occupational health legislation only allowed for negligible amounts of compensation, thereby stimulating the attempt to obtain legal recourse in the United Kingdom (see Box 3.1).

Finally, the role of the state goes beyond the enforcement of command-and-control regulations. In the first instance, it can use state licensing requirements and state procurement activity to affect corporate behaviour. It can also mandate company reporting on social or environmental issues, thereby creating greater market pressures for CSER (Aaronson and Reeves 2002; Fox 2004). In South Africa, the state has used or contemplates using these various measures most visibly with regard to its BEE programme. This programme has crucial pertinence to CSER.

BEE refers to the process intended to redress the lack of black participation and ownership in the South African economy resulting from apartheid. One of the most high-profile attempts by the state to promote BEE has been in the mining sector, given its prominent historical and economic role. A key element of these efforts was the promulgation of the Mineral and Petroleum Resources Development Act (28 of 2002), which was preceded by two years of intense, often acrimonious, interaction between the government and the established mining industry. Its implementation is still a matter of much debate and tension, and this has crucial implications for the industry.

The government's objective in this legislation was to implement state sovereignty over all mineral resources, representing a shift from the previous system, which allowed private ownership of mineral rights (Dale 1997). The Bill initially published in 2000 required existing rights holders to reapply for exploration or mining rights, and 'when considering the granting of a prospecting or mining right, preference must be given to historically disadvantaged persons' (South Africa 2000: 28). Not surprisingly, the established companies, represented by the Chamber of Mines, were unhappy with the Bill, particularly regarding 'security of tenure . . . and confusion over the issue of compensation' (*Mail & Guardian* 1 March 2001). By the time the revised Bill passed into law in October 2002, however, established industry representatives had publicly made peace with the new legislation: 'Industry concerns related not to this change in principle [regarding mining rights vested in the state], but rather to the nature of the transition' (Godsell 2002). This was to be specified by an empowerment charter for the industry, subject to a negotiated drafting process in a so-called tripartite sector partnership committee, which included representatives of labour and of established and emerging black mining companies.

However, when a draft of this charter prepared by government was leaked in July 2002, requiring that 51 per cent of the industry be controlled by black-owned companies within ten years, the markets reacted with a drastic sell-off of shares: the JSE resource index fell five per cent and the gold industries index shed almost twelve per cent. The market's response to the government's BEE proposals is best illustrated by a comparison of the share price of Anglo American, which has a relatively high stake in South Africa, with one of its main competitors, Rio Tinto, which has comparatively little: note the divergence of prices after July 2002 (Figure 3.2).

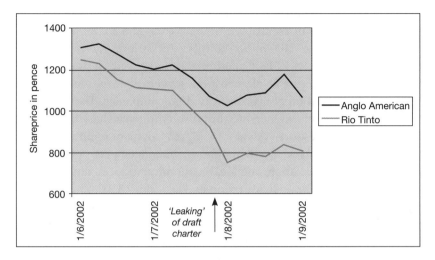

Sources: http://www.angloamerican.co.uk; http://www.riotinto.com.

Figure 3.2:   Share prices of Anglo American and Rio Tinto in mid-2002.

In a hasty damage-control effort, government issued a statement emphasising that the draft charter 'does not in any way represent official government policy' and that a multi-stakeholder task team would work towards the establishment of a final charter (*Business Report* 31 July 2002: 1). This led the Johannesburg-based *Sowetan* newspaper (16 August 2002: 11) to complain in its editorial, 'The mining houses still call the shots'.

However, it may be argued that the mining company power is only proximate; and the real constraint on the government's transformation agenda lies substantially with investors, who are prone to divest from companies perceived to be exposed to uncertainties and risk. Hence, shareholders are described as 'the most mobile of [the industry's] interest groups' able to 'destroy R25bn' within a day (*Business Day* 30 July 2002: 12). Hence also the repeated claims, by both industry and government, that 'transformation in the mining sector [is] necessary but should not undermine investor security or competitive returns' (*Business Day* 15 August 2002: 1).

The intense reaction, primarily by foreign investors, created a renewed commitment by government and the established mining companies to negotiate and search for compromises within the sector partnership committee. The outcome of these negotiations was the final charter published in October 2002.[4] It is significant in that, over and above providing a compromise on the industry's BEE equity targets (26 per cent ownership or control within ten years) and a commitment by industry to facilitate R100 billion to this effect, it provides for a much broader approach to BEE. Called the Broad-based Socio-economic Empowerment Charter, it allows for a scorecard to judge past and present transformation efforts of individual companies. These include not only black equity ownership, but also employee share ownership schemes, human resource development, employment equity (aspiring to 40 per cent black participation in management), preferential procurement, beneficiation, and local economic and social development in mining and labour-sending areas (see Box 3.3). This explicit broadening of the definition of BEE, coupled with negotiated methods for the state to measure and sanction company performance against these criteria, is a crucial development for the mining industry, as well as for the state's broader socio-economic transformation programme.

Box 3.3
Scorecard for the Broad-based Socio-economic Empowerment Charter for the South African Mining Industry

Human resource development
- Has the company offered every employee the opportunity to be functionally literate and numerate by the year 2005 and are employees being trained?
- Has the company implemented career paths for historically disadvantaged South African (HDSA) employees[5] including skills development plans?
- Has the company developed systems through which empowerment groups can be mentored?

Employment equity
- Has the company published its employment equity plan in accordance with the Employment Equity Act and reported on its annual progress in meeting that plan?
- Has the company established a plan to achieve a target for HDSA participation in management of 40 per cent within five years and is it implementing the plan?
- Has the company identified a talent pool and is it being fast tracked?

- Has the company established a plan to achieve the target for female participation in mining of ten per cent within five years and is it implementing the plan?

Migrant labour
- Has the company subscribed to government and industry agreements to ensure non-discrimination against foreign migrant labour?

Mine community and rural development
- Has the company co-operated in the formulation of integrated development plans as required in local government and planning legislation and is the company co-operating with government in the implementation of these plans for communities where mining takes place and for major labour-providing areas? Has there been effort on the side of the company to engage the local mine community and major labour-providing area communities? Companies will be required to cite a pattern of consultation, indicate money expenditures and show a plan.

Housing and living conditions
- For company-provided housing has the mine, in consultation with stakeholders, established measures for improving the standard of housing, including the upgrading of the hostels and their conversion to family units, and promoted home ownership options for mine employees? Companies will be required to indicate what they have done to improve housing and show that a plan to progress the issue over time is being implemented.
- For company-provided nutrition has the mine established measures for improving the nutrition of mine employees? Companies will be required to indicate what they have done to improve nutrition and show that a plan to progress the issue over time is being implemented.

Procurement
- Has the mining company given HDSAs preferred supplier status?
- Has the mining company identified the current level of procurement from HDSA companies in terms of capital goods, consumables and services?

- Has the mining company indicated a commitment to procurement from HDSA companies over a three to five-year time frame in terms of capital goods, and consumables and services, and to what extent has the commitment been implemented?

Ownership and joint ventures
- Has the mining company achieved HDSA participation in terms of ownership for equity or attributable units of production of 15 per cent in HDSA hands within five years and 26% in ten years?

Beneficiation
- Has the mining company identified its current level of beneficiation?
- Has the mining company established its base line level of beneficiation and indicated the extent that this will have to be grown in order to qualify for an offset of equity transfer requirements?

Reporting
- Has the company reported its progress towards achieving its commitments in its annual report?

Source: http://www.dme.gov.za/minerals/pdf/scorecard.pdf (accessed July 2003).

The final outcome of the negotiations may be interpreted, in part, as a convergence of CSER-related pressures on companies – many of which have an international origin – and government's BEE imperative. From a business perspective, the primary emphasis on the transfer of equity to black people could not easily be reconciled with the expectations that mining companies contribute to local economic development, community relations and environmental stewardship. Hence, the final charter and the scorecard may be seen – at least in theory – to represent the interests of a broader range of groups, premised on the incentive to broaden the initial emphasis on equity transfer as a primary element of BEE.

This connection between BEE and broader, international incentives is increasingly made in the public debate. For instance, the Minister of Minerals and Energy stated in 2003 that, though sustainable development or CSER was not an explicit topic of discussion during the negotiations surrounding the BEE scorecard, the BEE requirements should be considered crucial elements of sustainable development in South Africa (Mlambo-Ngcuka 2003). This perspective is shared by some mining company leaders who emphasise the link between BEE, sustainable development and long-term benefits to business in South Africa. AngloGold's chief executive argued:

> What the Charter is turning out to be is a test of the social licence. A business will only survive if it benefits all of its stakeholders over time – if people, the community, customers, employees and shareholders are left better off having an association with the company. I think it's a very good document and is going to make the South African industry more competitive, not less, and lead to greater wealth creation, not less. To draw on the gene pool of 100% of South Africa, not just white males, has got to be a good thing (Godsell, quoted in AngloGold 2002: 9).

Hence, even in the wake of severe acrimony, state imperatives are being adopted, at least in the rhetoric of some business leaders, as being in the enlightened self-interest of business. This dynamic and the extent and manner in which the new dispensation is affecting companies, even in these early stages, is considered below in the local case study.

The implications of externalising and subcontracting

Often industries respond to pressures to internalise the social and environmental costs of doing business by changing the way that labour is engaged and this usually takes the form of some kind of casualisation. In the South African mining industry, the subcontracting of a number of mining activities, including so-called core and non-core functions, has become more prevalent since the 1990s. Subcontracting here refers to a number of arrangements where a third party enters the employment relationship as intermediary between the mine and the workers. Often such intermediaries perform specialised functions, but in some cases they merely recruit and supply labour – that is, they act as labour broker. Companies often use this arrangement to prevent the direct employment of workers and the resulting responsibilities associated with a contract of employment, including minimum pay and benefits.

CSER reports are generally silent about issues such as subcontracting. Hence, we attempt to use the example of labour subcontracting to illustrate some of the contradictions caused by this form of externalisation. We draw on an analysis of historical texts as well as a more recent case study.

Historical manifestations

Subcontracting has taken place both on the surface and underground. On the surface, typical non-core functions such as catering, cleaning, security and maintenance of hostels have been subcontracted. Construction work on the surface has also been subcontracted. Evidence suggests that surface construction was already subcontracted at the turn of the twentieth century (Moroney 1978: 43). Traditionally, certain specialised underground work has also been subcontracted, for instance, the sinking of shafts and other forms of underground construction (Bezuidenhout and Kenny 1998).[6]

Before the mid-1920s, the subcontracting of core mining work occurred on a relatively widespread basis through the form of gang subcontracting. The contract system took on a specific racial character and built on the arrangement of underground mining work organised in teams (or gangs) of African workers supervised by white miners. In 1893, the editor of the *South African Mining Journal* wrote, 'The white miner is more a shift-boss than a miner proper, being required to take charge of gangs of natives, superintend work and get as much out of them as possible' (quoted in Callinicos 1980: 100). The white supervisor was usually assisted by a boss-boy in the supervision of work (Johnstone 1976: 159).[7] The contract system replicated this form of work organisation, but the white ganger had to take responsibility for supervising work and paying wages to the gang members, and even provided the explosives needed to perform the work. Remuneration was linked only to performance, without a basic salary, which carried the risks of non-payment and debt if targets were not achieved. This led to instability and mobility amongst the white workforce (Yudelman 1984: 105).

Despite pressure from the government, the system of using gangs of African workers supervised by white subcontractors did not disappear. By 1922, '[c]ontractors were a privileged and generally highly paid group of white miners whose earnings fluctuated with results achieved by "gangs" of black labourers they supervised' (Yudelman 1984: 192).

In an attempt to reduce the number of white mine workers during the profitability crisis in the gold mining industry in 1922, mine managers started to end contracts with these white gangers. This became a very important cause of the seminal 1922 strike (Johnstone 1976: 123, 159; Yudelman 1984: 105).

Contemporary resurgence: The East Rand Proprietary Mines case study

So successful were mining employers in phasing out subcontracting of core mining activities after 1922 that it seems only to have re-emerged in the 1990s. Certainly, there must have been instances where it was used on a limited scale, but the statistics provided by Standing, Sender and Weeks (1996: 302)[8] indicate that there is a new trend towards subcontracting of underground work. According to the latest reports, roughly fifteen per cent of all mineworkers, amounting to over 30 000 employees, are appointed on this basis (*Business Day* 10 October 2002). However, at some mines, such as the East Rand Proprietary Mines (ERPM), in the early 2000s nearly all employees were employed by contractors. Indeed, the case of ERPM, like the 1922 strike, illustrates the volatility that this form of externalisation can cause. Ironically, externalisation at ERPM was part of a process of BEE.

In 1999, Khumo Bathong Holdings was formed as a black empowerment company by Paseka Ncholo, a former Director of Public Services in the South African government. Khumo Bathong Holdings took over the loss-making ERPM after it had filed for bankruptcy. By the end of 2001, the mine employed about 4 500 people and produced 150 000 ounces of gold annually. The new mine management intended to increase output by half. In December 2001, the mine made its first profit after the acquisition (*Business Report* 16 October 2001, 4 March 2002). In February 2002, Khumo Bathong was in the news again when the company bought a three per cent stake in Durban Roodepoort Deep (DRD) for R68 million. The deal was financed by the Industrial Development Corporation. In March, Ncholo was appointed as a non-executive director on the board of DRD (*Business Report* 14 February 2002). Also in March, the company announced that it was negotiating a profit-sharing scheme with employees: 'We are asking our employees to take joint ownership of the mine by growing the mine's production through productivity levels at the stope face', Ncholo announced to the media. All profits made above a certain target would be split between the mine's shareholders, management and the mineworkers. At that time, venture capitalist Claus Daun owned 70 per cent of the shares, with Khumo Bathong owning the rest (*Business Report* 4 March 2002).

On the surface it looked as though the ERPM story was a successful tale of black economic empowerment in the making. However, by April 2001 the National Union of Mineworkers (NUM) was protesting against the hiring of employees at the mine by a labour broker. Protesters gathered to hand over a memorandum to Khumo Bathong. The union felt that these workers were paid much less than the industry average. Indeed, some workers allegedly received salaries as low as R700 a month. The union also alleged that the labour brokers sometimes took a cut of half the daily wages of some workers. A union spokesperson said at the time:

> In our view, if Khumo Bathong is concerned and interested in the welfare and prosperity of ordinary black mineworkers, it would desist from using this contractor who continues to brutalise workers . . . It is a known fact that contractors take short cuts in the rush for profit . . . The union will continue engaging the company on this matter and will not stop until the brutalising contractor is out, who in our view is given licence by management to perpetuate atrocities (*Business Day* 11 April 2002, 10 October 2003).

In August 2002 contracts at the mine were in the news again when it was reported that Ncholo had stepped down as chairman and director of ERPM after Daun had initiated a forensic audit into the mine's 'relationship with contractors and suppliers'. The audit focused on reported 'irregular payment practices and monthly payments to a senior manager by a supplier'. Three senior managers were suspended pending the outcome of further investigations. During this time, Ncholo entered into negotiations with Daun to buy out his 70 per cent of ERPM (*Business Report* 21 August 2002). Subsequently, DRD acquired ERPM with Khumo Bathong as a joint venture (*Business Report* 10 September 2002).

However, days before the takeover deal was sealed, Ncholo threatened to dismiss the mine's entire workforce of 4 000 employees for taking part in a two-day anti-privatisation strike. According to the NUM, the strike was extended to ERPM because employees 'were being underpaid by the labour broker contracted to the mine'. The labour contractor involved, Circle Labour and Accommodation, was warned by mine management that the workers would be fired if they failed to return to work. Technically, this could be done by cancelling the contract between the mine and the labour broker. A statement released by management read, 'A consequence of the termination of the contract would be that Circle must immediately remove its workers from ERPM's property' (*Business Report* 6 October 2002).

After losing five days of production, management acted on this ultimatum and terminated its contract with Circle. Management enforced a lockout and two former employees were killed and fourteen injured when striking workers were reportedly prevented by security personnel from 'vandalising the 109-year-old Boksburg mine'. The NUM threatened to 'finger other mines using labour brokers if the situation at ERPM was not resolved'. After the mass dismissal, the company immediately started to hire employees who had formerly been engaged indirectly as contract workers. According to reports, '2 800 employees would get their jobs back' (*Business Report* 8 October 2002; *Sunday Times* 13 October 2002). Ncholo said, 'We intend to double the pay of our lowest paid worker from R700, bringing our salaries in line with that of the industry' (*Business Report* 10 October 2002).

Following this incident, the government became involved by appointing the Commission for Conciliation, Mediation and Arbitration (CCMA) to ensure that the employment contracts and conditions of those workers appointed by the company complied with national legislation and minimum standards. Membathisi Mdladlana, Minister of Labour, reportedly 'expressed concern that some mine officials were using labour brokers to avoid paying the minimum wage agreed to by the Chamber of Mines'. A spokesperson for the Department of Labour said that the Ministry had found that wages paid to workers by the labour broker involved were 'well below the market norm and workers had accepted these out of desperation'. The human resources manager of Circle Labour responded, 'We supply the labour and the mine manages it. We therefore do not decide on wages' (*Business Report* 18 October 2002).

Indeed, the introduction of a third party into the employment relationship brings forth many uncertainties and legal loopholes in terms of company responsibilities. In the mining industry, labour contractors are often not only labour brokers, but they also have to provide accommodation for employees. This process and its social consequences are very difficult to regulate. Contractors are also notoriously difficult to monitor in terms of their compliance with health and safety regulations. For example, mineworkers often claim that contractors are sent in to mine areas that other employees deem unsafe (Bezuidenhout and Kenny 1998).

The language of corporate social and environmental responsibility, as well as BEE, often clouds processes of externalisation that go against all the principles of triple-bottom-line accounting and the internalisation of principles of sustainability into business practice. Like the unrelenting sourcing of migrant workers who still live in single-sex hostels, the growing trend of labour subcontracting in the mining industry externalises the cost of social reproduction to workers in precarious employment relationships.

Case study of platinum and chrome mining in the Rustenburg area

The so-called Bushveld Complex stretches across North West and Limpopo provinces and contains the world's largest reserves of platinum group metals as well as other resources, including chrome. The case study area is the mining region surrounding the town of Rustenburg, where platinum mining first commenced in the late 1920s (see Figure 3.3). It includes large mines owned by Anglo Platinum, Impala and Lonmin (the largest platinum companies in the world), as well as a smaller mine owned by Aquarius Platinum. In addition, the area contains the chrome mines of Samancor (a subsidiary of BHP Billiton) and Xstrata. In total, these mines employ between 70 000 and 80 000 workers, though this number fluctuates depending on industry and mine cycles. The case study research reported in this section is based on interviews with representatives from all of the mining companies in the area, as well as with community groups, NGOs, traditional authorities, and local and provincial government. Some informants requested anonymity and therefore their personal details have been withheld.

In line with general trends in South Africa mentioned above, the case study companies traditionally understood their social responsibility in terms of ad hoc charitable donations to good causes, motivated by a

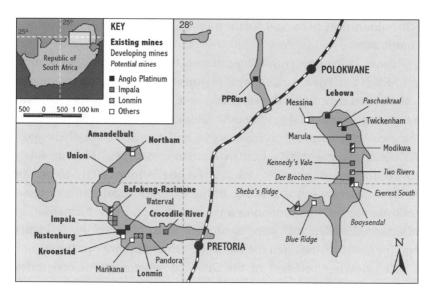

Source: Johnson Matthey 2003: 1.

Figure 3.3:   Map of South African platinum mining areas in the North-West province.

sense that it was the right thing to do. There was generally no integration between this form of CSI and company business plans. With the political changes in 1994, corporate donations became more formalised and strategic. CSI was increasingly motivated by the growing political imperative to be seen as a positive contributor to social development around the mines. One general manager remarked, 'Pre-1994, there was a different culture' (Interview, Pilkington, 25 June 2006). An interviewee from the local municipality argued, 'A lot of these things started when the ANC came to government; a lot of these companies wanted to become politically correct' (Interview, Modisakeng, 16 May 2003).

It is not easy to assess company CSI efforts in the area rigorously, as little structured information on these efforts is available and there have been few systematic evaluations. However, it is apparent that CSI represents significant investment in the area's social services. A rough estimate of CSI-related expenditure by companies in the Rustenburg region in 2002, based on company reports and interviewees' comments, would be about R20 million. Given that the Rustenburg local municipality's 2002 budget for capital projects was about

R30 million, the CSI budgets of the mining companies represent a major contribution.

However, there are crucial limitations to this traditional interpretation of CSER as CSI. For a start, a simple reason why CSI projects cannot make a significant dent in the development needs of the area is their general avoidance of informal settlements around the mines, which present the area with its most pressing social and infrastructure challenges. As noted by one mine's human resources manager, 'No one takes care of the squatter camps' (Interview, Botes, 4 June 2003). According to most interviewees, this is due to the uncertain legal status of these settlements with the companies unwilling to support the formalisation of informal settlements prior to an agreement between the residents and the landowners, often the Bafokeng Tribal Authority or the state.

The growing problem of the informal settlements demonstrates more fundamental limitations of the past CSER practices of companies. First, a key criticism of company CSI efforts is that they do not have any impact on their core business practices. This pertains to the growing informal settlements because reliance on migrant labour and large single-sex housing compounds are widely acknowledged to be a key cause for the growth of such informal settlements. In this respect, it is important to note that all case study companies have, since the mid-1990s, diminished their reliance on single-sex hostels. However, this reduction took place as part of a modernisation drive motivated by an emphasis on core competencies, whereby employee housing was considered expendable. Common reference is made to one chief executive's statement that the company was in the business of mining, not housing. The social implications of these changes did not feature prominently, much less were they part of a broader CSER strategy. One indication of this is that most company organisational structures dedicated to managing social issues around the mines have only recently considered housing issues as part of their brief. Hence, the manner in which the mines reduced their reliance on single-sex hostels has, in general terms, led to the further growth of informal settlements.

The second concern regarding past CSER activities pertains to inadequate co-ordination between companies and other stakeholders at the local level. Despite widespread acknowledgement that the social problems in the case study area could only be dealt with by means of improved co-ordination between all role-players, mining company

CSER efforts failed to support or even facilitate such co-ordination. Instead, companies sought to use their CSI initiatives to extract further competitive advantage. As noted by one company's CSI manager, 'Every company wants to be seen to be doing much more than the others are doing, so there is always that competition' (Interview, Bam, 16 April 2003).

Crucially, all case study companies have recently undergone significant changes with respect to the rhetoric and, potentially, the practice of CSER. To outside observers, the most prominent change has been the increase in public reporting on CSER-related issues in line with trends identified above. Hence a more holistic and integrated approach to CSER, often under the banner of sustainable development and including greater attention to social issues, is apparent in recent company reports.

Changes in corporate policies and reporting are also reflected in new organisational structures and budgets for CSER-related issues. The first significant organisational change pertinent to CSER was the emergence of dedicated SHE departments within companies in the late 1990s. However, the most crucial organisational changes with respect to CSER have occurred more recently in most companies. To illustrate, in 2002 Anglo Platinum established its socio-economic development department, dedicated to CSI projects, small business development and affirmative procurement, housing and support for sustainable habitats around the mines, HIV/AIDS, and stakeholder engagement. This represents a significant broadening of the definition of the company's social responsibilities, and it also involves significant expansions of human resources and dedicated budgets. The key driver for this change was the BEE scorecard. As noted by the department's corporate manager in late 2003, the main driver was the need to 'provide us with future mining licences' (Interview, Khambula, 2 April 2003). The BEE scorecard was also a key motivation for organisational changes in the other case study companies, as summarised in Table 3.2.

All interviewees concurred that the BEE scorecard was the most important catalyst for CSER-related change, though many noted that changes in this direction have already been occurring due to other incentives. These other incentives include growing pressure from local communities and local government and increasing expectations by international stakeholders, particularly investors and stock exchanges.

Hence there has been a confluence of motives, spearheaded most recently by the BEE scorecard. As argued by Lonmin's Director for Corporate Affairs, Tony Reilly:

> We have a combination of local pressure and legislation, most especially the BEE scorecard, coupled with our moral obligation and our common-sense view that says you need a stable environment with happy people [surrounding the mines], and running with that coincidentally in time . . . are the increasing pressures from the [financial] institutions in the UK (Interview, Reilly, 7 April 2003).

Table 3.2:   Organisational changes relevant to CSER in the case study companies, with the BEE scorecard as a primary incentive.

Company	Organisational change
Anglo Platinum	A new department dedicated to socio-economic development established in 2002; a new director for transformation (focused on the BEE scorecard) installed in 2003.
Impala	No management structures or posts, though committed board attention to the BEE scorecard.
Lonmin	New post of general manager for corporate accountability established in 2003; a board standing committee established for the BEE scorecard.
Aquarius	Environmental manager employed in 2003; much board attention to the BEE scorecard.
Samancor	No new management structures or posts (community issues have been included in the SHE department from the beginning); much board attention to the BEE scorecard.
Xstrata	Creation in 2002 of new post of general manager for corporate development dedicated to the BEE scorecard; a new director for transformation installed in 2003.

The extent to which changes in corporate reporting and structure actually lead to more responsible business practices at the operational level remains to be seen. One aspect of this is the perennial challenge of translating corporate policies into operational practices, as discussed above. One of the important indicators for this will be the inclusion of social criteria in mine managers' performance assessments over and above the environmental criteria that are already applied in some companies.

Conclusions

This chapter has illustrated how historical, political and socio-economic forces have led to diverse interpretations and manifestations of CSER in the South African mining sector. In particular, this understanding of the contextual, institutional factors underlying the definition and motives of CSER is counterposed to the assumption that there is an independent, market-based business case for CSER. Proponents of the business case for CSER, including many of the most prominent corporate leaders in the field, believe that voluntary measures to improve social impact will have positive effects on company profit margins, at least in the medium to long term (World Business Council for Sustainable Development 2000; Holliday, Schmidheiny and Watts 2002; International Finance Corporation, SustainAbility and Instituto Ethos 2002). Hence the International Council of Minerals and Metals commits members to the support of sustainable development to enhance shareholder value

The overarching conclusion of this chapter is that such claims regarding the inherent, voluntary nature of CSER need to be treated with caution. More specifically, such CSER-related promises, and reference to the business case for CSER in particular, cannot be relied upon independently of a consideration of institutional context, with emphasis on the role of the state.

For a start, the interpretation of CSER as CSI is historically defined. Some prominent South African mining companies saw such philanthropic activities as a measure to mitigate the worst impacts of apartheid and to ensure stable operating conditions into the future. It also allowed companies to portray themselves as benefactors, both prior and subsequent to 1994. CSI had little impact on their core business practices, however, particularly their reliance on migrant labour and single-sex hostels, significant components of the apartheid system. It is clear that no significant business case for CSER – in its broad sense beyond philanthropic initiatives – existed in apartheid South Africa.

As illustrated in the local case study, CSI initiatives have had little impact on the root causes of social problems surrounding the mines, many of which relate to the core business practices of the mining companies, especially employee recruitment and housing. The dominant interpretation of CSER as CSI, even after 1994, has meant that CSER has been a convenient sideshow to business as usual.

The potential for core business practices to be included in the definition of CSER grew with the increasing prominence of international sustainable development discourse. Represented by the proliferation of triple-bottom-line reports, this narrative has the stated objective of accounting for and internalising company social and environmental costs. However, recruitment and housing practices have generally been ignored in these reports, apart from some very recent exceptions. This indicates that the more recent sustainable development discourse has also been subject to an interpretation that minimises the need for significant change to business practice, thus giving credence to the greenwash criticism of CSER (see Chapter 2).

The business case argument for CSER has its roots in the belief that modernisation is generally conducive to improved social outcomes. This is most explicit in the term eco-modernisation, which refers to the potential environmental benefits of increased operational efficiency and competitiveness (Porter and Van der Linde 1995), but it is also prevalent in the broader CSER narrative (World Business Council for Sustainable Development, 2000). The case study research suggests, instead, that these incentives can indeed be damaging to the social outcomes of business practices. In the first instance, competition between companies, even as it pertains to their desire to project the most caring image, has obstructed improved collaboration between the various role players in the study area. A second example is the shift away from single-sex hostels. The overarching and guiding framework for this was a focus on company core competencies, without consideration of the social implications.

Furthermore, a critical assessment of CSER in the South African mining sector points towards the lingering implementation gap between corporate policies and practices at the operational level. While the corporate level seems keen to respond to stakeholder expectations, pronounce CSER policies and publish CSER reports, there seems to be insufficient commitment to force the corporate will onto the operational culture on the ground and this still seems dominated by production objectives. This is indicated, for instance, by the continued, general absence of social criteria – though not environmental criteria – in mine managers' performance assessments.

Concomitant with this critical view of mining company CSER narratives and practices, this chapter has also pointed to relatively recent trends towards a more sincere version of CSER. This entails a broadening of the definition of CSER to include core business practices, with a focus on nationally-important issues such as housing and employment equity. It also includes organisational changes that see CSER-related issues considered much higher in the management hierarchy than has previously been the case.

The key driver in this respect has been the state's transformation agenda encapsulated in the BEE scorecard. Premised on a negotiated policy-making process, the scorecard provides a definition of BEE that overlaps considerably with a version of CSER that considers South Africa's historical legacy. It also provides the key incentive, in that companies will be measured against its requirements in the process of transforming their old-order rights into new-order rights under the new legislation. On the basis of the BEE scorecard's contents, as well as the initial reactions of companies to it, this development may be interpreted optimistically as an opportunity to influence mining activity towards poverty alleviation and more sensitive community relations. However, bearing in mind the critique of the state's BEE programme as being biased towards the creation of a black elite, the implementation of the scorecard will require careful scrutiny in years to come.

Some corporate leaders have argued that contributing to the state's transformation agenda will be in the long-term interest of companies, interrelated as this is with South Africa's political and economic future, particularly in the case of mining investment. Much of this is probably public relations, especially to assuage shareholders, but it also points to business's seemingly inherent desire to perceive and mould change in a way that makes it seem voluntary (Dobbin and Sutton 1998). One aspect of this may be that emphasising the commonality of interests and the voluntary nature of change contributes to the ability to influence that change, as illustrated in the negotiations leading up to the BEE scorecard. Negotiation will also play a role in the actual implementation of the BEE scorecard with respect to individual company commitments and performance. Hence companies will play a crucial role in ensuring that BEE is indeed broad-based.

Notes

1. This chapter draws on Ralph Hamann's doctoral dissertation, which was submitted to the University of East Anglia in 2004. The thesis supervisors were Tim O'Riordan, David Fig and Simon Gerrard. Financial support was provided by the Ernest Oppenheimer Memorial Trust and the Harry Crossley Foundation. The chapter has also benefited from discussions with the other contributors to this volume and those listed in the book's acknowledgements.
2. Institute of Chartered Accountants of England and Wales. 1999.
3. A number of interviews were conducted with informants who preferred to remain anonymous. Their participation was conditional on their identity being protected.
4. See www.dme.gov.za/minerals/mining_charter.htm
5. Historically disadvantaged South Africans are legally defined to include black, Asian and coloured people, white women and the disabled.
6. Some of the larger subcontracting companies were themselves owned by the larger mining houses. Concor, for instance, was owned by Anglo American.
7. These boss-boys later became known as team leaders (Moodie with Ndatshe 1994: 44–75).
8. Standing, Sender and Weeks' statistics imply that by 1994 at least one of every ten underground workers in the gold mining industry was appointed on a subcontract basis. Unfortunately, the authors of the ILO report do not indicate whether traditional subcontracting practice, such as shaft sinking, is included in the statistics.

References

Aaronson, S.A. and J. Reeves. 2002. *The European Response to Public Demands for Global Corporate Responsibility*. Washington DC: National Policy Association.

Acutt, N. 2003. 'Policy, People and Petrochemicals: A Case Study of Voluntary Approaches to Corporate Environmentalism in the South Durban Basin'. Norwich: University of East Anglia (PhD thesis).

African Institute of Corporate Citizenship (AICC). 2002. *Socially Responsible Investment in South Africa.* Johannesburg: AICC.

Ali, S. and L. Behrendt. 2001. 'Mining and Indigenous Rights: The Emergence of a Global Social Movement'. *Cultural Survival Quarterly* 25 (1): 6–8.

Alperson, M. 1995. *Foundations for a New Democracy: Corporate Social Investment in South Africa*. Johannesburg: Ravan.

Anglo American Corporation of South Africa. 1998. *Anglo American Corporation Annual Report 1998*. Johannesburg: Anglo American.

————. 2000a. *Anglo American plc Safety, Health, and Environment Report 2000.* Johannesburg: Anglo American.

————. 2000b. *Anglo American's HIV/AIDS Policy*. Johannesburg: Anglo American.

————. 2002a. *Anglo American's Corporate Social Investment in South Africa*. London: Anglo American.

————. 2002b. *Resourcing our Future: Anglo American plc Safety, Health and Environment Report 2001*. London: Anglo American.

AngloGold. 2002. *AngloGold Annual Report 2002*. Johannesburg: AngloGold.

Auty, R.M. and R.F. Mikesell. 1998. *Sustainable Development in Mineral Economies*. Oxford: Clarendon.

Banerjee, S.B. 2001. 'Corporate Citizenship and Indigenous Stakeholders: Exploring a New Dynamic of Organisational-Stakeholder Relationships'. *Journal of Corporate Citizenship* 1: 39–55.

Bezuidenhout, A. and B. Kenny. 1998. 'Subcontracting in the Mining Industry'. *Innes Labour Brief* 10 (1): 30–36.

BHP Billiton. 2000. *HSE and Communities Annual Report*. London: BHP Billiton.

Boele, R., H. Fabig and D. Wheeler. 2001. 'Shell, Nigeria and the Ogoni: A Study in Unsustainable Development: II. Corporate Social Responsibility and "Stakeholder Management" versus a Rights-based Approach to Sustainable Development'. *Sustainable Development* 9: 121–35.

Callinicos, L. 1980. *Gold and Workers*. Johannesburg: Ravan.

Crush, J., A. Jeeves and D. Yudelman. 1991. *South Africa's Labour Empire: A History of Black Migrancy to the Gold Mines*. Cape Town: David Phillip.

Dale, M.O. 1997. 'South Africa: Development of a New Mineral Policy'. *Resources Policy* 23 (1–2): 15–26.

De Beers Corporation. 2000. *Safety, Health and Environment Review 2000*. Johannesburg: De Beers.

Dobbin, F. and J.R. Sutton. 1998. 'The Strength of a Weak State: The Rights Revolution and the Rise of Human Resources Management Divisions'. *American Journal of Sociology* 104 (2): 441–76.

Du Toit, C. 2001. 'CSI: A SAGA Status Report' in *The CSI Handbook 2001*, edited by V. Rockey. Cape Town: Trialogue.

Elkington, J. 1997. *Cannibals with Forks: The Triple Bottom Line of Sustainable Development*. Oxford: Capstone.

Fedderke, J.W. and F. Pirouz. 2002. 'The Role of Mining in the South African Economy'. *South African Journal of Economic and Management Sciences* 5 (1): 1–34.

Fine, B. and Z. Rustomjee. 1996. *The Political Economy of South Africa: From Minerals-energy Complex to Industrialisation*. London: Hurst.

Flynn, L. 1992. *Studded with Diamonds and Paved with Gold: Miners, Mining Companies and Human Rights in Southern Africa*. London: Bloomsbury.

Fox, T. 2004. 'Corporate Social Responsibility and Development: In Quest of an Agenda'. *Development* 47 (3): 29–36.

Godsell, B. 2002. 'Forging a Shared Vision on Future of SA Mining'. *Business Day* (Johannesburg) 2 July 2002: 9.

Hocking, A. 1973. *Oppenheimer and Son*. Johannesburg: McGraw-Hill.

Holliday, C.O., S. Schmidheiny and P. Watts. 2002. *Walking the Talk: The Business Case for Sustainable Development*. Sheffield: Greenleaf.

Institute of Chartered Accountants of England and Wales (ICAEW). 1999. *Internal Control: Guidance for Directors on the Combined Code* (the Turnbull Report). London: ICAEW.

International Finance Corporation (IFC), SustainAbility and Instituto Ethos. 2002. *The Business Case in Emerging Economies*. Washington DC: IFC.

Johnson Matthey. 2003. 'The Expansion of Platinum Mining in South Africa'. Available at www.johnsonmatthey.com, accessed October 2003.

Johnstone, F.A. 1976. *Class, Race and Gold: A Study of Class Relations and Racial Discrimination in South Africa*. London: Routledge & Kegan Paul.

Jones, J.D.F. 1995. *Through Fortress and Rock: The Story of Gencor 1895–1995*. Johannesburg: Jonathan Ball.

JSE Securities Exchange. 2003. *JSE SRI Index: Background and Selection Criteria*. Johannesburg: JSE Securities Exchange.

King Committee on Corporate Governance. 2002. *King Report on Corporate Governance for South Africa 2002* (King II Report). Johannesburg: Institute of Directors.

Lang, J. 1986. *Bullion Johannesburg: Men, Mines and the Challenge of Conflict*. Johannesburg: Jonathan Ball.

Lipton, M. 1985. *Capitalism and Apartheid: South Africa 1910–84*. Aldershot: Gower.

Mamdani, M. 1996. *Citizen and Subject: Contemporary Africa and the Legacy of Late Colonialism*. Princeton: Princeton University Press.

McWilliams, A. and D. Siegel. 2001. 'Corporate Social Responsibility: A Theory of the Firm Perspective'. *Academy of Management Review* 26 (1): 117–28.

Mining, Minerals and Sustainable Development (MMSD). 2002. *Breaking New Ground: The Report of the Mining, Minerals and Sustainable Development Project*. London: Earthscan.

Mining, Minerals and Sustainable Development in Southern Africa (MMSD-SA). 2001. *Draft Regional Report: Mining, Minerals and Sustainable Development in Southern Africa*. Johannesburg: MMSD-SA.

———. 2002. *Mining, Minerals and Sustainable Development in Southern Africa: The Report of the Regional MMSD Process*. Johannesburg: MMSD-SA.

Mlambo-Ngcuka, P. 2003. Speech to the Chamber of Mines of South Africa Conference on Sustainable Development in Mining, Johannesburg, 3 November 2003.

Moodie, T.D. with V. Ndatshe. 1994. *Going for Gold: Men, Mines, and Migration*. Johannesburg: Witwatersrand University Press.

Moon, J. 2002. 'Business Social Responsibility and New Governance'. *Government and Opposition* 37 (3): 385–408.

Moroney, S. 1978. 'Mine Worker Protest on the Witwatersrand: 1901–1912' in *Essays in Southern African Labour History*, edited by E. Webster. Johannesburg: Ravan.

Pallister, D., S. Stewart and I. Lepper. 1987. *South Africa Inc.: The Oppenheimer Empire*. Johannesburg: Media House.

Porter, M. and C. van der Linde. 1995. 'Green and Competitive: Ending the Stalemate'. *Harvard Business Review* 73 (5): 120–34.

Rockey, V. 2001. *The CSI Handbook 2001*. Cape Town: Trialogue.

Segal, N. 2000. *The South African Mining Sector: A Report Prepared for the South African Chamber of Mines*. Cape Town: Graduate School of Business, University of Cape Town.

South Africa. 2000. *Minerals and Petroleum Resources Bill*. Pretoria: Government Printer.

Spoor, R. 2003. 'The Social Consequences of Mining in the Past and in the Future'. Address to a Nexus dinner, Johannesburg, 18 June 2003.

Standing, G., J. Sender and J. Weeks. 1996. *Restructuring the Labour Market: The South African Challenge*. Geneva: International Labour Organisation.

Truth and Reconciliation Commission of South Africa (TRC). 2003. *Truth and Reconciliation Commission of South Africa Report, 21 March 2003*. Johannesburg: TRC.

Turrell, R.V. 1987. *Capital and Labour on the Kimberley Diamond Fields, 1871–1890*. Cambridge: CUP.

Waddock, S.A. 2003. 'Editorial'. *Journal of Corporate Citizenship* 9 (1): 3–7.

Ward, H. 2002. *Corporate Accountability in Search of a Treaty? Some Insights from Foreign Direct Liability*. London: Royal Institute of International Affairs.

Warhurst, A. and L. Noronha (eds.). 2000. *Environmental Policy in Mining: Corporate Strategy and Planning for Closure*. London: Lewis.

Wolpe, H. 1972. 'Capitalism and Cheap Labour-power in South Africa: From Segregation to Apartheid'. *Economy & Society* 1 (4): 425–56.

World Business Council for Sustainable Development (WBCSD). 2000. *Corporate Social Responsibility: Making Good Business Sense*. Geneva: WBCSD.

Yudelman, D. 1984. *The Emergence of Modern South Africa: State, Capital and the Incorporation of Organised Labour on the South African Gold Fields, 1902–1939*. Cape Town: David Philip.

Interviews

All interviews conducted by Ralph Hamann. Keeton and Kilani interviewed by David Fig and Ralph Hamann.

Bam, Gwen. Regional Manager, Corporate Social Investment, Impala Platinum, 16 April 2003.

Baxter, Roger. Chief Economist, Chamber of Mines, Johannesburg, 12 March 2003.

Botes, Ernst. Human Resources Manager, Eastern Platinum Mine, Lonmin, 4 June 2003.

De Hoop, Henk. Analyst, Bernard Jacobs Mellet, 11 April 2003.

Gcili-Tshana, Eric. Secretary, Health and Safety, NUM, 29 October 2001.

Hollesen, Paul. Manager, Social Development, AngloGold, 27 March 2003.

Ireton, Karin. Sustainability Manager, Anglo American plc, Johannesburg, 21 September 2001 and 27 November 2002.

Johnson, Clyde. Executive Director, Mining, Mvelaphanda Holdings, 24 October 2001.

Joseph, Michael. Manager, Community Affairs, Anglo Platinum, Johannesburg, 21 September 2001.

Keeton, Margie. Executive Director of Tshikululu Social Investments, which manages the CSI initiatives of a number of companies in the Anglo group, Johannesburg, 7 November 2001.

Khambula, Cyril. Group Manager, Socio-economic Development, Anglo Platinum, 2 April 2003.

Kilani, John. Environmental Adviser to the Chamber of Mines, Johannesburg, 14 November 2001.

Linnell, Richard. Head, Public Policy Unit, BHP Billiton, Johannesburg, 19 October 2001.

Mfupane, Glen. Secretary, Environment, NUM, 29 October 2001.

Modisakeng, Mpho. Director, Planning and Development, Rustenburg Municipality, 16 May 2003.

Pilkington, Richard. Divisional Director, Process, Anglo Platinum, 25 June 2006.

Pressend, Michelle and Doctor Mthethwa, Associates, GEM, 9 November 2001.

Reichardt, Markus. Manager, Environment, AngloGold, Johannesburg, 30 October 2001.

Reilly, Tony. Director, Corporate Affairs, Lonmin, 7 April 2003.

Rocha, Jacinto. Director, Mineral Rights, Department of Minerals and Energy, 22 October 2001.

Stacey, Julie Courtnage. Manager, Safety, Health and Environmental Policy Unit, Anglo American plc, 11 September 2001.

4

The chemicals industry

Shirley Miller

Brief profile of the South African chemicals industry

Emerging from a need to service agriculture and mining, the chemicals industry in South Africa formed part of local initiatives for import-substitution industrialisation. From the 1930s, there were attempts to apply new technologies to the chemical transformation of the enormous coal reserves in the country. Mining company Anglovaal, for example, obtained rights to develop a local version of the German Fischer Tropsch technology for conversion of coal into petroleum. However, it was not until the 1950s that the new apartheid state created a dedicated enterprise for this purpose, the Suid-Afrikaanse Steenkool-en Oliemaatskappy (SASOL, the South African Coal and Oil Company). Although the technology was very inefficient, polluting and expensive, it proved strategically useful to the apartheid state. South Africa had no indigenous petroleum resources, and the parastatal aimed at creating greater self-sufficiency. With the rise in the oil price in the 1970s – and the fall of the Shah of Iran with whom the apartheid state had enjoyed a close relationship and who had invested in a SASOL refinery – SASOL opened two more plants on the highveld coalfields. By this time, the sanctions movement had begun to bite and the industry's role moved from one of saving valuable foreign exchange to one deeply embedded in the survival and militarisation of apartheid. Strategic decisions in the industry were thus not always based on commercial considerations and the private sector followed the state in similar investment decisions (Crompton 1994).

Currently, although small by global standards, the South African chemicals industry ranks among the world's top 25 producers. Its contribution to the Gross Domestic Product (GDP) is five per cent, its contribution to local manufacturing is around twenty per cent, and its share of exports of manufactured goods is also around twenty per cent. Its output covers 300 types of basic or pure chemicals, and is present throughout the value chain, from raw materials to intermediate goods and end-user goods. Upstream investment is highly concentrated in a few capital-intensive firms (just under 80 per cent of investment in the industry), while downstream investment is characterised by more diverse participation and far lower capital investment, and provides a slightly larger contribution of the added value within the sector since it is here that more beneficiation occurs (National Economic Development and Labour Council 2003: chapter 2). The industry has a presence in five recognised sub-sectors: petroleum and petrochemicals, basic chemicals, other chemicals, rubber, and plastics.

The three major players in the upstream part of the industry have historically been SASOL, AECI (originally African Explosives and Chemical Industries but now known only by its acronym) and Sentrachem (part of Dow Chemicals since 1997). While SASOL has expanded and entrenched itself in the industry, AECI has downscaled substantially from a conglomerate supplying many commodity chemicals (employing 28 000 workers in 1982) to a speciality product and service solution company (currently employing 8 000). Dow has changed Sentrachem's profile, leaving synthetic rubber production and other traditional chemical operations in order to follow its specialisation in agri-sciences. Apart from Dow, key multinationals with South African chemicals operations include BASF, Bayer, CIB, Degussa, Henkel, Hoechst, Huntsman Tioxide, Rohm and Haas, and Shell.

Employing around 180 000 workers in 2001, the industry as a whole is experiencing similar trends to the rest of the manufacturing sector in South Africa. This includes declining employment levels – principally as a result of increased outsourcing of services – mergers and acquisitions, cheaper imports and increased mechanisation. In manufacturing, over 16 per cent of jobs have been lost since 1990, whereas in chemicals the loss was 2.2 per cent. This slower rate of loss can be attributed partly to a 34 per cent rise in employment in the plastics sub-sector, the only one not to shed labour. The phenomenon of outsourcing non-core services (maintenance, security, cleaning, catering, etc.) means that the same employees usually experience wage and benefit cuts, harsher labour regimes and more job insecurity. Responsibility for benefits, housing, health and safety, and medical care devolves onto smaller employers with lower standards.

Regulation and self-regulation

No single law or government department regulates the industry in relation to environment, health and safety. As a result, the regulatory function is fragmented, found in ten key pieces of legislation and administered by six different authorities. Of these, the two critical, overarching acts which determine the health and safety of workers and the environment are the Occupational Health and Safety Act (OHSA) (85 of 1993), and the National Environmental Management Act (NEMA) (107 of 1998). The OHSA has established a hierarchy of controls with respect to hazards which requires the elimination of the hazard itself rather than protecting workers with personal protective equipment. Similarly, the NEMA has seen a shift from end-of-pipe pollution control to prevention at source. Both share a preventive approach which imposes a duty of care, the right to information, the right to participation and the right to act. The manner in which these Acts are given effect is subject to some debate. For example, the OHSA limits the extent of this duty through the 'reasonably practicable' principle. Thus economic costs are also considered in determining an appropriate response to the risk.

Although the 1993 Act ushered in a new approach to health and safety, it required more intensive policing by the labour inspectorate. This was not immediately forthcoming: the 56 inspectors were insufficient for the task of implementing the new preventive approach and their specific expertise and mandates were diluted with the implementation of a one-stop approach to inspection. The minimal impact of the inspectorate limits the regulator's capacity to ensure that individual employers are complying with the laws or with their own management standards. Inspections end up being request-based rather than proactive or random. The growth in the number of small, medium and micro enterprises (SMMEs) in the sector is also cause for concern, since this results in lower health, safety and environmental standards in the industry, and is far more likely to fall outside effective regulation.

Regulatory instruments in health and safety also include mechanisms which are triggered by certain performance targets. For example, the

OHSA, covering occupational diseases and injuries, sets ratings for companies in terms of high or low drawing down of compensation for their workers. A high incidence of disease or accidents triggers bigger payment obligations on the part of firms. Union officials have noted that this system favours under-reporting so that firms are less liable for higher payments.

The industry is also promoting more voluntary initiatives in order to raise standards. This has grown with the gradual retreat of the state from command-and-control approaches in favour of regulation, due to the expansion of neo-liberal economic practices. The wave of centralised regulation in the 1960s and 1970s gave way in the 1980s and 1990s to approaches that favoured self-regulation by firms. More recently, the trend has been towards the development of co-regulatory approaches that rely on input by a variety of stakeholders, especially civil society (Utting 2002). Civil society has been exerting more pressure on the industry to improve its environmental and social performance, particularly since the Bhopal accident and the rise of the environmental justice movement.

Voluntary arrangements are difficult to define, and take on a number of forms ranging from programmes of self-regulation through to signed multi-stakeholder agreements. In the view of the International Federation of Chemical, Energy, Mine and General Workers' Unions (ICEM), voluntary agreements should be additional commitments rather than a substitute for legislation, monitoring and enforcement (International Federation of Chemical, Energy, Mine and General Workers' Unions 1997: 3). Not being binding, they are difficult both to track and to enforce (see Box 4.1). In South Africa, co-regulatory practices are possible within the provisions of the NEMA. Yet when the state tried to implement such agreements in the petrochemical sub-sector prior to setting minimal national standards, the agreements collapsed in a haze of civil society suspicion. This caused some commentators to note that 'voluntary agreements in the field of pollution control do not work in the absence of other related regulatory mechanisms' (Albertyn and Watkins 2002: 14). Voluntary agreements also depend on the ability of civil society to play a role in monitoring. However, in South Africa few unions or non-governmental organisations (NGOs) are endowed with technical capacities of the necessary order to co-regulate effectively.

Box 4.1
The Plastic Bag Agreement: The demise of the 'national flower'

Until 2000, most retail outlets in South Africa packed customer purchases in thin, seventeen-micron plastic carrier bags. Although the cost of the bags was included in the price of the goods and thus passed on to consumers, shoppers perceived these bags to be free. Consumers attached little monetary value to the bags since new ones were provided with each purchase. Three billion bags were produced annually, 60 per cent of them for retailers. Since systematic waste collection and recycling were limited in most urban townships, windblown plastic bags invaded road sides and informal corner dumpsites, and became attached to trees and fences. Government indicated that the accumulation of unsightly bags was adversely affecting the environment both in terms of living conditions and of tourism. Their omnipresence outside the waste stream earned them the title of South Africa's alternative national flower.

In 2000, the Minister of Environmental Affairs and Tourism – possibly caught off guard in Parliament during question time – put enormous stress on plastic bags as one of the country's most serious environmental problems. In following up, he published draft regulations which prescribed a minimum thickness of 80 microns for all plastic shopping bags.

Organised labour questioned the focus on plastic bags rather than other, more damaging, pollutants in South Africa. The plastic conversion industry is the one sub-sector within the chemical industry that has actually increased employment. The effect on investment in the industry and the prospect of considerable job losses both in the manufacturing and retail sectors led to the issue being referred to the National Economic Development and Labour Council (NEDLAC), a statutory body charged with review of laws affecting the economy. NEDLAC embarked on extensive research under the management of a tripartite (business-labour-government) committee. Legally the minister was obliged to take this report into account, but the regulations were gazetted before its publication.

Organised labour declared a dispute in terms of section 77 of the Labour Relations Act, which allowed for legal protest action. The clear procedures associated with the NEDLAC process facilitated interventions and meetings between the various parties, culminating in an agreement hailed by all parties as precedent-setting. This agreement provided for a five-year grace period during which 30-micron bags would be produced with a variance of 20 per cent, printing on bags would be reduced to facilitate recycling, there would be protection of workers' jobs in the industry and the establishment of a non-profit company to promote recycling.

Subsequently, a number of problems have arisen with the implementation of the agreement. The introduction of the new regulations has seen a reduction in purchase of shopping bags below the expectations of government and has resulted in short-time work and retrenchments in the plastic bag manufacturing industry. Job losses have continued and there are no evident signs of full-scale recycling as envisaged in the agreement. Some retailers have reneged on the agreement, and do not make a separate charge for their bags. Had there been a law instead of a voluntary agreement, these retailers would have faced considerable financial penalties.

The case of plastic bags illustrates some limitations of the voluntary-agreement approach. Individual firms can opt out. It also illustrates the importance of NEDLAC as a tripartite arena in which adherence to the rules of the game are important in securing an agreement. NEDLAC's weakness is the lack of participation of other sections of civil society which might have a valid interest.

Privately-implemented codes and ratings systems are also somewhat problematic. The South African chemical industry relies significantly on ratings systems of the International Standards Organisation (especially the ISO 14000 series) and the local National Occupational Safety Association (NOSA). In addition, it applies the methodology of the Responsible Care programme, internal to the global chemical industry.

Criticisms of systems such as the ISO 14000 series are that they are based on a self-declaration by industry. They only provide for the establishment of environment management systems and do not set benchmarks for specific environmental improvements, or standards, nor measure performance against tangible criteria. For these reasons the Environmental Protection Agency (EPA) in the United States has refused to reduce its regulatory oversight of those companies applying the ISO 14000 series (Sissell 2002). Although ISO 14000 is a popular choice among South African chemical companies for certification purposes, and often implemented in both directions of the supply chain, the costs of initiating and maintaining the system may be prohibitive to many of the smaller entrants into the industry.

NOSA certification also provides some problems. NOSA was established in 1951 by local business and the Compensation Commissioner. It provides for safety management systems that include audit procedures and occupational health and safety training. NOSA has been the major beneficiary of the Compensation Commissioner's discretionary power to disburse money from the Compensation Fund to promote health and safety. This funding has now been phased out. NOSA has extended its operations internationally and has a presence in Latin America, Hong Kong and Australasia. Huge discrepancies have been noted in terms of star-based ratings. For example, the highest NOSA award was presented to Middelbult Colliery on the morning before the horrific accident in which over 50 miners lost their lives. Subsequent inquiries revealed profound safety inadequacies at the mine. Similarly, Thor Chemicals was the recipient of the second highest star rating at the time that workers were dying from mercury exposure (see Box 4.2). Trade unions have thus constantly been critical of the NOSA standards, as has the Leon Commission on safety and health in the mining industry, which noted that they have become largely discredited in the eyes of those employed at the mines and in public perception. This is due to the very large disasters that continue to occur at mines with high star ratings, and the imperceptible impact on the overall level of fatalities and major injuries in South African mines. Despite Judge Leon's findings, little has been done to change the system, and recent high levels of fatalities in companies like SASOL have reawakened criticism of NOSA ratings. A key initiative in the industry has been the adoption of Responsible Care, which merits more detailed analysis.

Box 4.2

The case of Thor Chemicals

British chemical processing company Thor Chemicals first set up its operation in South Africa in 1963, four years after its foundation. Its British mercury-processing operation, when inspected by the Health and Safety Executive in 1981, 1983 and 1987 was found to have airborne levels of mercury twenty times higher than the acceptable standard. After the third inspection, the company faced an ultimatum: clean up or face prosecution. Thor closed its mercury operations in Britain and started focusing on South Africa where there was still a demand for recycling spent mercury catalysts. Thor imported mercury wastes from around the world, using its South African plant to incinerate them, and to extract the mercury to resell. In addition, Thor was manufacturing mercury-based compounds for biocides and battery fillers.

The recycling of wastes to extract mercury was not always successful and Thor invested in bigger and bigger plant, culminating in the commission of a rotary kiln incinerator to deal with a growing stockpile of waste. However, this could not process all the wastes. To clear the stockpile of mercury waste in its warehouse, Thor started dumping some of it into a storage dam. This led to the contamination of local springs and streams which fed into the nearby Umgeni River. In July 1988, the local water utility, Umgeni Water, began to report downstream readings of mercury a thousand times higher than the World Health Organisation standard for drinking water. Despite this being reported to the regulator, the national Department of Water Affairs and Forestry, nothing was done to investigate matters for over a year.

Protest was taken up by a rainbow alliance of black workers, peasants, white commercial farmers, students, green activists and Zulu traditional leaders. Workers at Thor were only represented by a trade union after winning a recognition agreement in August 1991. Medical tests revealed that many workers at Thor displayed mercury levels of 200 parts per billion (ppb), with 87 per cent above the notionally safe limit of 50 ppb. By February 1992, the first worker was admitted to hospital where he fell into a coma. This was followed by a similar incident in March. A third worker was hospitalised after going berserk at the plant. By April, an independent report on workers' health claimed that 28 per cent of all workers at Thor were likely to receive permanent damage from mercury poisoning. Pressure from media and the public led to a formal enquiry by the Department of Manpower in July 1992, which in turn led to the decision to institute criminal prosecution of Thor's top managers.

During the case, despite having access to international experts who could prove company liability, the prosecution effectively offered the defence a deal whereby Thor admitted limited negligence and was fined R13 500 (then worth US$3 700) in exchange for dropping the culpable homicide and other charges. Simultaneously, civil proceedings were brought in England on behalf of twenty South African workers, which resulted in Thor agreeing in April 1997 to a settlement of R9 million (US$1.5 million). This Thor did in order to avoid further punitive legal costs.

The South African government appointed a commission of inquiry into Thor Chemicals to decide on future management of the mercury waste. Reporting in May 1997, it recommended that the waste be incinerated. This was rejected by the environmental movement, which argued that incineration posed a threat to public health. In 2004, SRK Nyamazela Consulting was appointed by the Department of Environmental Affairs and Tourism to conduct an impact assessment on the clean up of the 3 500 tonnes of mercury waste. Thor contributed R24 million and the government R6 million, far from the predicted R60–80 million needed. Although this process was supposed to have been completed by early 2006, it has been stalled due to public disagreement about a sustainable method of conducting the clean up, with incineration widely rejected as a technology.

The Thor case raised a number of key issues: the importance of transparent and properly resourced environmental assessment, the need to overcome the fragmentation inherent in the state in terms of its regulatory functions, the need for workers to undergo training in health and safety independent of company processes, and the failure of self-regulation in the chemical industry.

Sources: Butler 1997: 194–213; Ward 2002: 2–5; Carnie 2004.

Responsible Care

When the catastrophic gas leak at Union Carbide's Bhopal plant in India occurred in December 1984, it killed thousands of workers and local residents and permanently injured up to 150 000 people. Full compensation to the victims has never been paid, but the accident provided a wake-up call to the chemicals industry to raise its operational and environmental standards, particularly in developing countries. Global public disquiet caused it to take action. It set out to do so by introducing its own system for environmental management, which it called Responsible Care. First to introduce the scheme was Canada in 1985 while South Africa waited until 1994 to follow suit. Today the programme exists in 46 countries, responsible for 85 per cent by volume of the world's total chemical output.

In South Africa the programme was initiated by the Chemical and Allied Industries' Association (CAIA), the membership organisation of chemical companies. It moved from fifteen adherents in 1994 at the outset of the programme to 110 in 2002, after which it was compulsory for all corporate members of CAIA to join. Responsible Care signatories account for 90 per cent of the annual turnover of the local chemical industry, and for one third of the industry's employees.

The methodology of Responsible Care involves firms reporting according to six management practice standards (MPSs) covering the following topics: health and safety of persons; storage and distribution of chemicals; transportation of chemicals; waste management and pollution control; community awareness and emergency response; and product stewardship. Compliance with the requirements of each MPS is evaluated through self-assessed quantitative indicators of performance (QIP) questionnaires. Each Responsible Care signatory is required to report on an annual basis on the MPSs. In terms of results, CAIA reports that there is increasing participation and compliance by member firms. It notes a decline in the disabling injury rate and the number of incidents involving chemical release in the storage, distribution and transport of chemicals. There has also been more reporting on waste generation, recycling and disposal.

However, there is a major problem with the information released by firms in the Responsible Care programme. Expectations that Responsible Care would go beyond official data collection in the industry seem to have been unfounded. The nature of the collection of data, their presentation and the lack of verification processes mean that it is difficult for other stakeholders to use them as indicators of performance. It is thus not possible to establish from Responsible Care's current published information whether any verifiable and significant positive changes have occurred with respect to occupational and environmental health and safety in the South African chemical industry.

For this reason the key trade union in the industry – the Chemicals, Energy, Paper, Printing, Wood and Allied Workers' Union

(CEPPWAWU) – has found it difficult to participate in the Responsible Care programme. It eschews any invitation to be part of the programme's Voluntary Advisory Forum aimed at raising concerns about the industry and commenting on the implementation of the programme. In principle, the union regards it as a waste of time to participate in an advisory body that cannot direct change, and which merely serves to legitimate and endorse. Its position is that there should be formal, transparent and comprehensive data-collection mechanisms, that baseline standards should be legislated in consultation with the union and other stakeholders, and that skills should be shared with smaller firms so that standards are universally applied across the sector. Only then, in its view, would voluntary arrangements be possible.

Nevertheless, the union has entered into an accord with the industry through its association, CAIA. This aims to improve health, safety and environmental performance in the workplace through capacity building, collection of information using quantitative indicators, their independent verification, a full review of the efficacy of Responsible Care, and the inclusion of labour's comments in all Responsible Care reports.

SASOL: A case study of a globalising chemical company

Originating in 1950 as part of the apartheid state's drive for fuel self-sufficiency, SASOL is today the country's largest chemical company and dominant in the sector. Until 1979 – when it was renamed SASOL Limited and listed on the Johannesburg Stock Exchange (JSE) – it remained a parastatal whose major purpose was to use the Fischer-Tropsch technology to convert coal to synthetic petroleum, offsetting international oil sanctions. It received enormous state subsidies – R6 billion of which remain unrefunded (*Mail & Guardian* 23 September 2005) – and protection, mainly due to its value in import substitution and sanctions busting.

SASOL's two industrial complexes were built close to rich coal deposits. The first, Sasolburg, entailed the establishment of plant on the southern banks of the Vaal River, 100 kilometres south-west of Johannesburg. The town of Sasolburg and its adjacent industrial plants forms one node of the notorious Vaal Triangle, which contains not only SASOL's oil-from-coal plant but also several open-cast coal mines, a coal-fired power station, an oil refinery, a steel mill (ISCOR at Vanderbijlpark, a nearby town), and several petrochemical and metallurgical plants. Most of these were built by the state and state-owned corporations, and some have since been privatised or semi-privatised. In the 1970s SASOL developed a second synthetic fuel node, called Secunda, alongside coalfields in the eastern highveld area. By 2000, SASOL was responsible for producing 40 per cent of South Africa's liquid fuel requirements, in the form of synthetic fuels produced from coal and natural gas.

SASOL's chemical operations began as by-products of and inputs into the synthetic fuel process. Today it is the largest petrochemical and explosives corporation in the country. It is a key producer of petroleum, diesel, kerosene, liquid petroleum gas, paraffin, fuel oils and gas. It has important interests in the coal industry. However, SASOL has also diversified considerably from its original synthetic fuel production mandate. Its interest in using natural gas as a feedstock for producing synthetic fuel has expanded, and it has been replacing coal as a feedstock with natural gas. The company has also become a major producer of ethylene, propylene, ammonia, phenols, sulphur, road tar, pitch, creosotes, alcohols, ketones, fertilisers, explosives and waxes.

SASOL developed towns, townships and single-sex hostel accommodation to house employees on racial lines to service the operations of these installations. Its notorious anti-union policy led it to use the military and third force elements to break strikes and it resisted recognition of non-racial unions until 1984. More recently it has had to move away from its past profile as a company dedicated to apartheid's survival, in order to operate in a new global and local context.

Currently SASOL is a global oil and gas company with interests in the Americas, Asia, Australasia, Africa and Europe. Its chemicals account for 60 per cent of group sales. Its international operations include gas-to-liquid plants in Nigeria, Qatar and Malaysia, with ethane and polyethylene production in Iran. Its acquisition of Condea gave it chemical production facilities in Europe, the United States and China. By 2003 it had listed on the New York Stock Exchange but it has confirmed that its primary listing remains in Johannesburg, unlike some depatriated companies which moved their head offices out of South Africa. It currently employs just under 25 000 people in South Africa, and a further 6 000 in other countries. From 2004, natural gas from Mozambique has been used as a supplementary feedstock for synthetic fuels (SASOL 2004a: 30) and the company began converting its Sasolburg plant to process natural gas as its hydrocarbon feedstock, a process that was completed by 2005 (SASOL 2005a: 32). It is unclear, however, how much of the natural gas is replacing coal-generated liquid fuels and how much ends up in other products.

Historically, SASOL suffered from a dismal environmental record. In a 1991 study of environmental injustices under apartheid, the town of Sasolburg and the neighbouring township of Zamdela were said to constitute 'perhaps the most industrialised and polluted city in South Africa . . . SASOL's outdated plant is reputed to be one of the most environmentally damaging factories in the world' (Cock and Koch 1991: 21). The 1998 Vaal Triangle Air Pollution Health Study (VAPS) found average levels of particulate to be 250 per cent of the acceptable level, and that this compromised child health as shown by disproportionate evidence of respiratory disease (Brümmer 2000). South Africa's contribution to greenhouse gas emissions constitutes between one and two per cent of the world's emissions. On a per capita basis, these are well above the global average and the averages of other middle-income countries. The principal generators of South African emissions are coal-fired power stations and the SASOL oil-from-coal process. These two sources are also responsible for the bulk (57%) of the methane emissions from coal.

What has impelled SASOL's drive to improve its social and environmental performance? This has been shaped by both external and internal imperatives. The external pressures include conformity with international regulatory measures such as the United Nations Framework Convention on Climate Change and the Stockholm Convention on Persistent Organic Pollutants. Listing on the New York Stock Exchange and the expectations of institutional investors influenced SASOL's need to conform to higher standards of environmental performance. Internally, the growing HIV/AIDS pandemic and legal obligations in terms of black economic empowerment (BEE) and employment equity have also shaped SASOL's sustainable development strategy. The King II Report has been influential on company non-financial practice, while increased civil society activism for environmental justice has put pressure on SASOL to attend to pollution matters more comprehensively.

The establishment of a Safety, Health and Environment (SH&E) Centre at its Johannesburg headquarters has clearly been a result of

SASOL's international expansion and the global rebranding of the company. Regional and national regulatory directives such as the European Union White Paper on Chemicals and the United States EPA's High Production Volume Chemicals Program are increasingly defining SASOL's operations. Scrutiny by global civil society (for example, in the form of a website entitled sasolwatch.com) has also contributed towards the company's desire for better record keeping and practical performance improvement. Some jurisdictions hold directors liable for accidents and environmental damage. In addition, the King II report prompted the development of an audit protocol 'to manage potential SH&E liabilities and risks' (SASOL 2003b).

SASOL has responded with a series of annual sustainability reports, leading to improved disclosure and transparency. It has established an SH&E Corporate Governance Committee, comprising the managing directors of its key operations and the executive director for sustainable development. Technical support is provided by intra-group forums on issues like water, waste, and health and safety. The Committee makes many decisions, but ultimate responsibility rests with the group's senior executive management.

In terms of voluntary initiatives, SASOL is a signatory to the Global Compact and reporting is in compliance with the Global Reporting Initiative (GRI). The company takes some pride in being an 'active participant' in the local Responsible Care programme (SASOL 2003b: 27), stressing its commitment to Product Stewardship within overall chemical management programmes. There has also been strong support for the implementation in the chemical and refinery sectors of environmental management co-operative agreements (EMCAs), and disappointment about their collapse (see Box 4.3). However, its view is that the company played no part in their failure: 'Despite our efforts to develop an EMCA that would include commitments beyond what is required by law, limited progress has been made, due largely to issues beyond our control' (SASOL 2003b: 11). The company looks to ISO 14001 for certification of its environmental performance in its South African operations.

In terms of reportable injuries, SASOL has adopted US Occupational Safety and Health Administration (OSHA) rules with a view to 'facilitate meaningful comparison with our industry peers and reflect our approach of adopting world best practice throughout the group'

(SASOL 2003b: 52). SASOL uses the Recordable Case Rate (RCR) to assess work-related injuries and fatalities. The RCR definition of a reportable injury includes all work-related fatalities, lost workday cases, and work-related injuries requiring medical attention beyond first aid, or involving loss of consciousness, restriction of work or motion, or transfer to another job. It is measured in terms of numbers of injuries per 200 000 work hours. SASOL has established a target of 0.5 RCR for the end of 2006. The RCR for the SASOL group has dropped steadily from 2.55 in 2001 to 1.03 in 2004, but this masks considerably higher figures for South Africa itself, even though 81 per cent of the SASOL workforce is located there. It is unlikely that the 2006 target will be realised. It is more feasible that SASOL may reach its secondary target of a 50 per cent reduction of serious incidents from the 2001 level.

In terms of voluntary initiatives, SASOL claims that over 80 per cent of its business units are ISO 14000 certified, including over 40 plants in South Africa (SASOL 2005b: 19). In addition, the company claims that it will have reached a target of 90 per cent Practice in Place (PIP) standards under the Responsible Care Codes of Practice by 2006, up from 60 per cent in 2002 and 81 per cent in 2004.[1] By 2005 every SASOL chemical enterprise was required to implement the Responsible Care Product Stewardship code (SASOL 2004b). Later that year, SASOL (2005b) claimed that it had achieved a 91 per cent rate of implementing the PIP standards across the group.

Box 4.3
Voluntary initiatives in the chemicals sector

Context

In recent years negotiated environmental agreements have emerged as a new policy mechanism, particularly in Organisation for Economic Co-operation and Development (OECD) countries. The increasing popularity of these kinds of mechanism appears to be driven by two converging trends: the growing importance of the private sector and the evolution of environmental policy. In theory, voluntary agreements represent a complementary set of mechanisms alongside traditional command-and-control or direct-regulation and market-based instruments.

In the South African context, general reference to partnerships and agreements has been made in a number of government policy papers, and formal provision for ECMAs has been made in NEMA. This provision recognises the use of administrative agreements for the purpose of promoting compliance with the principles of NEMA. However, the appropriateness of voluntary agreements in the current context is being debated. The debate centres on the issue of timing, given the current regulatory reform process. Is it appropriate to sign binding agreements before regulatory foundations and standards have been set for fundamental issues like air quality? What is the role of third parties, and what is the nature of their participation during different stages of negotiation? From industry's perspective, the uncertain regulatory context is a key motivation to explore the use of alternate policy mechanisms such as voluntary agreements. From the perspective of a number of NGOs and community groups, however, the regulatory context and history of weak enforcement is the very reason to caution against the use of these mechanisms.

Process

Notwithstanding the regulatory void and unresolved policy questions, a number of pilot agreements have been developed and two substantive EMCAs – one for the chemical industry and the other for the oil refinery industry – are now in draft form awaiting further direction from government. In essence, both draft agreements set out industry-wide commitments based on three themes: air quality, water conservation, and waste management. Implementation is envisaged through individual site environmental management plans. The agreements were developed on a voluntary basis between industry and government. As such, broader stakeholder input into the process was, until recently, almost completely neglected.

In parallel with the industry-led pilot processes, the Department of Environmental Affairs and Tourism (DEAT) published a draft discussion document in 2000. This sparked concern from several stakeholder groups and motivated a number of civil society groups to convene a policy workshop in Durban in August 2000. The proceedings of the workshop formed the basis of a civil society submission to DEAT. In early 2001 DEAT undertook to continue the process on a consultative basis. A revised document was commissioned and a two-day multi-stakeholder workshop was convened in October 2001 to identify key concerns from stakeholders and to elicit guidance on giving effect to section 35 of NEMA. While this represented the first substantive effort by DEAT to engage a broader set of stakeholders in the policy process, it raised questions about the representation and constituency of the stakeholders invited to participate in the process.

Both NGO and governmental stakeholders have expressed a fair amount of resistance and scepticism towards EMCAs. The root of this appears to be a loss of confidence in the leadership of the authorities and a deep mistrust of industry, compounded by a lack of transparency in the negotiation of pilot EMCAs. Linked to this is the fear that EMCAs might be used as a substitute for standards or for delaying the law reform process. Furthermore, there is a sense of confusion around the host of initiatives including environmental impact assessments, environmental standards, a series of new governance plans, international initiatives, and the relationship between all of these and EMCAs. The lack of clarity about where EMCAs fit within the regulatory framework is exacerbated by broader processes of change including the devolution of powers and the subsequent problems of capacity, consistency and institutional memory at all levels of government.

Prospects

Nevertheless, the potential benefits of voluntary agreements – such as promoting improved performance, making information available and promoting reporting and monitoring – have been recognised in principle. The principle of EMCAs has tentatively been accepted on the understanding that government guarantees that the law reform process be prioritised and the participatory framework clarified. The need for guidelines on the process of developing EMCAs is clearly apparent and DEAT has endeavoured to address the issue. At this point the fate of EMCAs remains unclear. While the potential exists for them to be used as a complementary policy tool, a number of critical issues need to be addressed, including the regulatory framework, administrative implications and participation.

The concept of using an administrative agreement as an environmental policy tool is very new in the South African context. The pilot EMCAs were complex and this in itself added to the scepticism around the goals of the agreement. It might be sensible, therefore, to pilot an EMCA using a simple framework with a single objective such as, for example, environmental reporting. Testing the concept on a small scale rather than the top-down, sophisticated approach implicit in the draft EMCAs is more likely to be successful and hence to build trust in the concept.

Furthermore, the requirements of section 35 of NEMA are broad and therefore provide a degree of flexibility in the way that it might be interpreted and implemented. As such, EMCAs do not necessarily have to follow the precedent being set by current pilots. A number of different institutional arrangements could be applied, for example:

- They could be used to complement permit applications, be required as a permit condition or complement EIA conditions of approval;
- NEMA does not prescribe that EMCAs must be sectoral – they could relate to a specific product or a particular process. They could be single agreements and local in scope or they could be multi-sectoral and geographic in extent;
- They could provide a mechanism for compliance with international conventions for which there is currently no legal framework;
- They could facilitate action on issues difficult to regulate such as energy efficiency and clean technology;
- They could be used to incorporate social objectives into environmental management plans.

The exclusion of civil society, provincial and local spheres of government, and organised labour from the negotiation phase of the pilot EMCAs ignored the principles of transparency, open governance and participation espoused in NEMA; and has exacerbated the lack of trust between parties. This approach has eroded confidence in the concept and is a setback to the introduction of formal voluntary agreements into the South African environmental policy mix.

Nevertheless, given South Africa's economic climate and the associated pressures on industry, there is reason to believe that mechanisms such as voluntary agreements are likely to play an increasing role in corporate environmental strategy. Appropriate design agreements have the potential to complement regulatory goals. However, they are not a panacea. Voluntary agreements represent only one type of policy mechanism, and they must function within a set of integrated and complementary tools including traditional regulation and market-based instruments. While voluntary agreements have the potential to facilitate new relations between NGOs, industry and government, this is premised on the assumption that they contribute to building mutual understanding and improving trust. It is clear that building trust requires transparency and an open and democratic process, and is therefore fundamental to effective and credible voluntary agreements.

In September 2004 an explosion at the Secunda plant caused ten fatalities. This created considerable disquiet in the labour unions and they blamed SASOL management for faulty pipes and inadequate safety measures. Further accidents, fires and fatalities occurred, involving sixteen recorded deaths between June 2004 and May 2005. SASOL commissioned Du Pont to undertake a safety audit during 2005 and this resulted in the identification of major management deficiencies on safety issues. Most significant was the linking of management performance bonuses to output rather than to safety criteria (*Business Day* 31 May 2005). The voices of union members are not reflected in company safety reporting and there is a strong sense among unionists that health and safety records are stronger when there are legal instruments and negotiated agreements, as for example at SASOL's mines.

Because of SASOL's high investments in coal, its carbon emissions are significant. However, the switch to Mozambican natural gas as a feedstock for the formerly coal-to-oil operations has meant a significant reduction in emissions since 1998. Even so, some observers have concluded that 'emissions will remain constant as expanded capacity absorbs the benefit of cleaner production' (Butler and Hallowes 2002: 19).

Local concerns about industrial emissions led to innovative interventions by a local NGO, GroundWork, in conjunction with the US-based Communities for a Better Environment (CBE). Using the bucket brigade air monitoring system,[2] they found sixteen hazardous air pollutants in Sasolburg, seven of which were carcinogenic. Levels for benzene, vinyl chloride and methylene chloride were particularly high. Although SASOL rejected both the test methodology and the results, it did acknowledge high levels of benzene. Fearing negative publicity, the company initiated a hazardous air pollutant monitoring programme from 2001 in various parts of Sasolburg, and claimed that 'almost all

of the samples . . . were within South African guidelines', although
they did find elevated levels for benzene in one sample (SASOL 2003b:
43). While the company acknowledged that industrial pollution was
a possible source of the benzene elevation, it also listed other possible
contributors such as traffic, petrol stations and residential fuel usage
including the burning of rubber, coal and plastic bags. Objective
toxic release inventories may be the only way to verify emissions
independently (Goldblatt 1997: 131), but these do not yet occur. South
Africa's Air Quality Act, which went into effect on 1 September 2005, is
likely to set higher emissions standards, particularly for areas identified
as air quality hot spots, such as the Vaal Triangle.

While SASOL has reduced its emissions, it nevertheless admits
that it has yet to fulfil permit requirements with respect to some
substances such as fluoride, particulates, sulphur dioxide, ammonia
and ammonium nitrate. Chlorine releases into the atmosphere have
also had negative impacts on neighbouring communities. The renewed
regulatory enthusiasm of the Department of Environmental Affairs and
Tourism, now equipped with a serious-minded inspectorate called the
Green Scorpions, needs to ensure that SASOL fulfils stricter emissions
standards.

Because of its listing on the New York Stock Exchange, SASOL is
keen to be included in the Dow Jones Sustainability Index, reserved
for the top ten per cent of listed companies rated on environmental
performance. However, the listing has remained elusive, partly because
of the company's poor investment in renewable energy. Said Dow,
'The company lacks a clear vision beyond fossil fuels at this point in
time, which is perceived as a constraint to sustainability with regard to
expected market developments in the renewable energy sector' (SASOL
2003b: 7). SASOL's rating in 2003–4 climbed to 74 per cent, but by 2006
it was down to 68 per cent. The company remains outside the top decile
of the index, a position to which it aspires (SASOL 2004b, 2006).

Responding to community pressure, SASOL established stakeholder
engagement mechanisms in both its industrial complexes. However,
their function and independence has been questioned: the forums have
focused on local non-industrial pollution, such as a project to reduce
pollutants arising from domestic coal fires. This focus is a source of
frustration to some members of the forums who feel that without

addressing industrial pollution, the main source of the problem faced by communities is being sidelined (Butler and Hallowes 2002).

The company makes no information available on occupational disease and thus the acute and chronic affects of chemicals at the workplace on employees are not included in their review of activities. South African law imposes specific duties in relation to hazardous chemicals, which include biological and environmental monitoring. The failure to place these important indicators of the health status of workers in the public domain is a serious omission and precludes any assessment of the health burden created by working at SASOL's operations in South Africa. SASOL's European and American chemical operations have superior results in respect of health, safety and environmental indicators. If SASOL upholds its stated intention to employ best practice across all its operations, this may have more positive effects for its South African enterprises.

Like most other South African businesses, SASOL has responded slowly to the HIV/AIDS epidemic, which has devastated the working population and their communities. South African business did not foresee the impact that HIV/AIDS in the wider environment would have on internal organisation, and thus failed to take proactive preventive measures. SASOL's strategic planning in the late 1990s only identified AIDS as a major threat to the economy rather than directly to the company (Dickinson 2004: 633). While the state was blamed for lack of co-ordination and leadership, a state-led response would in all likelihood have urged business to follow similar strategies towards HIV/AIDS as it is currently beginning to implement (Dickinson 2004: 635).

SASOL's initial response to HIV/AIDS took place on its mines where the prevalence among wage personnel was estimated to be about 37 per cent. The company dealt with the potential impact on productivity by initiating a 'reserve bench' of workers with key skills to facilitate the replacement of workers who were performing poorly, so as to sustain productivity. At the same time the problems of the affected workers were addressed through training, counselling and treatment of non-AIDS-related illness or entering the AIDS management programme which included anti-retroviral drugs. Stress was placed on working together with the trade unions on these issues (Innes, Dickinson and Henwood 2003: 9).

Within South African working communities, the workers as well as their families are vulnerable. High unemployment levels are exacerbated since each worker with HIV/AIDS 'plunges an extended family into poverty' (Dickinson 2004: 642). Communities acknowledge the importance of SASOL's AIDS policy but relationships with the company may become complex. Innes, Dickinson and Henwood (2003: 12) observed tensions 'between those who are grateful for the company's benevolence and those who would like to see community representatives take a more active and challenging stance towards partnership with the company'. Although SASOL has acknowledged the importance of extending anti-retroviral care to workers' spouses and families, it has preferred to enter into partnerships with government and other donors, rather than covering this expense. Most community representatives and unions feel that the company should take sole responsibility for providing anti-retroviral drugs to all employees and their immediate families (Innes, Dickinson and Henwood 2003: 13).

In some cases the company found that there was no financial difference between responding and doing nothing, but in units with higher prevalence there was a stronger case for intervention. Some managers recognised that it was politically unfeasible to oppose the provision of anti-retroviral drugs whatever the economic cost-benefit analyses revealed. Non-material benefits, such as the company's benevolent, caring image among workers, were seen as critical (Innes, Dickinson and Henwood 2003: 6).

From 1999 a corporate HIV/AIDS forum was established to co-ordinate the company's various initiatives. Guidelines were formulated in December 2000.[3] In 2002, SASOL's Group Human Resources Manager was placed in overall charge of the HIV/AIDS programme. The company engaged the services of a large international consulting firm to assist it in formulating its response to HIV/AIDS, resulting in the implementation of SASOL's HIV and AIDS Response Programme (SHARP). This assesses the potential impact of HIV/AIDS on its operations and it implements behaviour response initiatives and provides for care, including anti-retroviral drugs, through company medical insurance benefits. SHARP coordinators have been appointed in the business units. Regional steering committees, including trade union and community representatives, monitor its progress. A corporate-level steering committee is responsible for strategic review and external communications. Managers are assessed in terms of their performance in respect of HIV / AIDS-related indicators, in line with the way in which health, safety and environment has been given a higher profile in performance appraisals (Dickinson 2004).

While much has been achieved to date, there are still a number of problems. The increased outsourcing of functions has shifted the burden of AIDS from the company onto individual workers and their families. Treatment of spouses and retired workers is still a contentious issue. It is still too early to evaluate SHARP, and SASOL's AIDS record in China and other parts of Africa also requires scrutiny (Innes, Dickinson and Henwood 2003: 14).

SASOL's Employment Equity Plan, submitted in terms of legal requirements, indicated that the organisation intended to have people from designated groups – black, Asian and coloured persons, as well as white women and disabled persons – in at least 40 per cent of all leadership and professional positions in its South African operations by 2005, from a 25 per cent base in 2002. The position in 2004 is shown in Table 4.1. To redress the low levels of black senior managers, SASOL initiated the Accelerated Leadership Development Programme (ALDP) to fast-track the development of senior black employees to fill executive positions. May, Machaka and Roberts (2002: 6) found that in the chemical sector as a whole 'training plans are also racially skewed in favour of white employees'. An important area for consideration is the linking of firms' skills plans with employment equity plans.

Table 4.1: Representation of designated groups within managerial and non-managerial positions at SASOL, 2004.

Category	Designated groups		Designated groups excluding white women	
	No.	%	No.	%
Executives (41)	5	12.2	4	9.8
Senior Management (1 061)	145	13.7	99	9.3
Management (6 514)	2 719	41.7	1 705	26.2
Skilled and semi-skilled (15 843)	12 047	76.0	10 765	68.0

Source: SASOL 2004a, 2004b.

In terms of BEE, SASOL's approach has been to create viable new empowerment businesses in the mainstream economy (SASOL 2003a). In addition, it has established some joint-venture partnerships with black-owned companies such as Exel and Umkhumbe WeAfrika.

Until 2004, commercial agreements with other oil companies prevented SASOL from operating its own service stations: 85 per cent of its fuel production was sold to other oil companies and either branded as SASOL on forecourts or mixed with other fuel. These arrangements obliged SASOL to support Exel in opening over a hundred service stations. Only since 2004 has SASOL had a free hand in establishing its own branded outlets, in which its BEE partners enjoy participation.

SASOL signed the Liquid Fuels Charter in 2000, which committed the company to achieve 25 per cent black equity ownership in its liquid fuels business by the end of the decade. SASOL aims to extend black participation in an integrated liquid fuels business rather than confining it to certain parts of the value chain. However, CEPPWAWU, the major union organised within SASOL, has previously commented that while BEE companies may be gaining access to the market, this might be at the lower and more marginal end of the value chain (Chemical and Allied Industries' Association and CEPPWAWU 2002). The Liquid Fuels Charter was adopted as a result of state intervention rather than as a voluntary initiative on the part of industry. SASOL's non-energy liquid fuels empowerment initiatives include the development of fourteen downstream chemical businesses that employ more than 300 people. Five of these have BEE components.

When SASOL changed chief executives from one white male to another, there was considerable public and media comment on the absence of senior black executives in its board and upper management. This led to a questioning of SASOL's commitment to transformation. SASOL has countered with a plan to extend black ownership of its operations, and 'in due course' to increase black representation at board level (SASOL 2005a: 8).

In November 2004, SASOL announced that it intended to pool its liquid fuel resources with Petronas, the Malaysian oil company and owner of Engen (in 1986, following the US Comprehensive Anti-apartheid Act that required all American corporations to disinvest from South Africa, Mobil had sold its holdings in South Africa to Petronas). Should the merger go ahead, it would make the new company,

Uhambo, the largest liquid fuels business in South Africa. Uhambo would produce 48 per cent of South Africa's liquid fuels and market these across the whole of sub-Saharan Africa. SASOL would throw in its Natref refinery at Sasolburg, while Engen would contribute its Durban refinery. In September 2005, on the eve of appearing before the competition authorities, SASOL announced that Uhambo would make 12.5 per cent of its shares available to an empowerment partner, Tshwarisano LFB (Pty) Ltd. Should the merger not be found acceptable, SASOL undertook to sell 30 per cent of its liquid fuels business to Tshwarisano (*Sunday Times* 25 September 2005).

Tshwarisano (meaning 'pulling together' in SeSotho) is a broad-based consortium led by three prominent businesspersons – Penuell Maduna (former Minister of Justice), Hixonia Nyasulu (one of South Africa's most prominent women company directors) and Reuel Khoza (former chairperson of Eskom). They own 30 per cent of Tshwarisano. A further 47 per cent is owned by Exel, a business which comprises SASOL's previous empowerment partners. Five other consortia of black-owned businesses and NGOs, and trusts set up by SASOL to benefit employees and charities, will retain the remaining 23 per cent. Some of these consortia include trade union investment and pension funds, and there is a high degree of women's participation. SASOL agreed to pay R80 million to Tshwarisano's advisors, and a further R1.1 billion to help underwrite Tshwarisano's purchase.

Merger hearings at the Competition Tribunal proved controversial when it was revealed that the Department of Minerals and Energy's submission had been written by BP's lawyers. BP, Shell, Chevron and Total opposed the merger on the grounds that Uhambo would dominate inland fuel distribution and squeeze its competitors out of the market (*Mail & Guardian* 21 October 2005). In the end, the Tribunal found against Uhambo, and it was not allowed to proceed.

SASOL has also committed to affirmative procurement in respect of the purchase of goods and services from organisations owned and operated by historically disadvantaged groups. The value of these operations more than doubled from R640 million in the 2002 financial year to R1.495 million two years later. CEPPWAWU has acknowledged the importance of procurement, but warns that it must ensure that occupational health, safety and environmental standards are met. The company should also ensure that decent work is promoted, as well as compliance with legislation such as the Skills Development Act (Chemical and Allied Industries' Association and CEPPWAWU 2002).

When SASOL commissioned a corporate history in 1990, its author described it as 'a colossus with a soul' (Wessels 1990: 3). Originally, corporate social and environmental responsibility (CSER) spending was in the purview of the Managing Director and his wife. More recently these interventions have been formalised into line functions. After apartheid, the orientation of spending became more in line with 'the government's call for joint efforts in fighting poverty and developing our country' and a growing realisation of the need to redress the imbalances of the past (M. Mape, Manager, Corporate Social Investment, SASOL, personal communication, May 2003).

SASOL's CSER contributions make it one of the largest donors in the chemical industry and in the corporate sector as a whole. Projects are evaluated in terms of the five identified focus areas: education (45 per cent); job creation and capacity building (33 per cent); health and welfare (4 per cent); environment (4 per cent); and arts and culture (4 per cent) (see Table 4.2). A further ten per cent is held back for support in other areas like sport and crime prevention. Sustainability of the project is an important criterion and previous partnerships are also taken into account. The company involves its employees in its CSR investment through a forum which evaluates the proposals. Amounts under R500 000 are approved by the executive CSR sub-committee. Projects above R500 000 are considered and approved at board level. SASOL requires that a company representative sits on the project's board of trustees or management committee (SASOL 2003c). SASOL's investment takes place directly, through partnerships and associations such as the National Business Initiative.

Table 4.2: SASOL CSER areas and foci.

Area	Specific Focus
Education and training	Supporting mathematics and the sciences Developing educational infrastructure Providing resources and equipment
Job creation and capacity building	Developing entrepreneurs and small businesses
Health and welfare	AIDS awareness programmes and rehabilitation clinics

| Nature conservation and environment | Greening local communities
Protecting endangered species
Supporting bird watching |
| Arts and culture | Supporting musicians, orchestras, choirs and artists |

Source: Various SASOL Annual Reports.

SASOL's expenditure on CSER is not tied to its turnover or profit, as is demonstrated in Table 4.3. Its contribution to CSER leapt in terms of rand expenditure in 2002, but this brought it back in line with earlier (1998–9) levels as a proportion of its turnover and profit. Falling profits in 2004 meant that the proportion of CSER spend rose slightly, although remaining under one per cent of the whole. Increased CSER spending in 2001–2 has resulted in CSER being roughly the same proportion of turnover but lower in terms of operating profit. CSER has increased relative to employees' wages in the period under review.

Table 4.3: SASOL's CSER spending as a proportion of turnover, profit and wages, 1998–2004.

	1998–9		1999–2000		2000–1		2001–2		2002–3		2003–4	
CSER (rands)	23 m		23 m		25 m		75 m		79 m		80 m	
		CSER as %		CSER as %		CSER as %		CSER as %		CSER as %		CSER as %
Turnover	19.2 b	.12	25.8 b	.09	41.2 b	.06	61.6 b	.12	64.5 b	.12	60.1 b	.13
Operating profit	3.7 b	.62	6.4 b	.36	10.8 b	.23	14.7 b	.50	11.9 b	.66	9.3 b	.86
Employees' wages and salaries	3.3 b	.70	3.9 b	.58	5.0 b	.50	7.9 b	.95	9.0 b	.87	8.7 b	.91

Source: Constructed from data provided in SASOL Annual Reports.

Notes: $m=10^6$, $b=10^9$. In company literature the term corporate social investment (CSI) is used instead of CSER.

As a global player, SASOL has extended its CSER programme to its operations outside South Africa. In particular, there is recent emphasis on southern Mozambique, linked to the 865 kilometre natural gas pipeline which connects offshore finds to its plants in South Africa. SASOL has set aside US$5 million for community development in Mozambique, designated for communities living alongside the natural gas pipeline. Other initiatives in partnership with provincial leadership and communities in Mozambique have been directed towards education and training – for example, improvement to the Beira Industrial and Commercial School. This will not only enhance the country's skills base, but it will provide skills for SASOL's local operations.

In its US operations, SASOL's CSER takes the form of incentives to employees to donate their spare time to voluntary work in charities or schools of their choice. SASOL matches donations of time by up to US$3 000 per year and claims the value of these contributions to have been US$319 000 in 2003 (SASOL 2004b).

The question of how best companies can contribute to development is a subject of contention. Strategic interventions at local level deepen the reliance of those communities on the company. Not only is SASOL the major direct employer, it also is the *raison d'être* for many other economic activities and social services in, for example, its two South African hubs of Sasolburg and Secunda. Some see this direct investment in neighbouring communities as 'tantamount to patronage . . . If basic amenities are provided directly by local corporations, rather than as rights of citizenship, then the interests of communities will be aligned with those of the corporations' (Butler and Hallowes 2002: 45). Despite the accusations that these are company towns, relatively combative community organisations have emerged in both areas: Sasolburg Air Quality Monitoring Committee and Secunda's Voice of the Voiceless are concerned with environmental quality and continuing poverty levels.

SASOL was chosen by the NGO GroundWork and the University of KwaZulu-Natal's Centre for Civil Society as one of the recipients of the 2005 Corpse Awards, awarded to South Africa's 'deadliest corporations'. The Corpse Awards 'recognise worst corporate practice in producing environmental injustice' (GroundWork 2005: 1). In SASOL's case, the award was justified by SASOL's massive emissions of sulphur dioxide, hydrogen sulphide, volatile organic compounds, toxic wastes and carbon dioxide (57 million tonnes per year), as well as its lethal safety record.

Unions, too, have been pushing for better safety conditions at SASOL's plants and have participated critically in safety audits. The company acknowledges a 54 per cent union membership of its staff, organised by CEPPWAWU, the South African Chemical Workers' Union and Solidarity (the last with a largely white skilled membership).

The ability of civil society to stand up against industrial giants and to participate independently within company-instituted forums depends on the level of civil society organisation in that community. An essential support for community organisations is the development and enforcement of suitable environmental regulations which take into account both national environmental and development imperatives. Of relevance to the Sasolburg struggles is the emergence of a regional community environmental organisation, the Vaal Environmental Justice Alliance, launched in October 2005. This has emerged at a time when the state has, under pressure from civil society, begun to address the problems of air quality with the requisite urgency and decisiveness upon which campaigners have long been insisting.

In positioning itself as a global player, SASOL is under external pressure to improve its social and environmental performance. Membership of the Global Compact and other voluntary initiatives like Responsible Care obliges it to address issues which, in the past, it had neglected. The company can no longer look to the state as it did in the past, as sole shareholder, guarantor, protector, subsidiser and shield in relation to the labour market. The contemporary state has to play new roles guaranteeing BEE, employment equity, recognition of labour rights and environmental regulation. Although it is no longer cast in the role of apartheid sanctions buster, SASOL still has much leverage. As the petroleum price soars upward, the utility of its technology has been recognised as enormously advantageous.

As South Africa's largest public company by market capitalisation, the biggest player in the chemicals sector and the largest contributor in respect of CSER, SASOL's contribution to broader development goals will remain of great interest. A major challenge for the company will be to achieve better social and environmental standards of practice at home and to replicate this as it penetrates other developing countries that have poor human rights records or low labour and environmental standards.

Conclusion

The chemicals sector in South Africa has been shown to be significant and well-organised. However, its implementation of voluntary initiatives such as Responsible Care has been inadequate in terms of transparency, verifiability and public trust. This is particularly problematic under conditions of fragmented regulation, lack of capacity in government, and poor monitoring. It has underscored the importance of vigilant civil society formations on the fence lines of chemical companies, as well as trade unions that seek better working conditions and the linking of incentives to safety management rather than to output. Responsible Care has encouraged community awareness and emergency response committees in South Africa, but its implementation has been uneven and has attracted suspicion from communities where there is a history of poor relations with the industry stemming from the apartheid era. AECI established such a committee after a chlorine spill which hospitalised 90 local residents, but often these committees are seen as rubber stamps for industry (Acutt and Medina-Ross 2004: 309–10). CAIA's Voluntary Advisory Forum has been regarded as toothless by the chemical unions, which refuse to participate within the terms set by industry. Unless Responsible Care is revised to address some of the problems of transparency, accountability and participation, it will remain problematic and the credibility of the industry in addressing fundamental problems will be compromised.

In addition to the Responsible Care initiatives, chemical companies have adopted a number of other CSER initiatives. Acutt (2003) lists corporate membership of environmental groups, ecotourism sponsorship, support for environmental education, youth development and sports; as well as the provision of training and educational scholarships. However, these measures fail to address the central problem of the industry's record of safe management of the chemical value chain. They have not integrated social concerns sufficiently into normal operational practice. Therefore, despite the Responsible Care programme, the chemical industry has not sufficiently dedicated itself to a path of fundamental CSER. Such a path would involve making commitments to greater transparency, accountability and public participation in standard setting and monitoring. Real responsibility would also involve strengthening the state's regulatory capacity and encouraging smaller firms to uphold best practice. Until it is capable of making these kinds of commitments, the industry will continue to experience a deficit in public trust.

Notes

1. PIP standards determine whether companies have implemented six Responsible Care codes of practice – community awareness and emergency response, research and development, manufacturing, transportation, distribution, and hazardous waste management. Implementation is verified by independent third party evaluators.
2. This system is approved by the US EPA. Results are valid for the moment and place of sampling.
3. The development of policies was assisted by the national negotiation of a *Code of Good Practice on Key Aspects of HIV/AIDS and Employment* in NEDLAC (National Economic Development and Labour Council 2000: 5).

References

Acutt, N. 2003. 'Policy, People and Petrochemicals: A Case Study of Voluntary Approaches to Corporate Environmentalism in the South Durban Basin'. Norwich: School of Environmental Sciences, University of East Anglia (PhD thesis).

Acutt, N. and V. Medina-Ross with T. O'Riordan. 2004. 'Perspectives on Corporate Social Responsibility in the Chemical Sector: A Comparative Analysis of the Mexican and South African Cases'. *Natural Resources Forum* 28: 302–16.

Albertyn, C. and G. Watkins. 2002. *Partners in Pollution: Voluntary Agreements and Corporate Greenwash.* Pietermaritzburg: GroundWork.

Brümmer, S. 2000. 'Where Breathing is a Health Hazard'. *Mail & Guardian*, 2 June.

Butler, M. 1997. 'Lessons from Thor Chemicals: The Links Between Health, Safety and Environmental Protection'. In *The Bottom Line: Industry and the Environment in South Africa*, edited by L. Bethlehem and M. Goldblatt. Cape Town: University of Cape Town Press.

Butler, M. and D. Hallowes. 2002. *Corporate Accountability in South Africa: The GroundWork Report.* Pietermaritzburg: GroundWork.

Carnie, R. 2004. 'Clean-up of Waste at Thor to Start Soon'. *The Mercury*, 4 August.

Chemical and Allied Industries' Association (CAIA) and Chemicals, Energy, Printing, Paper, Wood and Allied Workers' Union (CEPPWAWU). 2002. *Accord Towards Improvement in Occupational Health and Safety, 19 September.* Johannesburg: CAIA and CEPPWAWU.

Cock, J. and E. Koch (eds). 1991. *Going Green: People, Politics and the Environment in South Africa.* Cape Town: OUP.

Crompton, R. 1994. 'The South African Commodity Plastics Filière: History and Future Options'. Cape Town: Industrial Strategy Project, University of Cape Town (unpublished draft).

Dickinson, D. 2004. 'Corporate South Africa's Response to HIV/AIDS: Why So Slow?' *Journal of Southern African Studies* 30 (3): 627–50.

Goldblatt, M. 1997. 'Registering Pollution: The Prospects for a Pollution Information System'. In *The Bottom Line: Industry and the Environment in South Africa*, edited by L. Bethlehem and M. Goldblatt. Cape Town: University of Cape Town Press.

GroundWork. 2005. *The Corpse Awards 2005: For South Africa's Deadliest Corporations*. Pietermaritzburg: GroundWork.

Innes, D., D. Dickinson and L. Henwood. 2003. 'Report of Business Responses to HIV/ AIDS in South Africa's Top 25 Companies'. Johannesburg: UNAIDS and UNRISD (unpublished report).

International Federation of Chemical, Energy, Mine and General Workers' Unions (ICEM). 1997. *Responsible Care – A Credible Industry Response? An ICEM Survey of the Understanding and Participation of Workers and their Trade Union Representatives in the Chemical Industry's Responsible Care Programme*. Brussels: ICEM.

Kirk, P. 2000. 'Clouds of Death over Sasolburg'. *Mail & Guardian*, 25 August.

May, C., J. Machaka and S. Roberts. 2002. *Economic Trends in the Chemical Industries and Implications for Skills Development*. Unpublished paper presented to the School of Economic and Business Sciences, University of the Witwatersrand, Johannesburg.

National Economic Development and Labour Council (NEDLAC). 2003. *Study into the Implications of Implementing the Globally Harmonised System of Classification and Labelling of Chemicals and Development of an Implementation Strategy for South Africa*. Johannesburg: NEDLAC.

National Economic Development and Labour Council (NEDLAC) and South African Department of Labour. 2000. *Code of Good Practice on Key Aspects of HIV/AIDS and Employment*. Pretoria: Department of Labour.

SASOL. 2003a. *Annual Report 2003*. Johannesburg: SASOL.

———. 2003b. *Sasolfacts* (April).

———. 2003c. *The Soul of SASOL 2003: Overview of SASOL's Corporate Social Investment Programmes*. Johannesburg: SASOL Group Communications and Public Affairs Department.

———. 2004a. *Annual Review 2004 and Summarised Financial Information*. Johannesburg: SASOL.

———. 2004b. *Sustainable Development Summary Report 2002–2004*. Johannesburg: SASOL.

———. 2005a. *Annual Review and Summarised Financial Information 2005*. Johannesburg: SASOL.

———. 2005b. *Sustainable Development Report 2005*. Johannesburg: SASOL.

———. 2006. *Annual Review and Summarised Financial Information 2006*. Johannesburg: SASOL.

Sissell, K. 2002. 'ACC fine-tunes RC 14001'. *Chemical Week*, 25 September.

Utting, P. (ed.). 2002. *The Greening of Business in Developing Countries: Rhetoric, Reality and Prospects*. London: Zed Books.

Ward, H. 2002. *Corporate Accountability in Search of a Treaty? Some Insights from Foreign Direct Liability*. London: Chatham House (Sustainable Development Programme Briefing Paper, 4).

Wessels, P. 1990. *Crescendo to Success: SASOL 1975–1987*. Cape Town: Human and Rousseau.

5

The food and drink industry

David Fig

Introduction

Food is important to all – to survive we need its nutrients. To secure its supply we need to engage in productive and service activities all along the food chain. Those not connected to the food chain need other resources to command access to its products. Its consumption goes beyond health and nutritional concerns and is invested with all kinds of cultural meanings, preferences and taboos. Its mass production has commodified it, leaving consumers dependent on global trading, pricing and marketing decisions far removed from their control.

The world experiences overproduction of food on the one hand and hunger on the other. Developed countries subsidise their food producers and stockpile what cannot be sold, while developing countries are faced with the question of ensuring basic food security – access by all their citizens to sufficient amounts of healthy food at all times. Yet, simultaneously, developing countries have to deal with the challenges of inequitable land ownership, mass unemployment, open access to more competitive imports, declining terms of trade, and steep food price inflation. The gap between the rich and the poor is growing.

This unevenness is a symptom of the commodification of food. Despite significant trade liberalisation, farmers in developed countries are still highly subsidised, having persuaded their governments to restrict market access, and to allow stockpiling and dumping. The intensification of agriculture has led to high-input factory farming, impacting on animal health and leading in some areas to the spread of diseases such as bovine spongiform encephalitis (BSE) and foot-

and-mouth. Applications of industrial chemical inputs and processes into agriculture and food production have also led to serious environmental problems such as water contamination, air pollution and soil degradation. The application of modern biotechnology to the food chain has raised questions about the environmental, medical and ethical impacts of genetic modification of crops, as well as challenges to the patenting of life forms by large corporations seeking to extend their control over the food chain. Products of the fast-food industry, whose franchising is only beginning to slow down after huge expansion, have supplanted more traditional and local foods, reduced nutrition, raised rates of heart disease, obesity and diabetes in developing countries, and have an extensive adverse ecological and social footprint. Modern patterns of industrialisation have led to serious climatic changes, impacting on agriculture and the availability of crucial inputs such as water, with Africa being particularly prone to higher levels of drought and desertification. Therefore, the challenges to the development of social and environmental responsibility in the corporate food sector are complex and numerous.

Although this chapter will largely discuss the food processing industry in South Africa, the picture cannot be understood without considering backward and forward linkages into agriculture and retailing. Each link in the food chain helps to form an understanding of a range of issues – from food security, nutrition and health to productivity, social equity and environmental sustainability. The sector has porous boundaries: it usually includes beverages and sometimes, but not always, tobacco. However, this study has taken cognisance of the tobacco industry because of its backward linkages into agriculture in the Southern African subcontinent, and because it makes particular kinds of claims to social responsibility.

South Africa has, since 1652, been a provider of agricultural commodities to the rest of the world. Its crop exports include wine, wheat, fruit, tea, tobacco, groundnuts and sugar. Meat, wool, hides and fish products also contribute to exports. The country's staple food crop is maize: 6.7 million tonnes are consumed annually, while production ranges from between two and ten million tonnes, depending on the vagaries of rainfall. Under drought conditions it becomes necessary to import, while in good years there is sufficient excess production to export.

The country's racist past continues to be reflected in its agrarian structures. The majority of black peasants had progressively been dispossessed by the late 1930s, and white farmers were allocated the most productive land. Currently there are approximately 60 000 commercial farmers, still overwhelmingly white. During apartheid they enjoyed preferential access to agricultural credit, were major beneficiaries of state irrigation schemes, and gained from price controls, protectionism and subsidisation. Black people were confined to cultivating just thirteen per cent of the land, and were effectively excluded from full participation in commercial agriculture. Efforts are under way to redress this racially skewed situation, but land and agrarian reform have been slow and have not yet made a radical difference to land ownership. The harsh legacies of slavery, indentured labour, migrant labour, sharecropping, labour tenancy, child labour and the tot system (in which a portion of wages was paid in alcohol) have all made their mark on social relations in the countryside. Currently, employers are resisting the implementation of a statutory monthly minimum wage of R714 (R872 in some areas) for farm workers, even though this is less than a living wage (South Africa, Department of Labour 2004).

Food and beverage processing has become a major part of manufacturing in South Africa. The industry developed in tandem with the needs of the mining industry, which grew after the discovery of diamonds (in the 1860s) and gold (in the 1880s). Technologies of food preservation improved during the nineteenth century, with canning and bottling making room for the application of refrigeration to safeguard fresh meat and fish products over time and distance. Advances in chemistry also assisted with food preservation problems, although in the late twentieth century affluent consumers began to question chemical residues in food and to develop a preference for more organic products. The South African food processing industry grew from local efforts at dairy production, at milling and baking of cereal products, and canning of fruit and vegetables. The mineral revolution also made it possible for foreign investors to gain scale advantages by setting up local plants: Unilever, Reckitt & Colman, Coca-Cola and others blazed the trail in the food sector. Levels of direct investment grew in the period after 1945, reaching a peak with the boom of the 1960s and contracting by the 1980s due to consumer boycotts and sanctions. By the mid 1990s, South Africa's democratic transition led to a new wave of investment in the sector. A number of local operations sold out to foreign brand leaders, particularly in the dairy and tobacco industries. Trade unionists have contrasted the harsher behaviour of some of these new entrants against that of longer-established transnational corporations.

This chapter attempts to assess the size, shape and importance of the food sector in South Africa. It examines how principles of corporate social and economic responsibility (CSER) are understood and applied in the sector. It raises strategic questions about the nature of partnerships in and around the sector. While it could not comprehensively survey every initiative in the sector, the study relied on published material from key companies, the business press, government, researchers and other stakeholders, as well as in-depth interviews with key role players from the corporate, trade union and research communities.

The food sector in the South African economy
As human beings living in the early twenty-first century, we generally consume very little that we cultivate ourselves. We have become dependent upon a vast agricultural and industrial production chain, which has global dimensions and keeps many millions of people employed.

Industry dimensions
South Africa has a significant place in global food production, with exports consistently exceeding imports. It currently derives over 2.8 per cent of its Gross Domestic Product (GDP) from agriculture and over 16.4 per cent of its GDP from manufacturing, of which food manufacturing accounts for five per cent and beverages for one per cent. This compares with 6.3 per cent of GDP from mining. Trade, including retail food sales, makes up a further 13.8 per cent of GDP (Statistics SA 2006: 5, Table A).

Manufacturing inputs in the food industry (packaging, chemicals, machinery) amounted to R24.8 billion in 1997, while the sector spent R3 billion on transport, R3 billion on financial and business services and R1.25 billion on energy and water (WEFA Consultants 1997). The value derived from activities comprising the food chain is thus considerable. Between 1990 and 2001, the food and beverage industry had average annual sales worth R59 billion. This culminated in sales of R83 billion in the year to June 2001, of which the beverage market was worth over R20 billion (Kirsten and Vink 2002: 9, Table 7; Statistics SA 2003).

Food manufacturing is often shorthand for the food, beverage and tobacco industry. The food component of this can further be broken down into the following sub-sectors: food production and processing; dairy; milled grains and starches; and baking, sugar and confectionery products. Each of the sub-sectors has its own institutional, social and economic dynamics, and data for each is collected separately under the Standard Industrial Classification System. It should also be noted that the sector does not include unprocessed foods such as fresh fruit and vegetables.

In general, manufacturing has experienced a decline, relative to the tertiary or services sector, as has the food, beverage and tobacco industry. Nevertheless, it remains the third-largest manufacturing sector by gross value of production (18%) after metals (23%) and petrol refining (around 20%).

Extent of employment
In terms of employment, the industry accounts for 3.9 per cent of all non-agricultural jobs in South Africa, and for 14.4 per cent of all manufacturing jobs. Numerically, this amounted to an estimated 185 728 jobs in June 2000 (Statistics SA 2000).[1] The calculation of the estimated workforce should be regarded with caution, however, since it does not account for workers in unregistered casual jobs or those in the informal sector, nor does it take into account those in related upstream or downstream industries. With these caveats, it should nevertheless be noted that the formal statistics indicate a declining trend in employment in the sector since 1990. Official figures have estimated this as a net loss of 52 000 jobs between 1990 and 2000, and a further 46 000 jobs between 2000 and 2003 (South Africa, Department of Trade and Industry undated). This could be attributed to factors such as a decline in consumption, the impact of mergers and acquisitions, the installation of less labour-intensive technologies, outsourcing of services, or the increasing use of unregistered casual labour through labour brokers. The decline occurred in all sub-sectors, but was sharpest in beverages and food processing (South Africa, Department of Trade and Industry; National Productivity Institute, 1990–96; Statistics SA, 1990–96; Statistics SA 1997–2000; Statistics SA 2000–03).

The formal wage bill has been estimated at just under R7.5 billion in 2003, with 55 per cent allocated to skilled occupations and 44 per cent to semi-skilled and unskilled workers. Breadwinners, on average, are likely to be responsible for five dependents each, and therefore the formal industry is likely to provide livelihoods for up to 930 000 people.

Employment conditions

It is extremely difficult to get a comprehensive picture of employment conditions in the industry. There is likely to be a wide range of different experiences. For example, Unilever claims not to pay unskilled workers below R3 000 per month (Interview, Hall, 9 May 2003), whereas the evidence in a sample of 397 respondents in the industry, contained in the 1999 October Household Survey, indicated that most weekly-paid workers who were surveyed (except in the beverage sub-sector) reported earnings of below R8 per hour (that is, less than R320 per 40-hour week). The survey indicated that only 75 per cent of workers in the industry are employed full-time (compared to 92% in the auto industry), with 12 per cent of women workers employed seasonally. Two thirds of the sample spent over 40 hours on the job (20% over 51 hours a week) (Statistics SA 1999). From this sample, it is possible to deduce that the majority of workers in the sector are earning below the minimum necessary to maintain a household of up to five dependents. In addition, the surveyed workers reported that benefits were rudimentary, with only 24 per cent of workers having medical aid contributions paid by employers, only 49 per cent having a pension contribution from employers, and only 57 per cent being granted paid leave (Statistics SA 1999). Conditions at work are said to deteriorate in smaller enterprises and in rural areas where there is less unionised labour and higher risks associated with unemployment (Interview, Masemola, 12 May 2003).

The Compensation Fund, which deals with occupational injury claims, reported 5 951 claims in the sector during 1995, of which 5 076 were the result of accidents involving machinery, lifts or vehicles while there were 23 fatalities that year (South Africa, Department of Labour 1999). Two years later, the figures were 4 472 claims out of a base of 263 762 workers, estimated at a frequency rate of 0.09. These figures indicate that, while not as dangerous as mining (frequency rate of 0.3), employment conditions in the industry are often unsafe, and injuries happen three times more frequently than in the chemical industry (0.03) (South Africa, Department of Labour 2001: Table 8B).

Production, ownership and concentration in the South African food sector

Productive activities

Food processing in South Africa is extremely diversified due to the variety of resources, crops and other agricultural commodities that the country produces. It includes the processing of dairy, fish, meat, fruit and vegetables, grain milling and baking, sugar refining, and the production of sweets and confectionery, tea and coffee, oils and animal feeds.

South Africa's climate varies across three main zones. The winter rainfall zone occurs in the Western Cape: it has a Mediterranean-type climate, allowing for the cultivation of grapes, olives, wheat, barley, hops and deciduous fruits. The grasslands occur in the central highlands, where maize, potatoes and sunflowers predominate. The sub-tropical zone in the KwaZulu-Natal, Limpopo and Mpumalanga lowveld areas is suitable for sugar, cotton and tropical produce. This climatic variation favours a wide range of secondary food processing industries, of a variety of sizes. Exports of canned fruit, vegetables and juices are well established, destined mainly for European and Asian markets. The sector also produces a wide range of processed foods for the domestic retail and food-service markets, as well as for agriculture, largely in the form of animal feed.

The beverage industry, particularly beer brewing and wine, has expanded continually. The sector has a wide product range, including conventional and sorghum beer, natural and fortified wines and spirits, as well as non-alcoholic soft drinks, which have experienced a recent boom (sports drinks, iced teas and bottled mineral water being some of the innovations). Despite expansion in the domestic market, the average per capita consumption of alcohol was 7.81 litres per year in 2003 and South Africa is therefore ranked relatively modestly by international standards. By comparison, the average per capita consumption for Australia was 9.19 litres, and for France 13.54 litres (World Health Organisation 2004: 11–12). Of total production in 2001, beers accounted for 45 per cent of the market, non-alcoholic drinks for 30 per cent, and wines and spirits for 25 per cent.

Wine is a relatively developed industry in South Africa, ranked seventh in terms of world output. With a global market share of 3.4 per cent in 1999, it produced three times the Australian harvest. There has been recent expansion in the number of cellars as well as export volume (22 million litres in 1992; 70 million litres in 1995; and 237 million litres in 2003). Despite its reputation for export, in 2003 only 25 per cent of total production went abroad. Wine employs about 50 000 workers, who support 250 000 dependants (South African Wine Industry Statistics 2003).

South African Breweries (now SABMiller) has become the world's second largest beer brewer, with interests in Africa, Central America, North America, Europe, India and China, selling brands such as Castle, Miller, Pilsner Urquell and Peroni. Its beer interests in South Africa continue to be managed by SAB Limited in Johannesburg, but it has received bourse listings in London and New York, and has located its head office in London. SAB Limited has over 95 per cent of the share of the local market in beer and usually manages to undercut and squeeze out budding rivals.

Overwhelmingly dominant in the soft drinks market, the Coca-Cola stable includes its own brands as well as those of Cadbury-Schweppes (purchased in 1999) and Appletiser (purchased in 2000). Coca-Cola distributes its products through a number of local bottling companies, most prominent of which is Amalgamated Beverage Industries (ABI) in Gauteng, which is majority owned by SAB (Ligthelm and Martins 1998; Van Seventer 1998; University of South Carolina 1999). Recent studies have estimated that the Coca-Cola system directly employed 16 500 bottling workers in 1998, but that 178 200 jobs were supported directly and indirectly by the same system in South Africa, amounting to a multiplier of eleven. Of the larger total, 42 per cent or 74 800 workers are located in the informal sector (University of South Carolina 1999: iii–iv). Rival company Pepsico failed in 1997 to establish local production after the lifting of sanctions, but some of its products bottled in Namibia enter the market through a customs union agreement. Nestlé recently entered the growing bottled water and iced tea markets. There are numerous local soft drink producers who together enjoy only a small fraction of the market.

In the case of tobacco, a single firm dominates, controlling over 90 per cent of a market in which one in every four adults smokes. This is British American Tobacco South Africa (BAT-SA), with its origins in the United Tobacco Corporation. In 1999 the parent group merged with Rothmans International (formerly Rembrandt), owned by the heirs of the late South African entrepreneur Anton Rupert, who retained a 25 per cent share in the British American Tobacco (BAT) group. BAT-SA is a wholly-owned subsidiary which employs 2 600 people, half of whom work in its two cigarette factories in Paarl (Western Cape) and Heidelberg (Gauteng).

Although not strictly speaking part of the sector, this study also sought to understand retail activities insofar as they impact on the food chain and prices. To this end, the focus was on Pick 'n Pay, one of the larger retail chains, and one which has been engaged in social responsibility activities for over three decades. Pick 'n Pay inhabits a retail landscape in which there are a few other large competitors (Shoprite-Checkers-OK group, Spar stores, Woolworths[2]). It sells fresh and packaged foods, and operates in-store bakeries as well as stocking non-food consumer items. With their considerable buying power and scale of operations, supermarkets are able to charge lower prices than convenience stores (referred to in South Africa as general dealers, corner cafés, spaza shops and tuckshops), and as a result command a large share of consumer spending on food.

Types of firm

This study was unable to assess CSER activities in the medium, small and micro business fields. Since at this scale there is little documentation, very limited participation in networks and less intensive trade union organisation, it was not easy to develop an accurate picture of such activities. At this scale, CSER is less likely to be significant and tends to be very localised with less pressure to improve corporate governance or environmental performance. However, this scale of activity may be significant at an aggregate level in its unwillingness or inability to conform to labour or environmental standards. Larger-scale firms have brand reputation concerns and more incentive and resources to devote to improving their corporate citizenship profiles. Nevertheless, smaller producers or service providers often have to conform to ethical and other responsibilities demanded by their larger partners. This is often the case in the food sector where larger corporations may demand that their smaller raw material suppliers do not engage in child labour, or do not supply them with genetically modified crops. Therefore, the small, medium and micro firms' positions will not be considered other than in relation to the larger corporations.

Ownership structure

Foreign wholly-owned subsidiaries in the food sector tend to respond to broader head office visions with regard to CSER. In most cases, this vision is an extensive one which has been carefully crafted, stresses the triple-bottom-line, and makes efforts to live up to codes of conduct on labour and the environment. However, our research also noted that with some of the newer entrants to the South African market there was a close correlation between weak CSER initiatives and poor or combative relationships with the workforce in the wake of mergers and local acquisitions. Since wholly-owned subsidiaries are responsible only to their head offices and not to local shareholders, there are no statutory obligations to report locally on their activities. Those who have been transparent about their activities, and who issue socio-environmental reports aimed at accurate accounting for these activities, are therefore to be commended. A further issue with respect to these firms is that, by virtue of being wholly owned, they are not in a position to offer shares in their companies in order to diversify ownership to enhance black economic empowerment (BEE).

Companies quoted on the JSE Securities Exchange include some of the larger players in each of the sub-sectors of the food industry. In May 2003, the JSE listed five beverage firms and nineteen food producers and processors under the category 'non-cyclical consumer goods'. Retail supermarket listings were placed under different headings: two were listed under 'non-cyclical services: food and drug retailers', while the remainder fell under 'cyclical services: general retailers'. Most of the listed companies in food and retail are firms engaged in meat or poultry production, grain milling, sugar milling and manufacture, fishing, agriculture, food and confectionery processing, or supermarket operation. Surprisingly few of the locally listed firms have CSER programmes in place. Apart from beverage companies SAB, ABI and Distell (30% owned by SAB),[3] retailers Pick 'n Pay and Woolworths, and sugar millers Illovo and Tongaat-Hullett,[4] the remainder of the listed companies on the JSE have no significant CSER profiles. The same group (without Distell) are the only food-related firms profiled in the latest edition of *The CSI Handbook* (Rockey 2002)[5] and the only listed firms to participate in membership of the South African Grantmakers' Association (SAGA).

The JSE is in the process of launching its FTSE/JSE Socially Responsible Investment index, which will develop measurements for corporate social and environmental performance. Although participation is intended to be voluntary, there is an expectation of a good response as firms seek to demonstrate their sincerity in supporting triple-bottom-line accounting. The index has potential to provide firms with a competitive edge. Leading firms in the sub-sectors may create a demonstration effect among their smaller rivals in setting the trend for participation (Newton-King 2002; Interview, Newton-King, 30 November 2002; *Sunday Times* 2003).

Listed firms are also one of the targets of the King II Report, a significant initiative by the Institute of Directors to improve corporate governance, with stress on sustainable development and triple-bottom-line accounting (King Committee 2002). King II followed on an earlier, narrower attempt which looked largely at boardroom ethics and practice. The report has met with wide acceptance among listed companies, the financial services community and the public sector, and its principles are also likely to have an extensive impact outside these entities.

While it is true to say that shareholder activism is not a strong feature of South African society, it is also true that there is a very vigilant financial press and growing pressure from the non-governmental organisation (NGO) community for financial, social and environmental probity.

Local unlisted firms are perhaps the most numerous in the sector. Some of these are sizeable and have significant market share, particularly in sub-sectors such as grain milling, where Genfoods-Premier and Pioneer (Bokomo-Sasko merger) are key role players. While Genfoods has directed its support to nature conservation initiatives, Pioneer has emphasised community development. Pioneer is an example of an unlisted firm which has aligned its corporate social investments with the principles of King II (Interview, Steyn, 30 April 2003). Unlisted companies are not obliged to report their results to the public – hence there is less leverage from public shareholders. Nevertheless, unlisted firms are not always immune to a range of pressures for transparency, not least from consumers.

Does the nature of ownership over-determine the CSER responses of firms? It is clear from the brief ownership typology above that the diversity in responses to CSER is fairly independent of the ownership structure of the firm. This will be confirmed in some of the more detailed appraisal of CSER practice below.

Concentration

The industry is characterised by a high degree of capital concentration. Of an estimated 1 800 firms in the sector, it is dominated by the 'top ten companies which are responsible for 68% of the industry's turnover' (Confederation of the Food and Drink Industries of the European Community 2002). High concentration occurs, as we have seen, in each of the sub-sectors. This usually means that there are a few dominant producers for each category, and in some cases a single dominant firm. This level of concentration creates the usual expectations of consumers and shareholders of large-scale enterprises and carries certain implications for the nature and extent of CSER activities. However, some of these expectations are likely to be resisted, particularly where they pose a risk to monopoly or dominant position in the sub-sector. For example, SAB has always vigorously resisted attempts by smaller firms to enter beer manufacturing. In discussions, notions of corporate responsibility in the sphere of extending BEE are restricted to diversification of service providers (distributors, taverners, etc.) rather than permitting new-entry competitors to access SAB's monopoly market share (Interview, Vukuza-Linda, 23 April 2003).

Meanings of and approaches to CSER in the South African food sector

In examining CSER in a highly diversified sector, it is important to understand how some of the practitioners interpret the way in which their activities achieve corporate and societal goals.

Visions and guiding documents

Firms that are seriously engaged in CSER invariably bind themselves to certain principled commitments or guiding philosophies. Some firms have issued their own codes. For example, in April 2002 Unilever (2002a) issued a revised Code of Business Principles which upholds values of honesty, transparency, diversity, human rights and legality, and sets out its obligations to different stakeholders and the environment. It includes sections on product development ('we will respect the concerns of our consumers'), competition ('vigorous yet fair'), anti-corruption, ethical responses to conflicts of interest, and steps necessary to monitor the code. At its Durban office, headquarters of the local operation and soon to be head office for the African region of Unilever, the code is given great prominence. A hyper-enlarged version graces the entrance and leaflets containing the document are distributed in the foyer. The company has also issued a mission statement on its sustainable agriculture initiative, but stops short of a refusal to prioritise organic farming methods over the cultivation of genetically modified organisms (GMOs) (Unilever 2002b).

As part of the Coca-Cola Promise, the company has issued ten explicit priorities against which 'clear, disciplined action' will be taken. These include values of diversity, human resource development, innovation, trusting relationships with 'all our constituents', rejuvenation and building of brands, good corporate citizenship, and 'clear leadership and innovation in sustaining the environment' (Coca-Cola Undated). As noted earlier, the corporation appoints locally-owned bottling firms to undertake production and distribution. In the promise this relationship is referred to in the following words, 'We will work with our bottling partners with clear respect for the independent nature of our relationship, actively supporting their efforts to evolve business structures that work best for them' (Coca-Cola Undated). Is this meant to imply that the bottlers are not bound by the Coca-Cola Promise, nor by standards of employment, environmental management and good citizenship set by the corporation? Unlike the Unilever code, the Coca-Cola Promise contains nothing explicit about ethics, corruption, transparency or human rights. It does speak of a 'focus on brand Coca-Cola' without considering the health implications of this high-sugar, high-caffeine product when explicitly marketed to young people.

SAB has a values statement which includes the assertion that 'We are a responsible corporate citizen' (South African Breweries 2002: 9). SAB networks in the United States where it is a member of Business for Social Responsibility, in the United Kingdom where it has joined AccountAbility, and in South Africa where it is a member of SAGA. In addition, it has a set of guiding principles that cover relations with various stakeholders, numbering future generations as part of this, in a way that allows for dealing with sustainable development, including the natural environment.

The Pick 'n Pay philosophy rests on a central metaphor which founder and chairman Raymond Ackerman derived from educators and mentors such as Professor W.H. Hutt (Department of Commerce, University of Cape Town) and Bernardo Trujillo (a US marketing

expert). Ackerman speaks of applying Trujillo's concept of four legs of
a table, supporting a healthy business: people, merchandise, promotion
(incorporating social responsibility) and administration. Thus, 'each
leg is vital to maintaining a healthy balance but the consumer atop
the table and the principles of consumer sovereignty are always
paramount, always providing the reason for the existence of the
structure below (Ackerman 2001: 62; Interview, R. Ackerman, 5 May
2003). Hutt's influence included erasing the difference between caring
and making profits. Says Ackerman, 'It is an absolute fact that the more
we ploughed into staff benefits, the more we gave to charity, the more
profits rose' (Ackerman 2001: 39–40). Pick 'n Pay estimate their social
responsibility programmes at 8 per cent of post-tax profit (Interview, W.
Ackerman, 5 May 2003).

Proctor & Gamble (P&G) is Cincinnati-based and has a portfolio
of around 250 brands, mostly non-foods, in the areas of detergents,
health, hygiene, beauty and baby care. However, it also markets some
food and beverage brands (Pringles being the most prominent in South
Africa), which amounted to 13.8 per cent of 2000–1 production by value
(Proctor & Gamble 2001: 31). P&G claims that its Principles, Values and
Statement of Purpose document is central to its organisation and that
the concept of sustainable development has been embraced in a way
that is consistent with this document (Proctor & Gamble 2001: 4, 12).
Part of the corporate culture is a comprehensive system of measuring
performance at all operational venues, so that most data are reported
on a global basis. Each business unit is responsible for the accuracy and
consistency of its own data, and collection systems are user-friendly.
This data-based approach assists in validating annual results in all the
measurable areas. Its performance led the Dow Jones Sustainability
Index to rate P&G first in the non-cyclical consumer products sector
in 2001.

Other corporations have aligned themselves with externally-
derived sets of principles. Among these, the King II Report is the most
significant benchmark in South Africa. King II is mindful of the classic
Brundtland definition of sustainable development, but offers its own
understanding of the concept of sustainability:

> In a corporate context, 'sustainability' means that each
> enterprise must balance the need for long-term viability and
> prosperity – of the enterprise itself and the societies and

environment on which it relies for its ability to generate economic value – with the requirement for short-term competitiveness and financial gain . . . (N)on-financial issues – social, ethical and environmental issues – can no longer be regarded as secondary to more conventional business imperatives (King Committee 2002: 91–2).

Drawing on work of the Commonwealth Business Council Working Group on Corporate Citizenship, the report outlines a set of principles underlying sustainability reporting and governance. It draws the attention of practitioners to existing codes such as the Global Compact, the Global Reporting Initiative (GRI), the Global Sullivan Principles and the AA 1000 framework (King Committee 2002: 226–75) and goes so far as to reproduce key information on these codes. In addition, the report recommends the implementation of standards such as ISO 9000 (quality control), ISO 14000 (environmental management), SA 8000 (social accounting) and OHSAS 18000 (health and safety) (King Committee 2002: 101). There is great stress on sound relations with stakeholders and on dealing with social transformation issues such as employment equity, diversity management, BEE and social investment.

Because the King II Report is home-grown, revises an already familiar Code of Corporate Practices and Conduct, and introduces local firms to a range of external codes, there has been a great deal of interest in its content. In the food sector, Pioneer Foods stated that they have aligned all their social responsibility objectives with King II (Interview, Steyn, 30 April 2003). British American Tobacco South Africa uses the AA 1000 and the GRI guidelines, but also explicitly incorporates the principles of stakeholder dialogue contained in King II (British American Tobacco South Africa 2002: 6). This trend is likely to be extended, and is by no means confined to the food and beverage sector.

Commercial benefit
CSER tends to be managed from within public, corporate or external affairs divisions as stand-alone operations while budgets for pure sponsorship are usually seen as part of the marketing division's activities. Nevertheless, there are considerable commercial gains to be made from CSER spending. Key gains include extending brand recognition and reputation enhancement.

Parmalat, which in recent years acquired a number of local dairy enterprises including Bonnita and Towerkop, has as one of its CSER emphases the question of children. 'Our milk products are to do with nutrition and child development, and so we find our support going to projects that are dealing with these themes', said Werda Biesenbach, Parmalat's head of corporate communications and editor of *Parmalat Pulse*. Parmalat also supports an environmental school which runs short courses for children from disadvantaged backgrounds. 'We see our products as close to the environment and to children, so we took time and trouble in selecting a project that would reflect these concerns' (Interview, Biesenbach, 29 April 2003).

Pioneer Foods links specific CSER project support to specific food brands in their stable. According to corporate affairs executive Faiza Steyn (Interview, 20 April 2003), 'We support early childhood development projects, because at a young age our beneficiaries can start to recognise our products'. Twinning projects with specific brands has paid off for Pioneer in terms of raising brand awareness and sales in particular communities. The business case for CSER has often been raised by proponents and has come to be one of its key drivers in the South African food sector.

Priorities for support

Tensions exist around the deployment of the limited resources that corporations devote to their CSER programmes. There is a surfeit of worthy causes and potential partnerships in a country like South Africa where the challenges of social and environmental transformation are considerable.

Companies tend to prioritise their stakeholders, starting with those who are in their employ and communities surrounding local plants. The South African Sugar Association (an amalgam of cane growers and sugar millers) devotes its attention to the sugar cane growing areas of KwaZulu-Natal and Mpumalanga provinces. Its activities include skills training, HIV/AIDS support, cholera prevention and extension support for small cane growers (South African Sugar Association 2002; Interview, Mills-Hackman, 9 May 2003).

Unilever's activities in South Africa date back to 1887 when the Sunlight brand was first registered. Exports began in 1890. W.H. Lever, known for building model worker housing at his Port Sunlight factory outside Liverpool, waited until the formation of the Union before establishing soap factories in Durban, Cape Town and Johannesburg in 1911–12. Lever Bros merged with the Dutch Margarine Unie in 1930 to form Unilever (Wilson 1954: vol. 1, 198–202). Its brands have become household names in South Africa. Unilever chose not to disinvest during the sanctions period, but the post-apartheid period has seen global co-chairman Niall FitzGerald invited onto President Thabo Mbeki's International Investment Council. Unilever has also seconded support to President Mbeki's International Marketing Council to assist in the process of branding South Africa.

Unilever's local CSER programme, administered through the Unilever Foundation for Education and Development, provides focused support to a few large projects. While a number of these have local application, there are also those located outside KwaZulu-Natal. 'Our strength is that precisely because we are a global player, we are multi-local as well as multinational', claims Corporate Affairs Director Ed Hall (Interview, 9 May 2003). The foundation amplifies existing corporate strengths in areas like marketing, ethics, water management and chemical engineering to endow centres of excellence in these disciplines at local universities. It uses company-based mentors and employee volunteers to support under-resourced schools, to build home-based AIDS-orphan fostering projects and clinics, and to participate in environmental education projects. The prestigious Nelson Mandela Scholarship project (consuming an investment of over R30 million) supports 50 postgraduate students to undertake degrees in the United Kingdom. 'While we are sometimes criticised as being elitist – since the funds could provide many more local scholarships – we firmly believe that one of the most fundamentally formative experiences in leadership training is study abroad', Hall argues (Interview, 9 May 2003). Returning students are not obliged to work for Unilever, but they are expected to return to apply their skills locally.

Nestlé is another multinational that has a very focused, limited list of key partners in its CSER operations. These include support for the eco-schools' programme in Eastern Cape province, for a community feeding programme (WARMTH) in Western Cape province, for pre-school education in Gauteng province, and for the environmental and development NGOs LEAP and EcoLink in Mpumalanga province (Nestlé South Africa Undated; Nestlé 2005).

Pick 'n Pay is less focused in its project support profile and backs an extensive range of community initiatives. These range from small-scale local interventions (a pensioner's birthday cake) to large-event sponsorship (the Pick 'n Pay Argus Cycle Race, attracting 35 000 entrants over 105 km), and even support for Cape Town's abortive bid to host the 2004 Summer Olympics. Store managers have some discretion over what to support, but larger decisions are left to head office. The Ackerman Foundation was also established recently to undertake philanthropic projects, but these are not necessarily linked to the priorities of Pick 'n Pay (Interview, W. Ackerman, 5 May 2003).

Foundations or integration?
The diversity of approach to CSER activities (scale, focus, spatiality) reflects the variety of interest of the role players in the sector. In some quarters there is a debate about whether a distinct CSER trust or foundation, such as that established by Unilever, segregates these activities from mainstream corporate functions. There is a strong argument that they should be integrated into normal line function activities. However, there seem to be few disadvantages in using a foundation approach, especially if there is clear CEO buy-in, expectations of employee voluntarism, good communications with other line departments, and solid alignment with corporate values and purpose.

Depatriation – is it a factor?
As we have seen, the food, beverage and tobacco sector contains a range of different corporate players, foreign multinationals, large listed and unlisted local corporations, and a range of small, medium and micro enterprises. The only example of depatriation in this sector has been that of SAB plc (now SABMiller), which gained its primary listing on the London Stock Exchange in March 1999. Once the core of its activities, the South African beer division (or SAB Ltd) is now only one component of a global beer empire. The company's South African CSER programme still maintains its own structure and priorities (Interview, Vukuza-Linda, 23 April 2003). Nevertheless, there is a strong correlation between depatriation and global adherence to new standards of corporate governance. Prior to 1997, CSER was dealt with in an ad hoc fashion, but from the time a primary listing on the London

bourse became imminent, SAB plc paid greater attention to developing a broader accountability and CSER function. There was a full review of corporate values, corporate accountability was incorporated into the firm's governance process, and a Corporate Accountability Working Committee was established in 1999–2000. Corporate citizenship reporting, confined mostly to the South African operations, began in 1997–8. By 2000–1 it assumed a triple-bottom-line format and was using GRI indicators. SAB plc adopted its group environmental policy on 17 April 2002. This commits the corporation to develop a group-wide environmental management system in line with ISO 14000 principles and has the long-term objective of independent certification of all its operations (South African Breweries plc 2002: 22).

How much of this new approach to governance and reporting can be attributed to the fact of depatriation? Quotation on the London Stock Exchange carries obligations for good governance and SAB Miller is now included in the Dow Jones and FTSE indices of the most socially responsible companies (South African Breweries plc 2002: 3). In its efforts to reposition itself as a global player, it is likely that these developments motivated the corporation to take governance and CSER issues much more seriously and to begin to adhere to world-class principles. Ironically, the ISO 14000 series is based on subjective standard setting and many environmentalists feel it is not sufficiently stringent in ensuring corporate minimisation of environmental impacts.

Controversies and challenges
Empowerment
Despite numerous empowerment deals in South Africa, this sector experiences such high levels of concentration that space for admission of new empowerment entrepreneurs seems limited. Foreign corporations (BAT, Unilever, Parmalat, SAB, Nestlé, P&G, etc.) have little incentive to hand over shareholdings of wholly-owned subsidiaries to empowerment groups. Some have an overwhelming monopoly (BAT, SAB) and would not want to encourage new competition with their own operations. Both Coca-Cola and SAB have, instead, placed emphasis on the types of partnership that they have created with distribution networks. For example, SAB prides itself on stimulating support for owner-drivers formerly employed by the company. Some companies have placed empowerment leadership figures on their global boards

(e.g. Cyril Ramaphosa, once secretary-general of the National Union of Mineworkers and of the African National Congress and now a prominent businessman in South Africa, is a non-executive director of SAB plc). Others, like Pick 'n Pay, have offered staff opportunities to take up equity in the company. The South African Sugar Association has set a target for black ownership of 30 per cent of total hectares of cane grown (Interview, Mills-Hackman, 9 May 2003). However, these gestures are not a substitute for addressing the key empowerment issue of substantial diversification of equity ownership in the different sub-sectors of the industry.

The larger fishing companies (Sea Harvest, I&J, Oceana) have retained the bulk of allocated quotas without having to cede much market share to smaller players. With a diminishing resource and accompanying redundancies, the reallocation of quotas is likely to have dramatically adverse consequences for traditional fishing communities.

Regulating the sector

Liberalisation of the South African economy helped to do away with the former marketing boards which dealt with particular agricultural commodities (Vink and Kirsten 2002). Part of their role was to set commodity prices in advance, usually over a one-year period. This assisted producers, processors, wholesalers and retailers to plan with a certain amount of stability and predictability.

Despite liberalisation of the markets, there is a profusion of regulatory instruments and institutions covering the food, beverage and tobacco industry. Industries like sugar and liquor are each governed by their own Acts of Parliament. Currently both the Sugar Act and the Liquor Act are being revised, and the South African Sugar Association and SAB plc are active in asserting their position before parliamentary portfolio committees and, in the case of sugar, at the World Trade Organisation (WTO). The tobacco industry is highly regulated and BAT-SA itself admits its products are risky and need 'sensible regulation' (British American Tobacco South Africa 2002: 34). In the case of tobacco the Department of Health is the primary regulator, whereas in the case of sugar this role is assigned to the Departments of Agriculture and Trade and Industry.

Tobacco is also keen to assist the regulators in ensuring that contraband and counterfeit products do not enter the market. To this end BAT-SA, acting through the Tobacco Institute of South Africa, works closely with the excise authorities, seconding personnel to the South African Revenue Services (British American Tobacco South Africa 2002: 35).

Food safety regulations and legislation are weakly enforced. Their administration is devolved to provincial and local government authorities. In 2002 the SABC3 television documentary team for *Special Assignment* undertook food tests on poultry bought from a range of outlets – from street stalls to supermarkets. The programme, which was aired on 26 November 2002, reported that all the chickens were contaminated in some way. The programme evoked widespread concern about food safety, prompting Woolworths to issue disclaimers validating the integrity of its cold chain and organic hormone-free and antibiotic-free products (*Sunday Times* 2002: 38).

While the mining industry has a single integrated safety inspectorate, and new dedicated regulatory agencies have been established for the electricity and telecommunications industries, there is no call for a one-stop regulatory agency for the food, drink and tobacco sector. Until that occurs, the industry will continue to deal with a proliferation of regulatory agencies, including national and provincial government departments and local municipalities. This carries implications for efficiency and global competitiveness.

Sugar
South Africans enjoy their sugar, consuming an estimated 31 kg per capita in the 2001–2 sugar year (Illovo Sugar 2002: 42). Sugar is a sweetener and a preserver of foods. It provides a cheap form of energy, tastes good and creates a temporary feeling of well-being. Its use in the food chain in South Africa is extensive. People add multiple teaspoons of sugar to their coffee and tea. Most canned vegetables and soft drinks contain high percentages of sugar. Part of the cuisine involves adding sugar to cooked vegetables. South Africans sweeten their dairy products, their fruit juices, their breads and their stews. They are large consumers of confectionery. The population suffers from high levels of obesity, dental caries, high blood pressure, heart disease and diabetes, but none of these health costs are borne by the industry.

This link is, of course, contested by the sugar industry, which is not only one of the most important funders of nutrition and dental research in South Africa, but is also involved in generic advertising and promotion of the product. The South African Sugar Association uses its own Nutrition Department to 'address misinformation about the link between sugar and health', targeting journalists, health workers and patients in state hospitals and clinics. It produces educational materials to 'correct the message about sugar and assist in the overall education of the patient'. It also sponsored a Nutrition Society of South Africa symposium on 'misinformation about sugar' that it feels is spread in HIV/AIDS education (South African Sugar Association 2002: 22).

Globally the industry has a vigorous lobbying style. Currently the United States Sugar Association is attempting to challenge the World Health Organisation's (2003) guidelines on healthy eating, which state that sugar should account for no more than ten per cent of a healthy diet. Unless the WHO revises this to 25 per cent, the United States Sugar Association, along with six other large food industry corporations, has undertaken to pressurise the US Congress to end its US$406 million funding for the WHO. The accusation is that the guidelines are based on faulty science. The WHO has rejected the sugar lobby's criticisms, claiming that a team of 30 independent experts had considered the scientific evidence and found its conclusions to be in line with the findings of 23 national reports that, on average, set targets of ten per cent for added sugars (Boseley 2003).

The local industry's dimensions are considerable. During 2001–2, it crushed 21.2 million tonnes of cane to produce 2.4 million tonnes of sugar, amounting to 1.8 per cent of the world production of 134 million tonnes. Just over half – 52 per cent – of domestic production was consumed in the domestic market. The industry's gross revenue was R5.4 billion, and it sustained '350 000 jobs, both directly and indirectly, mostly located in the rural areas of the country' (South African Sugar Association 2002: 3). Of those employed in the sector, there were 50 561 small-scale growers and 1 800 large-scale growers (South African Sugar Association 2002: 37). The industry's CSER programme is focused on areas of educational improvement, skills development, HIV/AIDS, cholera prevention, and an increase in the number of black commercial sugar cane farmers.

In contrast to the tobacco industry in its current phase, the sugar industry cannot admit that its product is the direct cause of health problems. As a product, sugar still enjoys an unassailable position in the hearts of consumers. Yet, sooner or later, as the obesity and heart disease pandemics mature, more thorough attempts may be made to control sugar's use. Will the industry wait until then to exercise its social responsibility in relation to the health of its consumers?

Tobacco

The tobacco industry now openly admits its product is risky. However, it argues that despite this the product is legal for adult consumers, and one quarter of South African adults continue to smoke. While not a major employer (2 600 people), the industry relies for its raw material on 600 local tobacco growers who provide around 46 000 jobs in Limpopo, North West and Mpumalanga provinces. The industry earns R11 billion a year, half of which it pays to the excise authorities. It claims that there are advantages in the country having a responsible industry, one that respects the ban on advertising, that co-operates in stopping sales to young people, and that encourages tobacco growers to end child labour (Interview, Crow, 29 April 2003; Interview, Millson, 29 April 2003). BAT, with over 90 per cent of the local and 15 per cent of the global market, works with the South African authorities to end the smuggling and counterfeiting of its brands. It equates its contribution to the fiscus through excise and VAT payments with a quarter of the country's current health budget or an eighth of the education budget (British American Tobacco South Africa 2002: 9).

In order to manage its social reporting and its CSER agenda, BAT-SA has appointed a social reporting team, which set about identifying its stakeholders and establishing externally facilitated dialogue sessions with them. These stakeholders included employees, suppliers, tobacco lobbies, regulatory agencies, retailers, consumer groups and health authorities. The Department of Health and a number of other health and medical agencies did not respond to invitations to participate in the process. Expectations of stakeholders were considered, with BAT-SA promising to take action on these and related concerns. Part of this was a re-examination of CSER priorities. Traditionally, predecessor firms like Rembrandt had strongly supported the arts, nature conservation, small business development and the Urban Foundation. As a result of the stakeholder workshops, BAT-SA has committed itself to redress historical social imbalances and current social needs. In line with this, it has initiated projects on BEE and HIV/AIDS.

Yet the overriding question is whether a tobacco corporation can be socially responsible, given that its product has been proven inherently harmful to human health. Can BAT-SA conduct CSER activities in a credible way? Its response: 'While tobacco can be a controversial product, it is also a very important industry, and we aim to be recognised as a responsible company in this industry' (British American Tobacco South Africa 2002: 9).

Genetically engineered foods and crops
Monsanto South Africa is a wholly-owned subsidiary of its US parent, based in St Louis, Missouri. Once responsible for the development of Agent Orange, a defoliant used with serious human consequences in the Vietnam War, Monsanto went on to invest in agro-chemicals and biotechnology. Backed by twenty-year patents, and beginning with soya, Monsanto rapidly commercialised genetically engineered (GE) cotton, canola and maize. The GE crops are resistant to Monsanto's proprietary glyphosphate herbicide, Roundup. US farmers who use these Monsanto seeds are contractually bound to use only Roundup to destroy the weeds around them. Within two years, by 1996, Monsanto was involved in 7.7 million out of the 12 million hectares of GE crops planted around the world. By May 1998, Monsanto had acquired Delta & Pine Land Co, the largest US cotton seed company, which had recently announced the development of a terminator technology, one which is genetically modified to sterilise seed after a single harvest. The farmer cannot grow seed and must purchase new seed, and related chemicals, commercially. Monsanto went on to acquire Dekalb (the United States' second-largest maize company), Holden's (responsible for up to 35 per cent of US maize planting), and AHP (the third-largest US herbicide and insecticide firm). By the end of the 1990s, Monsanto had become the largest agro-chemical corporation in the world.

Monsanto's entry into Africa was aimed not only at marketing its agro-chemicals, but also at promoting its GE crops. The company obtained permission to conduct field trials to test insect- and herbicide-resistant cotton in South Africa in 1994 and later engaged in field trials for other crops. It supported the first commercial release in the world of GE cotton to small-scale growers, in the Makhatini flats on the Pongola flood plain. GE white maize was released commercially for the first time in South Africa in the 2002 season. By late 2002, 350 000 hectares in South Africa had been planted with GM crops, up by 50 per cent in a single year. Over 175 field trials are under way in eight out of South Africa's nine provinces, and five commercial releases have been approved (Pschorn-Strauss and Wynberg 2002: 4).

In 1999 Monsanto acquired a majority shareholding of Sensako, a 40-year-old South African seed company which was formed in the agricultural co-operative sector and which had prior links to Dekalb (South African National Seed Organisation 1991: 14). Steady acquisition of other seed companies has given Monsanto strategic control over agricultural seed distribution in South Africa.

Resistance by consumers and governments to the commercialisation of GE foods and other crops has been extremely strong in the European Union (EU), Japan and India. The EU currently has a moratorium on commercialisation and imports, while Japan only allows imports for animal feed. At the beginning of 2003, India banned the importation of GE food in the form of aid, as Zambia had done in October 2002.

South Africa's pliant regulator, located in the national Department of Agriculture, has been permitting field trials without public disclosure of the contents of the risk assessments that are supposed to be conducted. This has been challenged by Biowatch South Africa in a landmark legal action under legislation governing access to official information. The case has been marked by an unusual development – the application by Monsanto to the courts to become a co-respondent with the Department of Agriculture. In a landmark judgement on 23 April 2005, Acting Justice Eric Dunn upheld Biowatch's constitutional right to access information, claiming that this was in the public interest. However, curiously, Biowatch was ordered to pay Monsanto's legal costs. In June 2005, Biowatch was given the right to appeal this decision.

Monsanto's CSER programme is extremely self-interested. It spends an undisclosed amount supporting a stakeholder organisation, AfricaBio. This organisation is involved in building support for Monsanto's position, as well as for genetic engineering (GE) in general. It conducts training across Africa, including in risk assessment, and has often posed as an independent NGO or a body representing small farmers, although its membership is largely drawn from corporate members and academics whose research is corporate-sponsored. Monsanto has also formed a partnership with the Industrial Development Corporation, the Land Bank and provincial agricultural authorities in support of the Makhatini cotton experiment.

The spread of GE in South Africa is controversial, and contested in particular in the NGO community and by the Food and Allied Workers' Union (FAWU), which has supported calls for a moratorium on field trials and releases (Interview, Masemola, 12 May 2003). Members of Parliament have recognised the shortcomings of the Genetically Modified Organisms Act (GMOA) (15 of 1998), and set up a stakeholder process led by the chairpersons of the parliamentary agriculture and environment portfolio committees. The Department of Environmental Affairs and Tourism (DEAT) has also indicated the need for a revision of the Act, while Monsanto and AfricaBio have expressed the view that there is no need for such a change (Interview, Mbengashe, 14 April 2003). As South Africa has ratified the Cartagena Biosafety Protocol, which governs trade in genetically modified organisms (GMOs), the GMOA has had to be amended to reflect South Africa's alignment with its international obligations. After a series of public hearings in which there was extensive representation by civil society organisations, the Agriculture Portfolio Committee of the National Assembly decided only to accept amendments proposed by the industry and the national Department of Agriculture. As yet, there is no segregation or labelling process to distinguish GMOs in the market.

GE crops are being resisted for a number of reasons. First, there is no conclusive evidence that their use over the long run will not compromise human and animal health and the environment. Second, there is strong resistance to the notion that living organisms may be patented, particularly among the Africa group at the WTO. Third, there is a concern that releases of GMOs into the environment will contaminate native races of plants and so damage biodiversity and the resource base which it sustains. Fourth, there is strong objection to the steady strategic control which the agro-biotech corporations have obtained over the food chain, in particular over maize, soya and oilseeds. Farmers resent having to forego seed saving and seed swapping, and must go deeper into debt to afford fresh seed for each harvest. Fifth, there is growing evidence that the claims of the industry that its crops are resistant to pests do not hold over time: insects are developing greater resistance to the pesticides introduced into GE crops. Sixth, claims that GE is what developing countries need to extend food production are regarded as spurious: food security depends not only on supply – and there is global over-production of food – but more centrally on households' abilities to access food. GE seed is more expensive and creates patterns of debt in developing countries while a technical fix is not necessarily a sustainable solution to the problem of food security.

The Monsanto Pledge states in part that 'the safety of our employees, the communities where we operate, our customers, consumers, and the environment will be our highest priority' (Monsanto, 2005: 2). Aware of its contentious activities, Monsanto has hired the World Business Council for Sustainable Development to assist it to report improvements to its emissions and use of resources (Monsanto 2005: 16). However, these kinds of improvements cannot mitigate the broader problems arising, for example, from the potential contamination of indigenous plant races by the release of GMOs into the environment.

Food pricing

Rapid food price inflation in South Africa during the course of 2001–2 could not entirely be attributed to the weak rand-dollar exchange rate. When retailers began to report very large profit increases, it became a matter of public interest. The former price regulatory mechanisms no longer applied, and by then food prices were largely determined by market forces including so-called import parity, where the maize price is determined in US dollars.

Despite this, the Minister of Agriculture at the time, Thoko Didiza, appointed a Food Monitoring Committee (FMC) under the chairpersonship of agricultural economics professor Johann Kirsten. The committee was charged with examining how the value chain functioned in staple foods and assessing whether opportunistic pricing patterns existed in the industry. The retail sector regarded this as needless interference and felt that the state should not intervene in shaping the market (Interview, W. Ackerman, 5 May 2003). However, FAWU found the deliberations of the FMC very disappointing. FAWU argued that excessive profit in the food retailing sector should be subjected to a windfall tax. Instead, the FMC concluded that high profits were not the result of market manipulation, nor of opportunistic profiteering. FAWU's view was that the South African Futures Exchange had confirmed that there was some room for speculative behaviour in the area of grain stocks. While farmers have gained, the bulk of the profit increased across the chain after leaving the farm gate. Retail gained, but the millers gained excessively (Interview, Masemola, 12 May 2003).

FAWU feels that the state should be more interventionist, especially with respect to the supply of maize at modest prices: 'While calls for re-regulation might seem out of touch with the times, the state could control any profiteering by creating parastatals across the value chain, in silage, milling, wholesaling and retailing of maize' (Interview, Masemola, 12 May 2003).

By October 2002 the situation had become acute and the Minister announced that, as a temporary measure, special white maize meal would be sold at wholesaler Metro Cash and Carry in 12.5 kg bags at a price of R25.99 when the market price for normal white maize meal had reached R47.39 per bag. FAWU and food researchers regarded this as a public relations exercise. They claimed that only three per cent of monthly maize consumption had been offered as part of this deal and also that the quality of the special maize meal (or sifted maize) was questionable and normally sold at a much lower price in any case (Interview, Masemola, 12 May 2003; Interview, Watkinson, 3 April 2003).

FAWU voiced its concerns about food price inflation in a resolution to the 2003 COSATU Congress. It called on government to establish parastatal companies across the chain of food production and supply which could accumulate food surpluses and release them during periods of scarcity. It further called for anti-hoarding measures, exemption from value-added tax for basic foodstuffs, accelerated land reform, and support for small-scale farmers and millers (Congress of South African Trade Unions 2003: 37–8). Earlier efforts by FAWU to ensure that these calls were included in the agreements arising from the June 2003 Growth and Development Summit were unsuccessful.[6] In the context of the trade union proposal for a universal basic income grant, it would be futile to implement this and simultaneously have it undercut by steady food-price inflation.

Conclusions

Although food security should be the responsibility of numerous role players in society, not least of government, there is a particular gap in this respect when considering the CSER programmes of the food and beverage industry. Exceptions include Nestlé, which supports Mpumalanga-based NGO EcoLink in addressing questions of rural food security through training in permaculture and food gardens, and Pioneer Foods, which gives support in kind to hunger relief projects in times of food stress. In general, however, the sector's CSER programmes do not deal strategically and systematically with the problem of hunger in society (De Klerk 2004). If anything, the level of retrenchment in the industry is such that the problem has become more acute. Greater reliance on outsourcing and contract or casual labour also has implications for the ability of workers and their dependents to fulfil their nutritional needs. The food and drink sector needs to focus more clearly on questions of consumer affordability of basic food needs within a CSER framework for the latter to have meaning and credibility.

Government has a constitutional responsibility to guarantee the 'right to have access to sufficient food and water' (South Africa 1996: s. 27). The 2000 Cabinet *lekgotla* (strategic planning session) decided that there was a need to implement an Integrated Food Security Strategy, and this was later adopted at a forum of national and provincial agriculture ministers and published in 2002 by the South African Department of Agriculture. Further work has occurred in setting up information systems and project identification and three pilot projects have been initiated at provincial level, which was anticipated would be rolled out to the rest of the country in due course. The government has interpreted the problem as one that should be addressed through demonstration projects. It has raised money for this approach through holding a Telefood concert, which was telecast internationally in conjunction with the South African Broadcasting Corporation (SABC) and the Food and Agricultural Organisation (FAO). However, a piecemeal project approach may only produce temporary, palliative solutions. Without addressing systematically the land question, skills, inputs, extension services, credit, food prices, HIV/AIDS and non-agricultural livelihoods, the food security of the South African urban and rural poor will remain elusive.

Another problem is that there is no industrial association for the sector as a whole that can engage strategically on some of these issues. We noted earlier that the sector is exceptionally diverse, with a variety of ownership models, scales of operation, kinds of production, and approaches to CSER. In general, the sub-sectors have their own institutional representation, one prominent example of which is the South African Sugar Association. One model for consideration is the

Brussels-based Confederation of the Food and Drink Industries of the European Community (CIAA), which represents the food and drink industry in its deliberations with EU structures. But would a broader sectoral association make any difference in South Africa? Is it possible that such a diffuse sector has more interests dividing it than uniting it? This chapter has tried to indicate the importance of the sector to the local economy, particularly when the multiplier factor is considered. Yet, unlike mining and chemicals, it is not yet organised in a comprehensive structure.

This is one of the reasons why it has been difficult to gather reliable statistics on trends in the sector. Information has to be pieced together and there are different measurement methodologies employed across the sector. This clearly provides a challenge to macroeconomic planners, as it does to analysts of the sector and to trade union organisers. In academic terms, the sector remains undocumented – there are no sectoral histories or analyses available to date in the public domain.

We have surveyed the range of CSER initiatives in the sector. The role of foreign corporations living up to global reporting and accounting standards sets the pace for a number of the larger local firms. We have seen the seminal influence of the King II Report. We have also seen some contradictory trends whereby corporations take little overall responsibility for the impact of their product, and may be utilising the Procrustean formulae of CSER to deflect attention from the fundamentals. We have highlighted the cases of sugar, tobacco and GE crops, but similar arguments could be made for alcohol.

Taken as a whole, CSER in the South African context is characterised by its diffuseness and lack of focus. This detracts from the overall impact that it might have achieved. It is only when the industry steps away from narrower self-interested visions, and begins to address the fundamental issues of product stewardship and social issues like hunger and food insecurity, that the sector will be judged to have made a positive and sustainable contribution to social transformation in South Africa.

Notes

1. Unsourced figures from the CIAA are 216 000, comprising two per cent of the economically active population (CIAA 2002: 14). Most recent figures of the Compensation Fund (covering the year 1999) showed that there were 242 762 workers registered in the food, drink and tobacco sector (South Africa, Department of Labour. 2003: Table 8B).
2. Woolworths is the South African equivalent of Marks and Spencer with which it has strong links. It has no ties with its namesake, F.W. Woolworth. Woolworths appeals to the more affluent end of the South African consumer market.
3. A merger of interests between Distillers Corporation's local operation and Stellenbosch Farmers' Winery. For a report on its social responsibility activities see Distell Group Limited. 2002: 25ff.
4. Individually and through the South African Sugar Association in which they are major players.
5. The same holds for the previous edition (Rockey 2001) in which there was also some participation by Guinness UDV, a foreign wholly-owned subsidiary of Diageo plc.
6. See www.info.gov.za/issues/gds/gdsagreement03.htm.

References

Ackerman, R. 2001. *Hearing Grasshoppers Jump: The Story of Raymond Ackerman as told to Denise Prichard*. Cape Town: David Philip.

Boseley, S. 2003. 'Sugar Industry Threatens to Scupper WHO'. *The Observer* (London). April 20.

British American Tobacco South Africa (BAT-SA). 2002. *Social Report . . . June 2002*. Stellenbosch: BAT-SA.

Coca-Cola. Undated. *The Coca-Cola Promise*. Available at www2.cocacola.com/ourcompany/theactions_include.html. Accessed 8 July 2006.

Confederation of the Food and Drink Industries of the European Community (CIAA). 2002. *Industry as a Partner for Sustainable Development: Food and Drink*. Brussels: CIAA.

Congress of South African Trade Unions (COSATU). 2003. *Resolutions of the COSATU Eighth National Congress*. Johannesburg: COSATU.

De Klerk, M. 2004. *Food Security in South Africa: Key Policy Issues for the Medium Term*. Pretoria: HSRC.

Distell Group Limited. 2002. *Annual Report 2002*. Stellenbosch: Distell.

Illovo Sugar. 2002. *Annual Report 2002*. Durban: Illovo.

King Committee on Corporate Governance. 2002. *King Report on Corporate Governance for South Africa*. Johannesburg: Institute of Directors.

Kirsten, J. and N. Vink. 2002. *Pricing Behaviour in the South African Food and Agricultural Sector: A Report to the National Treasury*. Pretoria and Stellenbosch: The Authors.

Ligthelm, A.A. and J.H. Martins. 1998. *The Informal Sector's Role in the Soft Drink Market in South Africa*. Pretoria: Bureau of Market Research, University of South Africa.

Monsanto. 2005. *2005 Pledge Report*. St Louis, Missouri: Monsanto.

National Productivity Institute (NPI). 1990–96. *Productivity Statistics*. Johannesburg: NPI.

Nestlé. 2005. *The Nestlé Commitment to Africa*. Vevey, Switzerland: Nestlé SA.

Nestlé South Africa. Undated. 'Community Programmes'. Available at www.nestle. co.za.

Newton-King, N. 2002. 'Introducing the FTSE/JSE Social Responsibility Index'. Presentation at JSE Securities Exchange, Johannesburg, 30 November 2002.

Proctor & Gamble. 2001. *2001 Sustainability Report*. Cincinnati: Proctor and Gamble.

Pschorn-Strauss, E. and G.R. Wynberg. 2002. *The Seeds of Neo-colonialism: Genetic Engineering in Food and Farming*. Pietermaritzburg: GroundWork.

Rockey, V. (ed.). 2001. *The Corporate Social Investment Handbook*. Cape Town: Trialogue, 4th ed.

Rockey, V. (ed.). 2002. *The Corporate Social Investment Handbook*. Cape Town: Trialogue, 5th ed.

South Africa. 1996. *Constitution of the Republic of South Africa, Act 108 of 1996*. Pretoria: Government Printer.

South Africa, Department of Agriculture. 2002. *The Integrated Food Security Strategy for South Africa*. Pretoria: Department of Agriculture.

South Africa, Department of Labour (DoL). 1999. *Compensation Fund: Report on the 1995 Statistics of the Fund*. Pretoria: DoL.

———. 2001. *Compensation Fund: Report on the 1997 Statistics of the Fund*. Pretoria: DoL.

———. 2003. *Compensation Fund: Report on the 1999 Statistics of the Fund*. Pretoria: DoL.

———. 2004. 'Farm Workers' Minimum Wage Increases'. Press Statement, 17 March. Pretoria: DoL.

South Africa, Department of Trade and Industry (DTI). Undated. *Manufacture of Food Products, Beverages and Tobacco Products*. Available at www.thedti.gov.za/econdb/manufrev/manufre1.html. Accessed 5 July 2006.

South African Breweries plc (SAB). 2002. *Corporate Accountability Report, 31 March 2002*. London: SAB.

South African National Seed Organisation (SANSOR). 1991. *SANSOR News: Newsletter of the South African National Seed Organisation* 1: 14.

South African Sugar Association. 2002. *Annual Report 2001/2*. Mount Edgecombe: SA Sugar Association.

South African Wine Industry Statistics (SAWIS). 2003. *South African Wine Industry Statistics 2003*. Paarl: SAWIS. Online. Available at www.sawis.co.za. Accessed 8 July 2006.

Statistics South Africa (Stats SA). 1990–96. *Employment and Salaries and Wages: Mining and Quarrying, Manufacturing, Construction and Electricity. Statistical Release P0242.1*. Pretoria: Stats SA.

———. 1997–2000. *Quarterly Employment Statistics. Statistical Release P0277 and P0277.1*. Pretoria: Stats SA.

———. 1999. *October Household Survey Results*. Pretoria: Stats SA.

———. 2000. *1999 October Household Survey*. Pretoria: Stats SA.

———. 2000–03. *Survey of Employment and Earnings. Statistical Release P0271 and P0275*. Pretoria: Stats SA.

——. 2003. *Manufacturing Statistics: Products Manufactured: Food and Beverages. Statistical Release P3051.1.* Pretoria: Stats SA.

——. 2006. *Gross Domestic Product: First Quarter 2006. Statistical Release PO4441.* Pretoria: Stats SA.

Sunday Times (Johannesburg). 2002. 'The Difference between Woolworths Food and What You Saw on *Special Assignment*'. 1 December.

——. 2003. 'Survey on Corporate Social Investment'. 9 February.

Unilever NV plc. 2002a. *Code of Business Principles*. Rotterdam: Unilever.

——. 2002b. *Growing for the Future II: Unilever and Sustainable Agriculture*. Rotterdam: Unilever.

University of South Carolina, Division of Research and Faber Center for Entrepreneurship, Darla Moore School of Business. 1999. 'Multinational Enterprise, Employment and Local Entrepreneurial Development: Coca-Cola in South Africa'. Unpublished manuscript dated 22 February.

Van Seventer, D.E. 1998. *The Economic Impact of the Coca-Cola System on South Africa.* Pretoria: WEFA Southern Africa.

Vink, N. and J. Kirsten. 2002. *Deregulation of the Agricultural Market in South Africa: Lessons Learned.* Johannesburg: Free Market Foundation.

WEFA Consultants. 1997. *Provisional Social Accounting Matrix*. Pretoria: WEFA Southern Africa.

Wilson, C. 1954. *The History of Unilever: A Study in Economic Growth and Social Change.* London: Cassell.

World Health Organisation (WHO). 2003. *Diet, Nutrition and the Prevention of Chronic Diseases.* Geneva: WHO.

World Health Organisation (WHO), Regional Office for Europe. 2004. *Global Status Report on Alcohol 2004.* Geneva: WHO.

Interviews

Interviews by David Fig. Biesenbach, Millson and Steyn interviews by David Fig and Rahmat Omar.

Ackerman, Raymond. Founder and Chairman, Pick 'n Pay, 5 May 2003.

Ackerman, Wendy. Director, Pick 'n Pay, 5 May 2003.

Biesenbach, Werda. Corporate Communications, Parmalat, Stellenbosch, 29 April 2003.

Crow, David. Managing Director, BAT-SA, 29 April 2003.

Hall, Ed. Director, Corporate Affairs, Unilever Foundation, 9 May 2003.

Masemola, Katishi. Deputy General Secretary, FAWU, 12 May 2003.

Mbengashe, Maria. Deputy Director General, DEAT, 14 April 2003.

Mills-Hackman, Joy. Development Manager, South African Sugar Association, 9 May 2003.

Millson, Simon. Director, Corporate and Regulatory Affairs, BAT-SA, 29 April 2003.

Newton-King, Nicky. Deputy CEO, JSE Securities Exchange, 30 November 2002.

Steyn, Faiza. Executive, Corporate Affairs, Pioneer Foods, 30 April 2003.

Vukuza-Linda, Nolitha. Corporate Relations Manager, SAB, 23 April 2003.

Watkinson, Eric. Researcher, NALEDI, 3 April 2003.

6

The impact of Black Economic Empowerment[1]

Roger Southall
Diana Sanchez

Introduction

Corporations operating in South Africa increasingly have to account for their actions. The editors of this collection trace this development from the 1970s when, in response to disinvestment campaigns by anti-apartheid activists, foreign corporations professed their adherence to external codes of conduct against which their activities could be measured, the intention being to demonstrate that their presence in South Africa was beneficial to black South African employees.[2] Subsequently, from the advent of democracy in 1994, corporations have had to respond not only to the growing global demand for accountability, but also to particular pressures emanating from the South African environment, notably those seeking social justice and redress for blacks after centuries of political oppression and economic exploitation by whites. Not surprisingly in this context, the drive for corporate social and environmental responsibility (CSER) has become closely meshed with that for black economic empowerment (BEE), a term which has at its heart notions about black upliftment and the deracialisation of patterns of wealth and ownership within the South African economy.

This chapter seeks to disaggregate the interrelationships between CSER and BEE. To undertake this task, we pose two central questions. First, to what extent is BEE seen as a fundamental aspect of CSER by established corporations operating in South Africa? And, second, to what extent do corporations which are substantially owned by blacks see the further pursuit of CSER as part of their remit – or to put it rather more simply, do they tend to act in a more or less socially and environmentally responsible way than their white or internationally-owned counterparts? However, before we proceed to explore these issues, it is necessary to wrestle with some basic definitions.

Defining black economic empowerment and corporate social responsibility

BEE is a term that entered the South African lexicon in the mid-1990s, yet continues to elude agreed definition. The 1994 Reconstruction and Development Programme (RDP) of the African National Congress (ANC) committed a democratic government to deracialise the political economy through strategies that equalise power relations between black and white, overcome extreme economic inequalities and abolish all discrimination based on race, gender or disability. In this context, the concept of BEE relates to the deracialisation of business ownership and control; while that of affirmative action is employed to end discrimination on grounds of race and gender with regard to education, the workplace, skills training and so on (African National Congress 1994: 93, 111, 115). Subsequently, as concerns arose that early attempts to promote the blackening of capitalism were leading mainly towards the enrichment of a tiny black elite, a minimalist definition of BEE – which centred around the promotion of black business – was increasingly contrasted with a maximalist position that emphasised the 'comprehensive restructuring of institutions and society . . . rather than the replacement of white individuals with black ones' (Edigheji 1999: 6). However, although visions of broad-based BEE were increasingly politically correct, they became so all-encompassing that they tended to be vacuous. Although this tension has never been fully resolved, a concerted shift back to a vision of BEE that revolves around issues of business ownership and control was recorded in the report of the Black Economic Empowerment Commission (BEE Com). Promoted by black business bodies and chaired by Cyril Ramaphosa (former leader of the miners' union and ANC general secretary, and now a leading businessman), this report was delivered to President Thabo Mbeki in April 2001. Its central thrust was that the state should promote a 'co-ordinated, simplified and streamlined set of guidelines and regulations

[that] would provide targets and demarcate roles and obligations of the private sector, the public sector and civil society over a period of ten years' (Black Economic Empowerment Commission 2000: 8).

The report was to be crucial in moving the government towards a more interventionist position. In his State of the Nation address to Parliament on 14 February 2003, President Mbeki promised a global transformation charter which would adopt a scorecard approach – 'covering ownership; management; employment equity; skills development; procurement; corporate social responsibility; investment and enterprise formation' – to guide the government in its partnership strategy and allocation of contracts, rights or licences to private business (Mbeki 2003).

President Mbeki noted that the scorecard approach had been developed in a charter negotiated by the mining industry and government in 2003. In fact, the leak of a draft mining charter drawn up by government which, among other goals, had set a target for mining operations to be 51 per cent black-owned within ten years had caused such panic that South African mining shares slumped overnight. This prompted a vigorous rearguard action by the industry which – after intense negotiations – resulted in the adoption of a charter. This, government conceded, considerably reduced empowerment targets that now required all mines to be 15 per cent black-owned in five years and 25 per cent black-owned in ten years. It also laid down a target of 40 per cent black management within five years, while promising flexibility through which achievement of goals regarding employment equity, community and rural development, worker housing and living conditions, procurement and beneficiation could be offset against each other (Southall 2004).

The president had stated that government was not seeking charters for every sector of the economy. However, the mining charter process set off a scramble – first in the financial services sector and subsequently in numerous other sectors that were clearly concerned about obviating direct official intervention – to hold discussions that soon resulted in a succession of charters. By 2005, fifteen sectors had finalised or were in the process of developing a charter. These espoused a broad-based scorecard approach. Although their particular targets varied considerably, they established standards for other sectors that lagged behind to emulate and shared a broad template that set goals for black ownership, management, employment equity, procurement, skills development, enterprise development and a residual target. Although the generic scorecard presented in the Department of Trade and Industry (DTI) codes of good practice does not specifically mention social or environmental responsibility, the residual element could be, and seems usually to be, allocated to CSER. Similarly, as the seventh edition of the Trialogue (2004a) *CSI Handbook* explains, other parts of the scorecard such as preferential procurement and small, medium and micro enterprise (SMME) development also encourage developmental actions from companies that can be supported through CSER programmes.

Although these charters possessed exhortatory rather than coercive status, they were designed to align the different industrial sectors to government policies and requirements which increasingly elaborated official definitions and standards of BEE and employment equity. Key among these were the Black Economic Empowerment Act (53 of 2003) which sets guidelines for charters, the Empowerment Strategy of the DTI released in March 2003, and the Codes of Good Practice released by the DTI in December 2004. These were expected to be applied in the development, evaluation and monitoring of BEE charters and initiatives; with the latter expected to be gazetted before the end of 2006. A black-owned company is defined as one with 50.1 per cent black ownership and a black-empowered company as one with 25.1 per cent black ownership. The latter definition, explained Deputy Director-General Lionel October of the DTI, would cater for joint ventures and would encourage white-owned firms to relinquish equity to black partners without fear of losing control (South African Institute of Race Relations 2003: 216).

According to Trialogue (2004a), industry charters have elevated the status of corporate social investment (CSI), particularly in those cases where it features as part of a company's transformation scorecard. For the first time, company boards are showing a real and active interest in CSI programmes as they seek ways to leverage them as part of their transformation process. Trialogue argues that CSI departments and projects are likely to continue receiving the recognition and resources required to make an impact, and it is expected that once industry charters have been finalised, clear CSI-specific sector indicators will be available.

The move towards charters gave impetus to the simultaneous development by the Johannesburg Securities Exchange (JSE) of a Social

Responsibility Investment Index (SRII), which was launched in May 2004. This initiative was spurred by the second King Report on corporate governance in South Africa (King Committee on Corporate Governance 2002) and by the simultaneous lobbying efforts of a number of local actors such as the African Institute of Corporate Citizenship (AICC). It sought to propel South African corporations towards advanced standards of corporate responsibility commensurate with those which have increasingly gained acceptance internationally, and hence to increase the flow of foreign investment to the country. And in South Africa, as the AICC suggests, the Socially Responsible Investment Initiative (SRII) is closely related to the broad BEE concept. In contrast to the global scene, where increasingly aware and informed consumers and investors have been the main drivers of SRI,[3] in South Africa the main impetus has come from the demand placed on business by government and labour to contribute to the transformation agenda (African Institute of Corporate Citizenship 2004). Indeed, the overriding motivation of SRI vehicles in South Africa (which focus almost exclusively on matters relating to empowerment and infrastructure) is that previously disadvantaged individuals derive benefit from investment in the form of improved standards of living and all that this encompasses.

Interestingly, the SRII sought to straddle the globally-preferred reference to corporate social responsibility and the preference of South African corporations for the term corporate social investment. As the editors of this book point out, the latter term suggests philanthropy rather than any obligation to compensate for past misdeeds or omissions under apartheid. As presented by Nicky Newton-King, Deputy Chief Executive Officer of the JSE, the core principles of the SRII relate to environmental sustainability, positive stakeholder relationships and upholding universal human rights. These established standards for good corporate performance extend well beyond the goals of BEE, yet nonetheless the key elements of the latter are integral to the philosophy of CSER that is presented. Hence in terms of positive relationships with stakeholders, firms are expected to demonstrate commitment to, inter alia, combating discrimination; promoting diversity (including gender and disability diversity) and employment equity, BEE (including company ownership and managerial positions of black people); prioritising local and affirmative procurement; and encouraging and monitoring equitable development of human capital. They are also expected to realise other objectives, such as the attainment of core labour standards, the promotion of social investment and the installation of appropriate HIV/AIDS policies which would contribute to the well-being of all employees and the wider community. Meanwhile, in pursuit of universal human rights, companies are expected to demonstrate adherence to the (now Global) Sullivan Principles (JSE 2002; Newton-King 2003).

In its second year of operations (2005), some adjustments had to be made to the index. For instance, companies face a bigger challenge to make it onto the SRII because the criteria against which they are now measured are more demanding than previously. According to Newton-King (2005), this is part of a developmental approach: 'This year, we were interested in understanding how companies had implemented SRI policies and strategies as opposed to last year when we focussed on whether companies had these policies in place.'

The adoption of the SRII by the JSE Securities Exchange undoubtedly flew in the face of the scepticism of many South African corporations, who were more likely to pay lip service to SRI than to ensure its determined implementation. Key to SRI's promotion was the insistence by the JSE and lobby groups that global trends demonstrated that CSER was good for business and long-term shareholder value, and that because investors were increasingly seeking companies with records of ethical behaviour there was a need to find an objective and accepted method for measuring the CSER performance of listed companies. Newton-King (2003) also argues that, in South Africa in particular, CSER is in the spotlight for various reasons – the importance attached to the New Partnership for Africa's Development (NEPAD); the need to address labour, affirmative action and health issues with greater focus; the holding of the World Summit on Sustainable Development in the country in 2003; and the fact that there is a corporate governance premium for emerging markets (for instance, investors are looking to invest in countries where profit margins are not likely to be eaten by corruption).

The moves towards more exacting demands with regard to BEE and CSER have clearly been complementary, yet different. Both set standards of performance to be achieved but, in contrast to the SRII which merely required companies to report upon what they were attempting to do to realise broad goals, the government's BEE legislation and the various charters established specific, time-bound targets to be achieved. Crucially, however, it would seem that while the issue of transferring ownership and control to blacks is the most central element in the government's conception of corporate responsibility, the philosophy of SRI/CSER being promoted by the JSE sees BEE as embodied in the wider notion of sustainable development. It will be argued below that these variant interpretations lie at the core of the difference between the ways in which established corporations and BEE companies regard themselves as vehicles of corporate responsibility.

South African corporates, corporate social responsibility and black economic empowerment

One hundred large South African companies surveyed by Trialogue Publications spent a total of R2.4 billion on CSI in the period 2003–4. This represents a nominal two per cent increase on the previous year's figure of R2.35 billion, but corresponds to a real decrease considering the recorded inflation rate for the year ending in March 2004 (Trialogue 2004a). Even for the 2002 data, which recorded a 7.8 per cent increase in CSI spending, Trialogue described the expenditure as a 'substantial and honourable contribution', yet noted that it was only half that provided by foreign donors and represented only one per cent of government's expenditure that could be considered developmental. Furthermore, the increase in expenditure in 2002 was below the rate of inflation. In addition, while five per cent of the leading companies had contributed 30 per cent of the total sample budget, 75 per cent of the sampled companies had contributed less than a quarter of recorded CSI (*Business Day* 24 December 2002).

CSI was defined by Trialogue as funding and projects by companies in communities that were external to their employees. Therefore, it did not refer to BEE performance in terms of ownership or employment equity, and hence indirectly endorsed the need for the development of the JSE's SRII. However, at this stage, the latter remains a limited tool for analysis since, in its eagerness to promote buy-in from its members, the JSE is restricting the information that it releases. It is therefore showcasing companies that have chosen to participate, declining to produce a ranking and (by default) leaving any strategy of naming and shaming to external commentators (JSE 2004).

Of the top 160 companies making up the FTSE/JSE share index that were invited to participate voluntarily in the 2004 index, only 74 agreed to do so and of these only 51 were judged to have met the qualifying criteria. This low level of inclusion meant that some very prominent companies were missing, either because they had failed to qualify (for instance, Sanlam, which claimed this was on a technicality), because they were adopting a wait and see attitude, or because, as in the case of Durban Roodepoort Deep mining company, they dismissed CSER as a fad and insisted that the interests of shareholders would always have to come ahead of those of stakeholders (*Financial Mail* 18 June 2004). Although the issue of black ownership was only one among other components of the index, the fact that eight of the companies listed in the index are also in the *Financial Mail*'s top twenty empowerment companies does initially suggest that the index results are tied to BEE performance.

Fifty-eight companies participated in the 2005 review (JSE 2005). Of those, 49 met the criteria. According to Newton-King (2005) even though the number of companies that took part in the 2005 review was lower than in 2004, the percentage of companies succeeding in getting onto the index was much higher than in the previous year.

> South African companies have done a great deal in the sustainability area and deserve to be recognised. While the number of constituents in the Index has decreased slightly from last year, we did expect this given that the criteria were harder to meet this year. The good thing to note is that many organisations are actively embracing the triple bottom line (Newton-King 2005).

However, because the raw data used to compile the index is not publicly available, information about how leading corporations choose to pursue BEE within a wider context of CSR must rely primarily upon highly selective and qualitative material, some of which is undoubtedly flawed by its greater devotion to public relations than to sober analysis.

In this regard, a guide to corporate citizenship in South Africa released by Trialogue and the AICC is helpful. Noting both an increasing public distrust of business (because of increased reports concerning corporate corruption, fraud, poor governance, and environmental and social mismanagement), Trialogue's guide defines the good corporate citizen as 'one that has comprehensive policies and practices in place, throughout the business, that enable it to make decisions and conduct its operations ethically, meet legal requirements, and show consideration for society, communities and the environment' (Trialogue 2004b: 8). This definition is distilled from a host of formal conventions, accords, standards and guidelines (ranging from the United Nations Universal Declaration of Human Rights to the FTSE4Good Index), as well as South African laws and precedents,[4] local corporate governance guidelines[5] and, not least, the recent flurry of transformation initiatives, notably the BEE Act (53 of 2003), the Employment Equity Act (55 of 1998), the Skills Development Act (97 of 1998, as amended in 2003) and various industry charters. The guide then discusses what it considers to be the key elements of good corporate citizenship, choosing to illustrate them by reference to case studies provided by leading companies.

Transformation

Noting the urgent need for the growth of a stable middle class, the narrowing of wealth gaps, the creation of a larger pool of qualified skills and growing the tax base, it is argued that business should indicate its commitment to creating broader-based ownership, assembling a representative workforce, equipping employees with skills and training, giving preference to emerging business as suppliers, providing products for subsidiary markets in the value chain, backing emerging enterprises, and improving the lot of underprivileged communities. The guide's summary comment is: 'Whilst a few progressive companies and industry sectors have made considerable effort in addressing transformation issues, most have made very little progress in this regard' (Trialogue 2004b: 49).

Company control

With less than five per cent of all publicly-listed equity in South Africa held directly by blacks, and indirect ownership by blacks of productive assets also very low, the improvement of this aspect of transformation is presented as a crucial element of good corporate citizenship. However, after early setbacks in empowerment initiatives (including the unravelling of various deals and the enrichment of just a few black executives rather than the attainment of a more broad-based transfer of ownership), the fundamental lesson has been learned – that 'ownership without direct involvement in business operations is rarely sustainable . . . [and] without active management control often negates the good intentions of BEE. Involvement is at best superficial, relationships are tenuous and loyalty to "the deal" is weak.' (Trialogue 2004b: 56). Slow progress has seen the government playing a more assertive role in driving BEE, but 'many large corporates are also exerting similar influence through their prescriptive practices' (Trialogue 2004b: 57). After a review of challenges and obstacles to ownership transfer, the key indicators for advance are listed as: the level and nature of BEE ownership, the robustness of the deal, the level of control, the arrangements for mentorship to enhance the involvement of black partners, and the synergies and business value that flow from any deal. The summary comment is that although 'almost all sectors of South African business still fall short of where they should be . . . the trends suggest that, despite a "false start", BEE ownership and control is now being taken more seriously' (Trialogue 2004b: 59).

Workplace equity

Employment equity is presented as the primary vehicle for BEE within the workplace. However, while strides have been made towards equality, there are still imbalances between the profiles of business and society. 'Clearly, specialist skills shortages make this difficult in some instances, but in general it is apparent that companies have not drawn fully on the potential skills pool at their disposal' (Trialogue 2004b: 64). If managed poorly, employment equity can create huge tensions. On the other hand, if imaginatively and successfully addressed it can enrich a company culturally while also opening up new markets. Measuring and tracking progress can easily be achieved, but companies should also consider qualitative indicators such as the identification of barriers to equity and ways in which these can be overcome, adoption of measures to secure buy-in from operational divisions, and the delineation of linkages between employment equity and skills development. Overall, while employment equity is now on the agenda of most companies, many 'have still not made sufficient progress', and 'small businesses have thus far not faced much pressure to transform' (Trialogue 2004b: 67). Only progressive companies are linking skills development and employment equity, while the majority of companies fear that expenditure upon skills training will leave them vulnerable to poaching by their competitors. However, employment equity is central to the charter movement, which is destined to grow (Trialogue 2004b: 59).

Skills and training

In recognition of the critical role skills and training should play in simultaneously promoting growth and BEE, the Skills Development Act and associated legislation now require companies to contribute a percentage of their total payroll cost to a National Skills Fund. This is controlled by 25 Sector Education and Training Authorities (SETAs) that make funds available to companies in their respective sectors. Companies then claim back compensation from their SETA for the training costs they incur. Trialogue (2004b: 68) praises this as 'an ingenious mechanism to encourage companies to spend money on skills development' which, because all companies pay the levy, goes some way to counter the free-riding problem where companies that do not spend on training poach from those that do. However, in part because of the internal inefficiencies of many SETAs, much of the accumulated money for training has gone unspent. Progress towards enhanced skills training therefore continues to rely heavily upon corporate self-motivation, with more progressive companies adopting comprehensive programmes that eschew short-term goals for a long-term perspective. In the South African context companies should also train their employees about issues like transformation and additional challenges such as HIV/AIDS. After a review of various indicators (such as the amount spent on training, the numbers trained, the spectrum of training offered), it is noted that although 'leading companies in this country understand the direct relationships between training competitiveness and productivity, and are spending upward of five per cent of payroll . . . smaller and less progressive outfits spend negligible amounts on formal training' (Trialogue 2004b: 71).

Procurement

Price inflation, inefficiency and reduced competitiveness were all costs of early efforts by government to coax the private sector into pursuing empowerment by giving preference to suppliers with correct credentials. These disadvantages of policy are now being recognised, yet the challenge remains for companies themselves to increase their purchasing from BEE firms without compromising their commercial objectives. Meanwhile, a particular problem is that of fronting in which white-owned and white-controlled companies erect black façades. This requires careful examination of the relationship between a supplier awarded a contract and the sub-contractors that actually do the work. 'A good corporate citizen examines how the company manages its procurement process, and the extent to which it is committed to embracing, encouraging and nurturing small and medium enterprise businesses and disadvantaged individuals', with such support possibly being offered out of a company's CSI programme (Trialogue 2004b: 83). Typical indicators of performance would include the existence of a policy on preferential procurement, the setting of measurable targets, quantitative measures of progress, and the promotion of additional work for small suppliers by sharing a company's preferential supplier database with other businesses. 'While a few companies have used procurement as a transformation lever for many years, most private sector businesses are only now beginning to recognize its worth' (Trialogue 2004b: 85).

The various aspects of good corporate citizenship that Trialogue and the AICC highlight are all elaborated by reference to case studies. Caltex Oil SA (now Chevron) and MTN are presented as driving transformation across a broad front; Anglo American proclaims itself as well on its way to achieving its target of 40 per cent historically-disadvantaged individuals in its management ranks within five years; Southern Sun, Old Mutual and Telkom present themselves as leaders in skills development and training; Shell Southern Africa and Telkom proclaim their procurement credentials; and so on. Yet while such infomercials provide testimony to the increasing need of corporations both to address BEE as part of CSER and to be seen to be doing so, the lack of comparative criteria renders generalisation problematic. While the introduction of the JSE's SRII is clearly an important step in this regard, its relative lack of emphasis upon ownership transfer suggests not only that this issue remains peculiarly sensitive but also that intimacy between BEE and good corporate citizenship is as yet far from universally accepted by corporate South Africa.

This would seem to be borne out by looking at the problem not from the perspective of SRI (as does the SRII) but from that of BEE, as presented by a ranking of the top empowerment companies compiled by the *Financial Mail* (2004, 2005). These indexes provide a Total BEE Score which is compiled by reference to individual scores for ownership, management, employment equity, skills development, affirmative procurement, enterprise development and social development. For both years, the index ranks Telkom (with a total BEE score of 69.58 for 2004 and 80.07 for 2005) as the top empowerment company; and Energy Africa (with a BEE score of 4.47) at the bottom in 2004 and Advtech (with a total BEE score of just 1.25) at the bottom for 2005. However, as the *Financial Mail* explains, these indexes are not a definite and exhaustive indication of the BEE status or activities of companies. There is some room for error, clearly allowed by the fact that for the majority of companies information was not available to provide scores for either enterprise or social development. However, for our purposes what is most interesting is a rather loose connection between social development (measured by CSI as a percentage of profits) and overall BEE performance. This can be illustrated by reference to BEE scores obtained by the most generous firms in terms of CSI for both years (see Tables 6.1 and 6.2).

Table 6.1: **Corporate social investment compared to** *Financial Mail* **BEE ranking, 2004.**

Company	CSI as % of profits	BEE ranking
Woolworths	18.6	54
Putco	17.0	78
Grintek	15.5	11
Wesco	15.3	61
KWV	14.2	104
CS Holdings	12.2	9
Iscor	6.9	7
Nedcor	3.9	13
Edcon	3.3	65
Phumelela	3.2	27
Harmony	3.0	18
Kumba	2.5	8
BJM	2.4	60
Enviroserv	2.4	21
Kersaf	2.2	22

Telkom	2.0	1
Sun International	2.0	19
Sasol	1.8	48
SAB Miller	1.7	55
Assmang	1.6	71
19 other companies	1.0 – 1.5	3, 10, 12, 14, 20, 37, 38 39, 41, 42, 47, 57, 59, 82, 89, 101, 115, 121, 134
25 other companies	0.1 – 0.9	4, 5, 16, 24, 28, 30, 32, 43, 56, 63, 64, 75, 83, 87, 88, 91, 94, 104, 110, 117, 132, 133, 145, 164, 190
136 other companies	No Information	

Source: Financial Mail 2004.

Table 6.2:   Corporate social investment compared to *Financial Mail* BEE ranking, 2005.

Company	CSI as % of profits	BEE Ranking
Cape Empowerment Trust	29.17	8
Merafe Resources*	10.0	9
Dimension Data	6.39	33
Mustek	6.35	14
Angloplat	6.13	105
Highveld Steel	5.62	68
Clientele Life	5.00	82
Primedia	4.52	21
Pick 'n Pay	3.78	61
Phumelela	3.70	2
Foschini	3.04	34
Barnard Jacobs Mellet	3.03	72
Edcon	2.37	37
Trans Hex	2.35	35

Investec	2.31	27
Ispat Iscor	2.29	50
Distell	2.20	51
Prism	2.09	60
WBHO	2.03	69
Sun International	2.00	24
27 other companies	1.0 – 1.9	4, 16, 39, 43, 48, 49, 58, 76, 116, 132, 136, 1, 30, 41, 12, 52, 59, 62, 71, 19, 45, 18, 23, 10, 36, 81, 28
27 other companies	0.0 – 0,9	3, 7, 32, 44, 53, 29, 95, 6, 103, 75, 31, 26, 38, 46, 57, 110, 22, 25, 86, 47, 17, 20, 13, 85, 5, 11, 54
111 other companies	No Information	

* Formerly SA Chrome and Alloys.
Source: Financial Mail 2005.

Although for both years the overwhelming majority of top CSI spenders made the top half of the *Financial Mail*'s empowerment index, there was no strong association between the two measures. For 2004, of the top ten CSI spenders, only two made the top ten BEE firms, and only four of the latter made the top twenty CSI spenders, even though, admittedly, the overwhelming majority (48 out of 64) of companies reporting CSI expenditure were among the top 100 BEE performers. For 2005, just three of the top ten CSI spenders made it into the top ten BEE firms and only three of the latter made the top twenty CSI spenders, although with a lower spending average since just two companies spent higher than ten per cent in 2005. Similarly, as occurred in the previous year, in 2005 the great majority of companies (69 out of 74) reporting CSI made it into the top 100 ranked according to BEE. It is also noticeable that for both years only three of the top ten CSI spenders were companies that met the SRII criteria. For both years, the majority (136 out of 200 in 2004 and 111 out of 185 in 2005) of the country's top BEE companies as measured by the index did not report any CSI, and hence probably did not regard social investment as part of their social responsibilities at all. Admittedly, the lack of overlap between the tables may reflect some inconsistency in annual reporting. Yet if this is the case, it would only seem to confirm that overall, South African firms retain a far narrower conception of good corporate citizenship than is being proposed by groups such as Trialogue and AICC.

In contrast to the above, a survey undertaken by the Centre for Development and Enterprise (CDE) in 1999 indicated that many South African companies viewed spending on BEE as a type of social investment, an interpretation which was shared by the South Africa Foundation (1999) who sponsored the survey. A more recent survey conducted among 25 leading firms by the Foundation similarly indicates increased spending upon empowerment, with this now more firmly interpreted as CSI (*Sowetan* 11 August 2004).

For the moment the evidence remains confusing. Clearly, the established corporations are demonstrating greater responsiveness to government's demands that they pursue BEE. In so doing, they define this as an aspect of wider CSR. Yet the extent to which they have absorbed either or both BEE and CSI into their bloodstream remains to be determined.

Black economic empowerment firms and corporate social responsibility

After more than ten years of democracy, the South African economy remains dominated by white-owned firms, both foreign and domestic. Considerable coverage is given in the media to black empowerment deals, yet the level of black ownership and control of the corporate structure remains remarkably limited. Despite the vast fortunes accumulated by a handful of emergent black tycoons, 'the upper class in South Africa [still] consists of a small, wealthy and mainly White segment of the population [whose] members dominate the top echelons of business and institutions and own a large proportion of all privately held corporate stock' (United Nations Development Programme 2003: 73). Indeed, in September 2003, although blacks held an estimated 14.1 per cent (or R214.4 billion) of the market capitalisation of companies listed on the JSE, their direct ownership amounted to no more than 1.6 per cent (or R23.6 billion) (*Financial Mail* 2004). The basic problem, of course, is that blacks lack capital, and hence, to be enabled to participate in a capitalist economy on anything approaching equal terms with whites, they either have to be given or loaned capital by the private sector, granted favourable opportunities by the state, or club together as multiple individuals in order that small savings can be consolidated into meaningful amounts that can be invested. In practice, all three routes are being followed, although in recent years (as noted above) the government has taken a much more assertive role in seeking to promote BEE, notably by pressurising the private sector to achieve ownership and employment equity targets via various charters.

Given this continuing dramatic racial inequality, emergent black capitalists are presented ideologically by the ANC as a patriotic bourgeoisie. Historically, the ANC theorised that the overthrow of apartheid would inaugurate a national democratic revolution (NDR) devoted to the attainment of a united, non-racial, non-sexist and democratic society in which the defeat of national oppression would lead to the development of a black capitalist class and the major growth of intermediate, black middle strata. However, because it was vital to ensure that these developments overcame the gross social inequalities of the past and worked to the ultimate benefit of all, it was deemed necessary that newly advantaged elements from among the previously oppressed should be subjected to certain controls, exerted from below by the working class and through the leadership of the party, to ensure that the long-term goals of the national liberation movement could be realised. Even if, as noted previously (Southall 2004), the theory of the NDR is shot through with ambiguities, what is important here is to note that it legitimises emergent black capitalists as patriotic.

When deconstructed, two meanings appear to attach to the term patriotic. First, there is the implication that the emergence of a black capitalist class as a product of changing racial ownership patterns is an historical good in itself. Hassen (2003: 2) describes the idea as a profound one, 'uprooting the legacy of apartheid through creating a pool of activist capitalists that, in the parlance of the Congress tradition, would be part of the "motive forces of change". The grouping of capitalists would undertake business, invest in the country and create jobs . . . making capitalism more humane and sharing the benefits of capitalist accumulation.'

Second, there is the implication of reciprocity between black capitalists and the racially disadvantaged communities from which they have come. This latter meaning readily lends itself to notions of SRI and / or CSI. However, it does not resolve a severe tension between the two aspects of patriotism in that the emphasis upon capital accumulation in the first can be interpreted as running counter to the social obligations implied by the second. Or to put it another way, black capitalists – many of whom are hugely indebted by virtue of empowerment deals financed by long-term loans and other liabilities – might well be tempted to say that their primary responsibility is to accumulate capital and advance black ownership of the economy. Insistence that black-owned companies should undertake additional burdens of social responsibility is likely to obstruct that goal and to render their often already fragile hold on capital more perilous. From this perspective, SRI and/or CSI is for white-owned firms, for only they need to atone for sins of the past. Even so, further distinction between types of BEE investment will demonstrate that this narrow approach is strongly contested, in theory at least, notably by the trade union movement which has more broadly based conceptions of both BEE and CSR.

Privately-owned BEE companies

Lack of reliable statistics renders generalisation about the extent to which privately-owned BEE companies engage in the funding of communities which are external to their employees – the definition of CSI offered by Trialogue – extremely perilous. For instance, although failure to report does not necessarily mean that no such expenditure has taken place, of the 25 most extensively black-owned firms out of the *Financial Mail*'s top 200 empowerment companies, only seven reported any CSI. Of these seven, two (Grintek and CS Holdings) ranked among the top six CSI companies overall, while ranked only seventeenth and eighteenth out of the top black-owned 25 companies.[6] For the 2005 ranking, only four of the ten most extensively black-owned firms report any CSI, with the highest being as little as 1.41 per cent. However, for all their limitations, such figures suggest that CSI does not rate highly among the objectives of privately-owned BEE companies.

Nonetheless, such BEE companies make payments to their black stakeholders. For instance, in a review grandiosely entitled 'Black Empowerment Titans Give Something Back', *Business Day* (19 December 2003) reported that Tokyo Sexwale's Mvelaphanda Holdings distributed R80 million to its stakeholders 'in a bid to ensure that empowerment filtered through to the previously disadvantaged investors'. This was described as 'one of the biggest cash distributions made by an empowerment company', yet the beneficiaries – who were shareholders – included the Umkhonto we Sizwe Military Veterans Association, the Steve Biko Foundation, the Johannesburg Child Welfare Society, Cotlands, the Women's Development Bank Investment Holdings (Wiphold), the Widows of African National Congress Veterans, and Makana Investments. According to the Military Veterans' Association, the money would help capacitate organisational structures, attend to the needs of veterans and their orphans, and create job opportunities. Wiphold proceeded to pay out R5.8 million in early 2003 to a not-for-profit trust dedicated to the support of women in rural areas. However, although described as generous payments to disadvantaged communities through social investment programmes, these actually appear to be returns on investments made by organisations or trusts. Consequently, while their outcome may indeed have been socially beneficial, it is not clear that they constitute CSI as defined by Trialogue.

In contrast, Sekunjalo (listed second out of the *Financial Mail*'s top 200 empowerment companies) is reported as having contributed to the Manto Tshabalala-Msimang Healthcare Bursary Trust (for students from poor areas wanting to study in the fields of health and science) as well as having supported the development of musical talent among disadvantaged communities through a series of sponsored jazz concerts, an activity which would appear to overlap heavily with advertising, as would Mvelaphanda Sports Investments' R15 million sponsorship of the national soccer first division in May 2004 (*Business Day* 19 December 2003 and 10 June 2004). Sekunjalo also claimed HIV / AIDS training and counselling for its employees as CSI, whereas this would more appropriately fall under the heading of human resources. Likewise, New African Investments Limited (ranked 128th in the top 200 BEE companies despite not providing information on CSI) is reported to have spent R10 million rebuilding two schools in Limpopo, and as helping to launch an AIDS orphanage in Zuurbekom (*Business Day* 19 December 2003). Yet such financial contributions appear extremely small compared to profits and would not seem to challenge the overall picture that BEE firms' expenditure on CSI is very limited.

Randall (2003) has opined that the government's recent thinking has shifted from individual to community empowerment in order to render BEE more broadly based. In this regard, the key principle of the empowerment strategy is to fast-track the entry of historically marginalised communities into the mainstream of the economy, and hence much emphasis is given to the involvement as equity holders of employee trusts, trade unions and other black groupings. Yet, Randall argues, while the goal of sharing the economic benefits of these transactions among more blacks is laudable, it detracts from the creation of a strong, self-standing class of black capitalists. In contrast, other observers view the ANC as determined to promote the strong black capitalist class which Randall desires, alongside the rapid development of a new, expanding black middle class, which would then take responsibility with government for the effective transfer of wealth to the rest of the country (Haffajee 2003; Southall 2005). This is an interpretation that is largely shared by an emergent patriotic bourgeoisie which views its overwhelming responsibility as being to accumulate capital and to promote the development of black society through investment and deracialisation of the economy. CSI and/or philanthropy can come later.[7]

Black-owned pension funds
In the late 1990s, institutional investors deployed assets of over R1 000 billion, or around 50 per cent of South Africa's total asset value. Of these, pension funds (including provident funds) accounted for around R600 billion, owning 60 per cent of the equity listed on the JSE. By 2000, some 8.4 million pension fund members were contributing around R52 billion annually, and pension funds had climbed to R694 billion. By 2003, it was estimated that pension fund assets totalled over R800 billion. Overall, pension fund contributions amount to some 14 per cent of total formal sector remuneration in South Africa, which ranks fourth in the world for per capita pension asset funds after the United Kingdom, Switzerland and the Netherlands (Naidoo 2001: 69, 2003: 32). The background to this impressive level of accumulation lies in the apartheid past, when prescribed asset legislation was used to generate investment. The Pension Funds Act (24 of 1956) made it compulsory for every pension fund to place at least ten per cent of its total assets in government stock and another 40 per cent in other prescribed stock (such as National Defence Bonds, ISCOR, SASOL and homeland development corporations). These figures peaked in 1977 at 22.5 per cent and 55 per cent respectively (Naidoo 2003: 32). In short, pension

funds were utilised to underwrite white political power. However, in 1989, under enormous pressure from capital, the apartheid government abolished prescribed assets in order to keep pension funds out of the hands of any democratically elected successor (Naidoo 2003: 32).

Pension fund assets clearly offer massive potential for BEE and patriotic SRI. However, on average, total investment as a share of GDP has fallen from an average of 26.4 per cent per annum in the 1970s to around 15 per cent today. One reason for this low rate of investment is a massive outflow of capital from the private sector (R206 billion between 1994 and 2002), which largely counterbalances the inflow (R264 billion during the same period) (United Nations Development Programme 2003: 13–14). This is explained at least in part by the decision of a number of leading South African corporations in which pension funds have invested to relocate their headquarters abroad. Nonetheless, it remains the case that pension funds constitute a tremendous stock of assets that could be used to finance development and promote equitable and sustainable growth if they were to be deployed appropriately. This was recognised, inter alia, by both the RDP, which argued that pension fund boards should be transformed to render them 'more socially responsible' (African National Congress 1994: 112), and subsequently by the BEE Commission, which recommended that both government and the private sector should commit to investing specified percentages of their total assets in projects of national priority and that union pension funds should be similarly directed.

Despite such recommendations, the pension fund industry remains unrestrained by official prescriptions demanding BEE or SRI. To be sure, amendments to the Pension Funds Act in 1996 laid down that member-elected representatives must comprise at least 50 per cent of boards of pension fund trustees. Yet while this is an enormous potential step forward for labour, in practice few members' representatives have the necessary time, information and skills to evaluate the advice given to them by professional asset managers, who are closely aligned to the financial sector, in particular insurance companies.

Anthony Sampson (2004: 265–75) records how pension funds in Britain have become ever less accountable to their members. Traditionally they dealt in government stocks, yet from the 1950s onward they invested in industrial shares in order to keep pace with inflation. Their holdings became so big that they became increasingly involved with the corporations in which they invested, and could not sell their shares without rocking the whole market. Their interests aligned with heads of corporations, who had become increasingly preoccupied with share price, resulting in chronically short-term thinking, even though their investors, potential pensioners, had long-term horizons. Yet when pension fund values collapsed, the professionals were keen to pass responsibility on to trustees, who were overwhelmingly part-time amateurs dependent upon advice.

The performance of the South African pension fund industry appears to have been little different. By May 2003, the value of pension funds was reported as having slumped by R75 billion since the beginning of 2002, with trustees blaming asset managers for failing to see that the stock market was overvalued and that a higher proportion of investments should have been held in cash and bonds. In turn, asset managers blamed trustees for tying their hands, although their standing was little helped by a series of scandals which, suggesting evidence of fraud and impropriety in some pension funds, saw savings of thousands being eroded (*Business Day* 28 May 2003; *Business Report* 17 September 2003). Yet blaming trustees carries little weight, for most are passive, and the industry's principal advice to them is that they should find asset managers they can trust (*Business Report* 13 May 2003). Indeed, international experience points to the enormous obstacles which confront trustees who attempt to impose restrictions upon pension fund investments. For instance, American unions which sought to get their members' pension funds to disinvest from corporations that had investments in apartheid South Africa ran into stubborn resistance (Southall 1995: 191). How much better, then, can South African trustees, whether they represent union or broader interests, expect to fare if they attempt to direct pension fund investment to longer-term and more socially responsible horizons?

According to Empowerdex, blacks owned nearly ten per cent of the total share value (R143.5 billion) of the top 115 companies listed on the JSE (British Broadcasting Corporation 2002). However, in contrast, BusinessMap argued that a more realistic figure was two per cent and that black-owned stakes in pension and other funds which were not actively managed for black shareholders could not be counted as real empowerment (*Business Day* 10 December 2002). Even so, taken together, black and union membership of pension funds is impressive and, despite the difficulties encountered by trustees, should be able to shift the industry towards strategies favourable to both BEE and SRI. There are four dynamics which are working in this direction.

First, following the various scandals which rocked the pension fund industry, the Financial Services Board – the statutory institution that oversees the non-banking financial services sector in the public interest – announced that it would be issuing new governance measures which would be largely based upon the King Report on corporate governance (*Business Day* 28 May 2003).

Second, although the Financial Services Charter envisages an apparently adequate ownership target of 25 per cent total black ownership by 2010 (of which at least ten per cent must be direct), it adopts a balanced scorecard approach in which ownership, procurement and human resources are together given a weighting of just under 60 per cent, which was considerably less than the then proposed 90 per cent in the government guideline (*Business Day* 20 October 2003). Indeed, in the scorecard released at the end of 2005, these three components had been reduced to a 70 per cent weighting. Even so, asset managers in the sector have demonstrated increasing commitment to empowerment in order to gain access to the billions held in funds for government, parastatals and unions, and there has been a growing number of deals whereby asset managers have sought to position themselves favourably. For instance, in 2003 Alexander Forbes sold 30 per cent of its financial services assets to Cyril Ramaphosa's empowerment consortium, Millennium Consolidated Investments (*Business Day* 12 December 2003). Prior to that, Nedcor had similarly announced that Reuel Khoza's AKA Capital would take a controlling 33 per cent stake in BoE Asset Management; Coronation Fund Managers had joined with Kagiso Trust Investments to form Kagiso Asset Management; and FirstRand had sold 40 per cent of asset manager Wipcapital, the financial services arm of Wiphold, for R20 million (*Business Day* 5 November 2002). By mid 2003, more than half of the top 28 asset managers had black ownership of more than 25 per cent (*Business Day* 6 March 2003, 19 June 2003). This flurry of activity was said to have been activated by the expectation that the public investment commissioners, who manage about R220 billion in pension funds for government, parastatals and unions, were likely to put out a R70 million tender for investment on the stock market (*Business Day* 5 November 2002).

Third, although it is cognisant of all the complexities relating to pension funds, the trade union movement is determined to increase its say over how retirement funds are used. The Congress of South African Trade Unions' (1997) September Commission recommended that retirement funds should hold at least twenty per cent in prescribed assets in order to promote long-term industrial growth and employment, that organised labour and representatives of policy holders should be given representation on the governing structures of insurance companies in which they have a stake, and that unions should take full advantage of the legislation requiring that at least 50 per cent of trustees should be worker representatives in order to influence investment policy and promote social responsibility. President Mbeki subsequently rejected the plea for government to impose a standard socially-targeted investment rule for all funds and suggested that only union-controlled funds should be so prescribed. Nonetheless, COSATU has continued to campaign for its goals, which meld well with possibilities that state-owned institutions such as the Industrial Development Corporation and the Development Bank of Southern Africa might play a greater role in identifying and promoting appropriate socially desirable investment projects (Naidoo 2003).

Fourth, retirement fund managers are coming under increasing pressure, especially from union trustees, to engage in both BEE and SRI. In a brief prepared by Fifth Quadrant Consultants (2003), it was reported that there was a clear correlation between union influence and the level of attention paid to SRI – although the latter was rarely more than ten per cent, and usually less. Managers viewed SRI as more risk-prone than other investments and hence more likely to conflict with the trustees' fiduciary obligations to maximise investment returns for their members. Nonetheless, they were prepared to pursue SRI opportunities if these were deemed to be economically sound and if they offered genuine possibilities of empowerment; although Quadrant expressed the view that while the latter was worthwhile, it should not be classified as SRI. Managers further reported that trustees had not really applied their minds to their potential power as institutional shareholders and continued to delegate full responsibility for investment decisions to themselves, although on the whole they regarded this positively, arguing that the issues raised by investment were too complex for trustees' engagement. Finally, Quadrant reported high awareness of empowerment criteria and indicated that it was common for trustees to place up to twenty per cent of investment with empowerment managers.

Overall, it would seem that while the pension fund industry is responding positively to government leverage with regard to BEE in order to promote its own security and expansion, its commitment to CSER/SRI is extremely limited and is only likely to be promoted in response to increased pressure, especially from union and worker trustees. However, the difficulty of ensuring that those who make investment decisions for trade unionists do so on behalf of the latter rather than in their own interests is demonstrated by the short, but already chequered, experience of union investment companies.

Union investment companies
The very considerable financial assets, mostly retirement funds, generated by the trade unions led in the early 1990s to the development of trade union investment companies. Early ventures included NACTU Investment Holdings, the Mineworkers' Investment Company, SACTWU Investment Holdings, and FAWU's Ikwezi company; followed fairly soon by the launch of SADTU Investment Holdings, Kopano Ke Matla (COSATU's investment arm), SARHWU Investment Holdings and NUMSA Investment Company. These investment arms were notionally quite separate from their owning unions, although normally union office bearers were nominated to serve on the trusts which, since they held all the shares in the investment companies, appointed the boards of directors. The income received by the trust was then distributed to union members or their families by way of, for example, education bursaries or housing loans. In many ways, the union investment companies were clear successors to many earlier worker-based self-help initiatives, such as co-operatives, yet they were distinguished by the substantial amounts of money they had to deploy. This meant that the unions were courted by the merchant banks and finance houses, which offered their services for investment. In turn, the unions wondered why they should not use their assets as vehicles not only for broad-based BEE but also for restructuring the nature of the South African political economy (SALB Special Correspondent 1996). The outcome was to be highly controversial.

For their protagonists, union investment companies were vehicles for progressive social change, worker power and black empowerment.

Prior to 1994, the major trade union federation, COSATU, had been committed alongside many in the liberation movement to the struggle for socialism. However, in practice, the negotiated transition – which in essence gave political power to the ANC while whites remained in charge of the private sector – confirmed the continuing capitalist basis of the economy. Even so, the changing landscape provided significant possibilities for economic restructuring, and in this context, as one trade unionist turned director put it, there were major assets, resources and opportunities up for grabs. In short, opportunities for relatively rapid accumulation exist. The issue then becomes, who accumulates what? If accumulation was simply left to the patriotic bourgeoisie, it would be to the detriment of workers, who would be passing up the chance to influence patterns of wealth distribution and capital formation. Unions should not suddenly become capitalist, but engage in collective ownership and economic activity, 'surely . . . a legitimate activity for unions and any other groups of people that have been discriminated against under apartheid' (Dexter 1999: 82–3). Rather than simply criticise, trade unionists should seize the democratic moment to participate strategically in broad economic empowerment, and launch new institutions that would promote the interests of working people generally. More specifically, union investment companies would help labour to transform the economy, facilitate transfer of skills to the disadvantaged, assist regional economic integration and, importantly, create jobs. Furthermore, they could prove a means whereby ownership of the means of production could be transferred to workers – in short, to help socialise the economy (Copelyn 1997; Golding 1997; Vlok 1999).

The counter-argument proposed that union investment companies, at least as hitherto conceptualised, were unlikely to benefit workers significantly, but were likely to weaken any struggle for socialism. It could not be assumed, warned one commentator, that the radical and militant tradition of South African trade unionists would automatically prevent them from repeating the excesses of business unionism experienced elsewhere. Various trade unions in both the United States and the United Kingdom had argued that globalisation and neo-liberalism had so eroded the basis for worker struggle that the best way to tackle declining union membership was for unions to offer an array of services, such as access to private medicine, as well as in a number of instances launching businesses to make money. Yet while creative strategies were needed in the new era, experience proved that such ventures were likely to depoliticise and demobilise workers, distract unions from fighting for better wages and jobs, encourage investment in morally dubious enterprises, and favour the interests of union barons over those of the membership at large (Faulkner 1999). Trade unions should not merely seek to build social capitalism, but should use their collective investments to build union strength and working-class political organisation, transcend intra-capitalist circulation – for example, by co-investing with the state to de-commodify the delivery of basic goods and services – and link up with unions and progressive organisations in investment initiatives internationally (McKinley 1999).

Yet the debate was far more pragmatic than it was ideological. How, in practice, were union investment companies going to benefit workers? Would not the speculative nature of some investments put workers' money at risk? Was it possible to be a business manager or director and serve trade union interests at the same time? How should such managers and directors be paid? And, inevitably, would not conflicts arise between unions and their investment companies, notably when profitability demanded that workers be sacked (Collins 1997)? However, the most thoughtful interventions stressed that the very significant financial assets available to the trade union movement meant that some form of collective investment was an inevitability, and that consequently the devising of social investment and accountability rules were essential in order to prevent unions being undermined by wrong investment choices. Ultimately, it was this line of thinking that characterised COSATU's policy statements, which pressed for union investment companies to link profit making to six goals, namely:

- promoting a social sector of the economy to influence investment patterns to generate real productivity and jobs;
- strengthening democratic governance within enterprises;
- using profit for worker and communal benefit;
- tying assets to community and worker ownership to inhibit the flight of capital;
- finding creative ways to redistribute productive assets; and
- establishing social forms of production as a step on the way to socialism (COSATU 1997).

The debate about union investment companies is understandably more about worker empowerment than black empowerment explicitly, yet it clearly envisions a broad-based form of empowerment which bonds the interests of worker/union shareholders to those of the wider community generally. Social responsibility, according to this mantra, should be inherent in union investment in a way that it is not in capitalist investment. Yet how has union investment worked out in practice? And how socially responsible has it been?

The immediate answer is quite simply that it is difficult to say, for there is a dearth of empirical studies describing how union investment companies have operated. In these circumstances it is difficult to venture more than a few generalities.

First, the companies themselves justify their existence as beneficial to workers and their communities while exuding determination to maintain their financial viability. John Copelyn, one of the most influential union investment pioneers, has stressed how, when in 1992 he became manager of Zenzelini Clothing, a company formed by the South African Clothing and Textile Workers' Union (SACTWU) to employ workers retrenched by a major textile company, he was obsessed with making it pay. It succeeded in paying off its debt, offered new skills and stable employment to half the union members who had lost their jobs, and used profits to fund home-based carpet production within the local community. Subsequently, SACTWU's promotion of investment companies yielded hundreds of millions of rand which, through its Education Trust, had by 1997 provided bursaries for 2 500 children of SACTWU members at a cost of some R5 million (Copelyn 1997: 77–8). At present, the SACTWU Trust's key projects extend across tertiary bursaries, matric tuition, HIV/AIDS issues, shelter and counselling for survivors of domestic violence, a children's resource centre, and sport, recreation and cultural initiatives. Likewise, the Mineworkers' Investment Company (MIC), launched in 1995, claimed by 2000 to have distributed R52 million to social initiatives, notably bursaries and educational programmes, and had committed itself to an additional R34 million over the next four years (Mineworkers' Investment Company 2000; Alsafe Undated). Meanwhile, although similarly ambitious, neither the National Union of Metalworkers of South Africa's investment companies nor South African Railways and Harbour Workers' Union's investment holding company had yet been able to make payments into their trusts (Vlok 1999). Overall, however, given that most investment companies are not listed, it remains difficult to state with any certainty to what extent they are honouring their good intentions, or what proportion of their profits they may be making over to social investment.

Second, trade union investment companies have linked arms with both established and empowerment capital to enter diverse investment areas, most particularly media, financial services, and information and technology. For instance, SACTWU owns 51 per cent of Hosken Consolidated Investments, which in turn has a major stake (66%, apparently through Midi-TV) in eTV, and either a 49 per cent or a 52 per cent stake (according to the source one consults) in Mettle Limited, a financial services company. In July 2002, Mettle purchased a 50 per cent holding in Johnson Crane Hire. SACTWU Investment Holdings owns 2.5 per cent of Cape Talk Radio. Controversially, it has also invested in Vukani Gaming Corporation and Sun Hotels. The MIC not only shares a major interest with SACTWU Investments in Midi-TV (via Sabido Investments), but has a 25 per cent (R200 million) stake in Primedia Outdoor, with whom MIC had successfully acquired control of Highveld Radio in 1996. SARHWU Investment Holdings, which had invested R217.5 million in Sanlam's Development Fund, and thereby gained control over an array of substantial holdings in ventures as diverse as Mercantile Bank and Rent-A-Bakkie, sold off almost R100 million of its investments in late 1998 in order to focus upon information technology and financial services. COSATU's Kopano Ke Matla has a 50 per cent interest in Prosperity Insurance, and a 35 per cent interest in Nicor Outsourcing, which aims to provide IT solutions for government, parastatals and their associate interests. The NUMSA and SARHWU Investment Trusts both have holdings in Brimstone Investment Corporation, described as a leading empowerment consortium linking union to community interests. Brimstone acquired a 20 per cent (R260 million) interest in People's Bank, a subsidiary of Nedcor in mid 2000.[8]

What has raised concerns within the union movement is not merely how union investment finance is becoming entangled with established corporate capital and to what end, but how this has enabled some former trade unionists to become extremely wealthy – both Copelyn and Golding have become millionaires. There are many, too, who think that investments in such activities as gambling are peculiarly inappropriate.

Finally, the few attempts by union investment companies to work closely with government have proved controversial. For a start, many have seen a contradiction between COSATU's opposition to privatisation and any move by unions' investment companies to purchase privatised assets. In any case, the major example of such a deal worked out disastrously when the government, which had sold Aventura holiday resorts to Kopano ke Matla (COSATU's investment arm) in 1998, had to resume ownership after Aventura's creditors threatened to foreclose following non-payment of debts (*Business Report* 29 November 1998; Helen Suzman Foundation undated).

A consolidated review needs to be conducted before any soundly-based conclusions about the overall performance of the union investment companies can be pronounced. However, this very preliminary analysis suggests that their potential for promoting either or both broad-based BEE or SRI has only been modestly realised. It remains the case, as the *South African Labour Bulletin* opined in 1999, that union investment needs a clear political strategy and policy guidelines if it is to play a meaningful role in bettering workers' lives (SALB Special Correspondent 1999).

Conclusion

Historically, few corporations in South Africa recognised obligations beyond those they owed to the state or to their shareholders, save insofar as the growth of international pressure propelled them into adopting practices that were more friendly towards black employees. However, in the present era they have to respond to pressures from government on the one hand and from diverse lobbyists on the other to implement policies promoting black empowerment and corporate responsibility respectively. Overall, this is a positive development for South African capital still has much to do to overcome its easy alignment with the brutalities of apartheid. Even if corporations' embrace of the process has been induced as much by fear of government sanction as by forward-looking vision, it is to be welcomed insofar as it indicates that the corporate sector is now taking the project of BEE seriously. However, the danger is that while, correctly, corporations are defining BEE as an integral aspect of CSER, they may claim to be fulfilling their wider social obligations merely by doing what, increasingly, they are required to do by government. There are many critics who claim that the implementation of BEE is principally creating a black corporate elite rather than empowering the wider black community. The further danger, surely, is not only that a narrowly-focused commitment to BEE will be paraded as evidence of corporate virtue, but that it will be at the cost of a much wider vision that sees corporate citizenship as embracing good governance and socially and ethically responsible behaviour generally. Established capital increasingly recognises that implementing BEE is important for future expansion and profitability. The impression remains that it is yet to view CSER in the same way.

For their part, black-owned corporations are most immediately concerned with accumulating capital and establishing their viability. Their attitude seems to be that, by being wholly or significantly black-owned, they are inherently patriotic and that, unlike established white-owned corporations, they do not have social debts to pay. In any case, many of them are tied to wider social interests via the trusts and community or union interests that in part own them. Yet the returns that BEE companies make to such entities have an inherently ambiguous character for while the funding of bursaries and numerous worthwhile community projects may be commendable, such funding may be more akin to payments to shareholders than to SRI. To be sure, community and union-based collective funding of black-owned industry may be an important step towards the elaboration of a vision of socially responsible stakeholder capitalism that avoids the excesses of both the colonial and contemporary American corporate models. Yet that would require BEE companies to recognise that patriotism is not enough, and that they too should embrace an expansive vision of corporate citizenship to achieve both profit and responsibility.

Notes

1. The authors would like to thank the Conflict and Governance Facility of the European Union programme in South Africa for its financial support for the research for this chapter.

2. The Codes of Conduct were promoted initially by the Swedish and British governments and subsequently by the Reverend Leon Sullivan, a black American civil rights activist, who elaborated fair employment principles to be followed by US corporations. A European Economic Community code followed in 1977 and a Canadian Code in 1978 (Southall 1995: 132–6).

3. An SRI is defined as an investment that combines investors' financial objectives with their commitment to concerns such as social justice, economic development, peace or a healthy environment.

4. Including the South African Constitution and the Bill of Rights, the Basic Conditions of Employment Act (75 of 1997), the Labour Relations Act (66 of 1995), the Occupational Health and Safety Act (85 of 1993), the National Environmental Management Act (107 of 1998), the National Water Act (36 of 1998), and directors' fiduciary duties.

5. The second King Report, the JSE Listing Requirements, and the JSE SRII.

6. Total black ownership (direct and indirect) of Grintek is recorded as 35.2 per cent and of CS Holdings as 34.1 per cent.

7. Except insofar, perhaps, as it promotes the social standing of magnates, as for instance through Patrice Motsepe's ownership of the Premier Soccer League club Mamelodi Sundowns.

8. The information presented in this paragraph was compiled from a host of Internet sources.

References

African Institute of Corporate Citizenship (AICC). 2004. *Socially Responsible Investment in South Africa*. Johannesburg: AICC, 2nd ed.

African National Congress (ANC). 1994. *Reconstruction and Development Programme: A Policy Framework*. Johannesburg: Umanyano.

Alsafe. Undated. 'Alsafe: A Division of Mathomo Group Limited'. Available at www.alsafe.co.za/about.html.

Black Economic Empowerment Commission (BEE Com). 2000. 'Presentation Prepared for the Portfolio Committee on Trade and Industry'. Available at www.pmg.za/docs/2000/appendices/000913BEE.htm.

British Broadcasting Corporation (BBC). 2002. 'Black Industrial Muscle Swells in SA'. Available at news.bbc.co.uk/2/hi/business/2410387.stm.

Collins, D. 1997. 'An Open Letter to Johnny Copelyn and Marcel Golding'. *South African Labour Bulletin* 21 (1): 79–80.

Congress of South African Trade Unions (COSATU). 1997. 'The Report of the September Commission on the Future of the Unions to the Congress of South African Trade Unions'. Available at www.cosatu.org.za/congress/septcomm.htm.

Copelyn, J. 1997. 'Seizing the Moment: Union Investment Companies'. *South African Labour Bulletin* 21 (2): 74–8.

Dexter, P. 1999. 'Union Investment Companies: Business Unionism or Union Business?' *South African Labour Bulletin* 23 (6): 82–4.

Edigheji, O.M. 1999. 'Re-thinking Black Economic Empowerment in Post-Apartheid South Africa'. Paper prepared for the TIPS 1999 Annual Forum, Glenburn Lodge, Muldersdrift, 19–22 September.

Faulkner, S. 1999. 'Investing in Ourselves: A Cautionary Tale'. *South African Labour Bulletin* 23 (4): 18–22.

Fifth Quadrant Consultants. 2003. 'Role of the Unions in the SA Retirement Industry'. Available at www.naledi.org.za/pubs/2003/retirement1.pdf.

Financial Mail. 2004. 'Top Empowerment Companies 2004'. Available at www.free. financialmail.co.za/projects/topbeecos/tables/top200a.html.

———. 2005. 'Top Empowerment Companies 2005'. Available at www.free.financialmail. co.za/projects05/topempowerment/tables/top185.html.

Golding, M. 1997. 'Pioneers or Sellouts? Exploring New Lands'. *South African Labour Bulletin* 21 (3): 85–90.

Haffajee, S. 2003. 'Tomorrow's People'. *Mail & Guardian*, 14–20 November.

Hassen, E-K. 2003. 'Black Economic Empowerment: What Gains?' *Naledi Policy Bulletin* December.

Helen Suzman Foundation. Undated. 'Sweets for my Sweetheart'. *Focus.* Available at www/hsf.org.za/focus_16/f16_Sweets_sweetheart.html.

Johannesburg Securities Exchange (JSE). 2002. 'The FTSE/JSE SRI Index and Corporate Social Responsibility: Philosophy and Criteria'. Available at www.jse.co.za.

———. 2004. 'SRI Index'.

———. 2005. 'SRI Index'.

King Committee on Corporate Governance. 2002. *King Report on Corporate Governance for South Africa, 2002* (King II Report). Johannesburg: Institute of Directors.

Mbeki, T. 2003. 'State of the Nation Address to the Joint Sitting of the Houses of Parliament, Cape Town. 14 February'. Available at www.info.gov.za/ speeches/2003/03021412521001.htm.

McKinley, D. 1999. 'Union Investment Strategy: Socialist Unionism or "Social Capitalism"?' *South African Labour Bulletin* 23 (6): 85–90.

Mineworkers Investment Company (MIC). 2000. 'The Mineworkers Investment Company'. Available at www.mic.co.za/mic/home_mic_hist.html.

Naidoo, R. 2001. 'Can Pension Funds Dance to a Working Class Tune?' *South African Labour Bulletin* 25 (2): 69–75.

———. 2003. 'Pension Funds: Investing in Growth and Employment'. *South African Labour Bulletin* 25 (2): 32–3.

Newton-King, N. 2003. 'Corporate Social Responsibility: An Exchange's View'. Available at www.jse.co.za.

———. 2005. 'Despite Tougher Criteria, Companies Still Outperform on Latest SRI Index'. Press release. Available at www.jse.co.za.

Randall, D. 2003. 'Put Small Business Back in Empowerment Equation'. *Business Day* 29 July.

SALB Special Correspondent. 1996. 'Union Investment: New Opportunities, New Threats'. *South African Labour Bulletin* 20 (5): 33–9.

———. 1999. 'Code of Conduct: Superficial Tool or Effective Policy Device?' *South African Labour Bulletin* 23 (4): 30–4.

Sampson, A. 2004. *Who Runs This Place? The Anatomy of Britain in the 21st Century.* London: John Murray.

South Africa Foundation. 1999. *Corporate Social Investment in South Africa: Viewpoint.* Available at www.safoundation.org.za/fhome.html.

South African Institute of Race Relations (SAIRR). 2003. *South Africa Survey 2002/2003.* Johannesburg: SAIRR.

Southall, R. 1995. *Imperialism or Solidarity? International Labour and South African Trade Unions.* Cape Town: University of Cape Town Press.

———. 2004. 'The ANC and Black Capitalism in South Africa'. *Review of African Political Economy* 31 (100): 313–28.

———. 2005. 'Black Empowerment and Corporate Capital'. In *State of the Nation: South Africa 2004–2005,* edited by J. Daniel, R. Southall and J. Lutchman. Cape Town and East Lansing, Michigan: HSRC and Michigan State University Press.

Trialogue. 2004a. *The CSI Handbook.* Cape Town: Trialogue, 7th ed.

———. 2004b. *The Good Corporate Citizen . . . Pursuing Sustainable Business in South Africa.* Cape Town: Trialogue.

United Nations Development Programme (UNDP). 2003. *South Africa: Human Development Report 2003.* Oxford: OUP.

Vlok, E. 1999. 'Plant Now, Harvest Later: Pressures Facing Union Investment Companies'. *South African Labour Bulletin* 23 (4): 23–9.

7

Responsibility from below in the era of AIDS

David Dickinson

Introduction

South Africa is currently at the epicentre of the AIDS pandemic and the disease is affecting all aspects of South African society. Antenatal HIV sero-prevalence surveys at public sector clinics have shown a rise in prevalence from 0.7 per cent in 1990 to 29.5 per cent in 2004 (South Africa, Department of Health 2005). The country's second national household sero-prevalence survey indicated that 16.2 per cent of the country's adult population (15–49 years old) is living with HIV/AIDS. The primary means of HIV transmission in sub-Saharan Africa is unprotected heterosexual sex, with the highest rates of prevalence found among sexually-active adults (UNAIDS 2003a). Poverty is regarded as an important co-factor in the likelihood of infection because of resulting behavioural and biological factors (Marks 2002; Nattrass 2004). The virus's destruction of the immune system results in increased illness and eventual death within eight to ten years of infection unless treated with anti-retroviral (ARV) drugs (UNAIDS 2003b), yet such treatment has been beyond the means of most South Africans. Despite the government's belated decision in November 2003 to provide anti-retroviral drugs in the public sector, the planned roll-out will not be fully operational until 2008 (South Africa, Department of Health 2003).

The response of corporate South Africa to HIV/AIDS has been slow, partial and erratic (Dickinson 2004a). Frequently, company responses have been driven from below by middle and low-level managers rather than as a strategic issue by top management (Dickinson and Stevens 2005). The earliest responses came from the mining industry in 1986 as a result of the detection of four per cent HIV prevalence rates among Malawian migrant workers (Brink and Clausen 1987). Outside the mining industry the first major company to respond was Eskom, the state-owned electricity corporation, which adopted an HIV/AIDS policy in 1988. In the late 1990s and early 2000s, other large South African companies launched comprehensive HIV/AIDS policies, or consolidated their previous ad hoc responses (Global Business Council on HIV/AIDS 2001; Randall 2002). In August 2002 Anglo American announced drug provision for all its employees on the grounds that such an initiative was cost-effective. Since then a number of other large companies have made similar announcements.

It is widely acknowledged that the HIV/AIDS epidemic will impact significantly on South African business in terms of markets, investor confidence, and workforces and the skills they embody (Clarke and Strachan 2000; Rosen et al. 2000; UNAIDS 2000; Whiteside and Sunter 2000; International Labour Organisation 2001; Barnett and Whiteside 2002). In addition to responding to the effect HIV/AIDS could have on operations and profitability, the disease has become an important area for corporate social responsibility (CSR)[1] and corporate social investment (CSI).

Corporate social responsibility, corporate social investment and HIV/AIDS

Bezuidenhout et al. (2003) suggest that, broadly-defined, CSR includes a commitment to sustainable development and a willingness to respond to stakeholders as well as shareholders – in other words, concern about how profits are made. Within the South African context, addressing this question raises uncomfortable issues around the role of business under apartheid. The Truth and Reconciliation Commission (TRC) concluded, 'Business was central to the economy that sustained the South African state during the apartheid years' (1998: 58). Many key issues for CSR – such as education, job creation, health and training – are pressing because of unequal development under apartheid.

In contemporary South Africa, CSR is usually narrated in two ways. The two narratives have a similar starting point: CSR has (or at least should have) shifted from being mere corporate philanthropy. One narrative, exemplified by Bezuidenhout et al. (2003), argues that companies have come under a range of pressures – accelerated by the re-entry of South Africa into the global economy – that constrain their freedom and promote a broad concept of CSR as concern about how profits are made. The second narrative, exemplified by Trialogue (2004) sees a shift to more narrowly-defined CSI, in which corporate giving makes business sense with returns in the form of image, employee morale, social stability and – in a voluntary[2] nod towards broader CSR – its contribution to corporate citizenship.

Thus, CSR/CSI can be explained in a number of overlapping ways – as reparation, as a necessary response in a more accountable environment, as charity (without asking too deeply why good causes exist), and as good business sense. These various explanations justify or explain HIV/AIDS-related CSR or CSI activity. Companies include HIV/AIDS within their CSR/CSI practice for reasons generic to their overall CSR/CSI activity as well as for those specific to the epidemic. Business practices – notably the construction of the migrant labour system (Phillips 2004), but also income inequality, the spatial concentration of poverty and unequal access to health care (Cohen 1999; Marks 2002) – can be regarded as important co-factors that fuel the HIV/AIDS epidemic. There is clearly increasing pressure on companies around HIV/AIDS, such as reporting frameworks, workplace rights and treatment for employees and their families (Fakier 2004). Certain aspects of the HIV/AIDS epidemic provide worthy causes to which companies can respond, AIDS orphans being a case in point.[3] There are also strong arguments regarding the business sense of responding to HIV/AIDS both within and beyond the company (Rosen et al. 2000; UNAIDS 2000; Whiteside and Sunter 2000; Barnett and Whiteside 2002). The impossibility of effectively mounting a purely workplace-based response to HIV/AIDS is easily illustrated by the sexual nature of transmission: the workforce cannot be ring-fenced and the embeddedness of workers in families and communities means that they will be affected in various ways by the AIDS epidemic even if they are not themselves infected (Brink 2003). The ways in which these arguments sometimes overlap can be illustrated by corporate involvement in supporting AIDS orphans. Appeals for companies to assist AIDS orphans mobilise not only heartstrings but also fears: innocent and adorable children now, but – if we don't respond – unsocialised and dangerous adolescents later. This fits three CSR/CSI narratives – charity or worthy giving, sound investment, and necessary responsibility.

HIV/AIDS, official corporate social investment and corporate social responsibility from below

Companies are responding to HIV/AIDS, in and beyond the workplace, for a range of reasons (Dickinson and Stevens 2005). Their responses include the broader concept of CSR – increased reporting of HIV/AIDS, provision of healthcare to workers (and sometimes their families), evaluation of the migrant labour system, and more subtle influences on workplace cultures brought about by confronting stigma and discrimination. Their responses also include more narrowly-defined CSI as corporate giving that yields a return. Trialogue's (2004) survey of 100 companies indicated that 70 of them supported HIV/AIDS initiatives beyond the company, averaging 16 per cent of the total CSI budget.

The scale of the epidemic and the need that it generates, especially among poorer sections of society, will place increasing pressure on CSI, or, as it will be referred to in this chapter, official CSI – that is, corporate giving organised by company CSI units. Important as it is, this chapter is not about official CSI per se. Rather, it explores the nature of HIV/AIDS-related CSR from below, how it differs in content and operation from official CSI, and the differences and tensions between the two forms of company-based, community-focused HIV/AIDS activity. It examines how the AIDS epidemic has seen company employees taking the initiative in responding beyond, as well as within, their own workplace to HIV/AIDS.

Designating company-backed and company-funded HIV/AIDS activity outside of the company as official CSI and employee-initiated activity as CSR from below has the potential to further complicate the debate around CSR and CSI. Companies generally choose the term CSI. By contrast, employee-led HIV/AIDS initiatives in communities are clearly not perceived primarily as good business sense – even if they are – but stem from feelings of commitment, compassion or responsibility. By and large, CSR from below is conducted by individuals who have come together within companies to organise workplace responses to HIV/AIDS. Often these responses have been ahead of – or indeed have become – the formal company response to the disease (Dickinson 2003; Dickinson and Stevens 2005). Their activity beyond the workplace is similarly grassroots in nature and generally operates quite separately and differently from official company CSI HIV / AIDS activities. Figure 7.1 illustrates official CSI and CSR from below in the context of HIV / AIDS.

Official CSI projects are run out of wholly or partly specialised units that report to management and the board. This process is perhaps most clearly exemplified when the corporation's CSI entity is referred to as the Chairman's Fund. By contrast, CSR from below emanates largely from workplace HIV / AIDS structures, which are often initiated through employee actions and reliant on volunteers or quasi-volunteers in the form of peer educators (Dickinson 2004b, 2005a, 2005b).

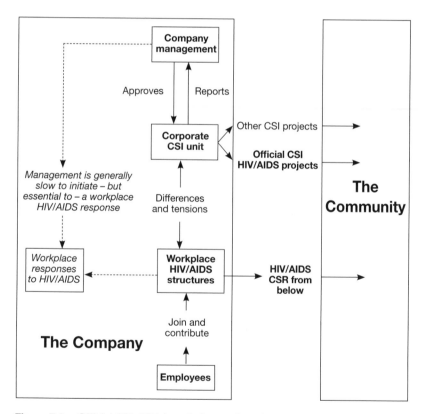

Figure 7.1:   Official CSI, CSR from below and HIV/AIDS.

Case studies

The companies

This account of CSR from below is drawn from research conducted in three South African companies. The names of the case study companies given below are pseudonyms while anonymity was guaranteed to the interviewees.

The first case study company, Deco, is a large, diversified group with over 25 000 South African-based employees operating primarily from a number of industrial sites that dominate surrounding communities – effectively company towns and townships. Research in this company between 2000 and 2004 was primarily focused on its internal response to HIV/AIDS, but during the 80-odd interviews that were conducted with a range of employees, questions on the relationship with the community frequently emerged as a significant issue. This was reinforced by the seriousness with which community-based HIV/AIDS projects were taken in meetings of the company's corporate AIDS forum and divisional HIV/AIDS committees that I attended. Discussion in these meetings highlighted the gap between Deco's CSI office and members of the forum, even though both were contributing to community activities around HIV/AIDS.

The second company, Healthco, is a private health care provider with some 20 000 employees, the majority employed in a country-wide network of hospitals. During 2003 and 2004, I conducted approximately 40 interviews with a colleague, Marion Stevens from the Centre for Health Policy at the University of the Witwatersrand, among company employees, mainly nurses, in four of the company's hospitals. Healthco encouraged hospitals to establish community-based projects as part of the organisation's response to HIV/AIDS. Given the nature of the industry, it was perhaps not surprising that a great deal of HIV/AIDS activity was being organised at these hospitals. However, what was illuminating was just how much of it was run independently by employees with values and sometimes activities that ran counter to managerial culture and objectives.

The third company, Manco, is a medium-sized manufacturing company with some 250 employees in Gauteng. I conducted research at the company in 2004 as part of a wider project on medium-sized manufacturing companies and HIV/AIDS. What was striking in this research was how tensions around official CSI and CSR from below were played out despite the close proximity of the workplace actors – in contrast to the large firms where vast gaps in physical distances and company geography[4] often separated people.

The idea that employees were doing their own thing emerged during research in these three companies. It soon became apparent that many employees involved in HIV/AIDS programmes had only the vaguest contact with those responsible for the company's CSI policies and programmes, and felt that the company's approach was inadequate and that action was urgently needed. I followed up these issues with questions on the way in which employees were organising, how they mobilised resources, and how they articulated their workplace-based activity to the needs of communities.

Many of the individuals interviewed were busy. In addition to their work responsibilities, they had taken on the issue of HIV/AIDS and imposed few boundaries on their commitment to this. However, without exception, they welcomed the chance to talk about what they were doing. Their stories were often heady mixtures of deep commitment to people – expressed in actions as well as words – and deep criticism – laced with cynical comments about colleagues and superiors – of the organisations in which they worked. In collecting these accounts, for which anonymity was guaranteed, it was clearly an advantage to be an outsider. It was also necessary, if the narrator was to open up, for the researcher to empathise with their frequently amateur, occasionally quixotic, but always profoundly genuine attempts to make a difference. When you listen, you also learn. I was deeply impressed by what I heard and saw.

A passion for people nobody else is helping

Many of the employees involved in HIV/AIDS workplace programmes were not in strategic positions. Nor, with a few exceptions, did they think strategically about their response to HIV/AIDS. When interviewed, managers would typically attempt to grapple with statistics, risk and the overall size of the problem that AIDS presented. By contrast, lower-level employees active in HIV/AIDS work would forefront direct and immediate needs, frequently supported by examples as to why they were actively involved. One nurse explained the success of hospital-based HIV/AIDS committees in Healthco by saying, 'It's simple. People get bombarded with stats [about HIV/AIDS], but what they really want to know is, how they can help?' This is not to say that managers only took a dispassionate view of HIV / AIDS. A number of managers in Deco explained how their Christian beliefs meant that they needed to consider the suffering resulting from AIDS. At the same time, however, they were extremely careful to separate what they could do in their personal lives and their role in the company, the former being informed by their faith and the latter by business needs.

Individuals frequently explained their involvement in HIV / AIDS activities within and beyond the workplace as a result of their passion for people, although this was often explained in somewhat clichéd terms. Those with a passion for people are likely to seek out jobs that involve assisting others – and are often less likely to climb managerial hierarchies successfully as this requires quite different attributes – and consequently will become more involved with people facing difficulties. In Deco, a Human Resources (HR) officer in a small division explained how she had moved into HR from her previous administrative position because she realised that there was 'a huge gap in people's lives. They have problems at home which they bring into the workplace, but they've no place to go with their problems, whether they're marital, financial, children, depression. And [now] we have to include AIDS.' Consequently, she had helped to establish the company's Employee Care Centre and had aggressively driven AIDS awareness.

A major component of hospital work is helping people who are ill, though within the private health care system of Healthco patients are often relatively privileged. This was not the case for many hospital workers – especially subcontracted cleaners, laundry workers, canteen staff and security – who, while working in a hospital, did not have the financial resources to afford medical aid. Frequently, they would seek assistance from nurses whom they worked alongside or who had established a reputation for being willing to help. Industrial nurses in Deco faced similar situations. Workers came to their clinics with AIDS-related symptoms for which they were able to provide little more than painkillers and advice. Referrals to sources of anti-retroviral drugs were meaningless because such employees were unable to afford medical aid.[5] One of these industrial nurses bitterly contrasted this experience with perceived managerial inaction over HIV / AIDS: 'They [managers] don't have to look the patient in the eyes [and turn them away]'.

Thus, particular positions within the working environment expose individuals to the problems of others, problems which frequently extend beyond the immediate cause of contact. For example, an industrial nurse realises that treatment is unaffordable, or an HR officer realises that absenteeism stems from family difficulties. Such positions expose people to social stresses, such as the AIDS epidemic, from which they might otherwise be insulated in their daily lives.

But this is not the only way in which those responding to HIV/AIDS in companies are exposed to the social stress of HIV/AIDS. Every person, whatever their status at work, is embedded within society. However, the extent to which they are exposed to HIV/AIDS or other social problems depends on the particular community (or communities) within which they are embedded. HIV infection is strongly correlated with socio-economic status (Cohen 1999; Johnson and Budlender 2002; Marks 2002). When interviewing peer educators – the lowest position in company HIV/AIDS workplace programmes – respondents would routinely talk of AIDS deaths in their families and the number of funerals of young people in their townships as factors motivating their involvement in HIV/AIDS activity. Such direct, collectively-based experience of AIDS was much less common among managers, though it sometimes involved individual members of lower socio-economic groups with whom they were in daily contact – typically domestic workers or the tea lady – who they knew to be HIV-positive or who had died of AIDS. Such contact raised awareness of the disease, but tended to translate into individual responses, such as securing anti-retroviral drugs for the employee, rather than systematically mobilising resources for those infected or affected by AIDS.

If proximity, either by exposure or status, to the social groups bearing the brunt of the AIDS epidemic provided a push factor in promoting action around HIV/AIDS by company employees, the lack of response to the epidemic by government provided a pull factor for workers to take direct action to alleviate the impact of HIV/AIDS. A Deco employee coordinating a group of peer educators in one of the company's operations explained that 'people are sick in the community, but the government is doing nothing'.

Not enough to be in the club

The thrust of this chapter is that, for many employees, their company was not doing enough when it came to HIV/AIDS in the community. Limited company involvement stems from a number of factors. One of these is a pragmatic calculation on the part of senior management that while the company's image on HIV / AIDS is important, it is based on a relative, rather than absolute, measure. As long as the company is in the same position as others there are unlikely to be any negative image implications. A senior Deco manager explained this with surprising frankness: 'It's now a corporate image issue, but if we're late [in responding to HIV / AIDS] we're not going to be killed for it. Who's ahead on this issue? [i.e., nobody]. So we're in the club. There is little competitive image difference on HIV / AIDS.'

Another fear is that it would be difficult to draw a line around company involvement in the community (Brink 2003; Dickinson 2004a). The failure of government to respond has strengthened this fear with companies often reluctant to bear costs which they feel should be the responsibility of government. An industrial nurse explained that, when she had suggested her company should help local clinics respond to HIV / AIDS, she had been told by her manager that 'we can't move in and do government's work'. This was despite the fact that, as she pointed out, 'in the past Deco's social workers went out [into the community] to help our own [i.e., white] people'. She went on to explain that she thought the company's head office was spending money 'on the wrong things'.

Helping communities

Unlike company management, employees do not control discretionary funds. Despite this restriction, those employees responding to HIV / AIDS were able to locate and allocate a range of resources to communities. A number were giving time to community-based HIV / AIDS projects quite independently of their work for the company. Thus, one white nurse had given talks on HIV / AIDS to her sons' Scout group, while a black nurse outlined the range of advice and support groups operating out of her Soweto church. The time spent on such activities shaded into company time on occasion. A catering manager in one of Healthco's hospitals explained that, having now settled into the job, he was in a position to delegate tasks and make time to fundraise for a feeding scheme that he would run under the banner of the hospital's HIV / AIDS committee.

The use of company time – despite often busy schedules – was also required to mobilise other resources. The most high-profile of these were collections from company employees. In Healthco hospitals, collection bins were placed on wards by members of the HIV/AIDS committee for staff to donate gifts that would be taken to the community projects, if necessary using a hospital driver. In one of Deco's divisions, the HIV/AIDS committee circulated a list of articles for employees to donate to an AIDS orphanage, with secretaries acting as collectors.

Such initiatives were publicly supported by management, but volunteers had to negotiate with their immediate supervisors for the time required to run such efforts. An admissions clerk in a Healthco hospital explained that finding time to be involved in the HIV/AIDS committee was difficult: 'I'm very busy. My boss knows [that I take time off to be involved], but she's understanding. It depends on your head of department'. Other unit managers were identified as preventing staff from attending meetings of the HIV/AIDS committee, thus limiting their ability to participate in its activities.[6]

Another source of resources was the company itself. On occasion this took the form of direct requests from management. At Deco, the HIV/AIDS committee got management permission to include a number of community-based HIV/AIDS counsellors in their training sessions at company expense. More commonly, it involved utilising resources that would otherwise go to waste. Hospitals can provide a wide range of products needed by community-based HIV/AIDS organisations, and a number of Healthco hospitals donated their condemned linen to community projects. Other, less obvious, items could also be put to use, ranging from carpet tiles ripped out when Healthco's corporate office was revamped to the collection of cardboard that was sold to recycling companies. This last initiative enabled one hospital HIV/AIDS committee to raise R500 per month for its community projects.

Such items were of only marginal value to Healthco, but the process of redistributing from company to community was not restricted to items that would otherwise be thrown away. One ward manager used the hospital photocopier to produce training manuals for a home-based care group that the HIV/AIDS committee was supporting. In Deco, an industrial nurse explained how she had learned to reallocate funds within her budget, allowing her to purchase drugs for HIV-positive clinic attendees which she otherwise would have been unable to provide. A senior nurse in Healthco told us how she had been able to provide a community hospice with saline drips which they could not otherwise afford. As we spoke she received a call requesting additional supplies. It was a matter, she explained to us, of allowing a young man with AIDS to die in the hospice rather than be transferred to a state hospital some distance from the informal settlement where he lived. The nurse called in a favour and, after the interview ended, went to pick up the saline sachets from the store and drove over to the hospice.

Reaching communities

Any process of redistribution requires not only resources but also a recipient and a distribution mechanism. Official CSI, while having a ready – if not adequate – supply of funds, often faces difficulties in the process of distribution. While a company's CSI unit might be run by individuals who have some contact with organisations needing support, these personal links are likely to be limited. As a result, official CSI projects have to rely on possible beneficiaries contacting them and, if there is to be some justifiable criteria for allocation, presenting a case. In the case of HIV/AIDS, a disease that disproportionately affects the poor, such a system may well present considerable barriers – something to which the company's own requirement of a return on its social investment adds. One result of these barriers and conditions is a tendency for companies to focus on a small number of already well-organised and relatively well-resourced HIV/AIDS projects while many other smaller, less well-organised projects are unable to access resources.

CSR from below struggles in terms of locating resources, often requiring the expenditure of considerable volunteer or company time, but in terms of distribution there are fewer barriers and constraints in redistributing resources. There is, of course, no need to consider any return for the company, though there may well be one, and they have multiple channels available to them through membership of HIV/AIDS committees and on occasion former employees who have remained in contact with committee members. Frequently, members of HIV/AIDS committees knew of projects requiring support through their churches. This provides a very direct route to grassroots activity that more formal structures find difficult to locate. A nursing sister running one of Healthco's hospital HIV/AIDS committees explained, in relation to possible community projects, that 'we can only go so far; there's a danger that we'll be swamped [by the number of possible projects to support]. We have to say we can't do them all'.

Of course, the relative efficiency and effectiveness of HIV/AIDS projects in the community can be questioned. However, what are really at stake are different forms of evaluation and screening. Well-run official CSI uses a formalised set of criteria to evaluate applicants, while badly-run official CSI simply hands over a cheque to the organisation that pulls hardest on the heartstrings or has the best contact with the CSI office. CSR from below uses the local knowledge of its members to assess the value of potential projects. Where employees or former employees are active in community-based HIV/AIDS work, there are additional – informal – checks, largely unavailable to official CSI, concerning the efficiency, effectiveness and governance of a project.

Such direct dealings with community projects put CSR from below initiatives in something of a grey zone, with their activities independent of the company's own official CSI structures. In some cases, attempts to work with official structures had been attempted, but then abandoned in frustration. At Deco, the training of community peer educators by the company had initially been seen as something that could be pursued through the Community Development Officer but after four postponed meetings they bypassed him and coordinated directly with the local clinics. There was a perception among some HIV/AIDS committee members that official CSI was a window dressing operation where sidelined employees ended up and where, since the company had little understanding of the community, words substituted for action. At a meeting of Deco's Corporate AIDS Forum, a representative of the CSI unit explained that they no longer called their activity 'outreach programmes' but rather 'partnership programmes with the community and other stakeholders'. By contrast, while CSR from below did not have a well-developed vocabulary to describe what happened, there was a clear sense of mission.

Official corporate social investment and corporate social responsibility from below: Conflictual or complementary?

An important question is whether a sense of mission, and the resulting action, that formed CSR from below is complementary to or in conflict with official CSI. At Healthco, senior management had conceptualised hospital-run community activity around HIV/AIDS as something that would generate good publicity for the company – effectively a marriage between official CSI and CSR from below. Yet, in a number of cases it had clearly run ahead of what management thought was ideal. At the same time, a corporate request for hospital HIV/AIDS committees to put forward names for an annual award for community HIV/AIDS work, which would be presented at a high-profile, publicity-gaining gala event, had had a disappointing response.

This failure to synergise employee activity around HIV/AIDS in the community and the company's inability to project an appropriate image ended on occasion in conflict. One of Healthco's hospitals sources many of its patients from the Teso community that, collectively, holds rights to land and mineral deposits. Not surprisingly, when approached by representatives of this community, hospital management tried to respond. One approach, based on the whim of a senior figure within the Teso community, was for the hospital to buy a minibus and convert it into a mobile education unit that would tour communities to provide basic health education. This would include the importance of personal hygiene, such as washing hands with clean water before preparing food. The proposal had been quickly approved by Healthco's head office and the brand-new, still-unused, minibus education-mobile was in the hospital car park when we conducted interviews. The hospital manager was clearly undecided if this constituted something to be proud of or if he had participated in commissioning a white elephant.

Completely separately, the hospital's HIV/AIDS committee had become deeply involved in a nearby squatter camp, primarily through supporting a Catholic nursing sister who ran a clinic in the settlement. The entire committee had walked through the camp and witnessed how, among other aspects of poverty, 'people had to survive without water . . . they have to buy water at R1 a litre. It's not clear where it comes from [i.e., whether it's safe or not]'. They had approached hospital management and reached agreement to fund water tanks that could help alleviate the situation. The problem was that the squatters were on land owned by the Teso community, who refused permission for the water tanks to be installed on the grounds that this would help make the squatter camp permanent. Hospital management were not willing to take the matter further. From then on, management and the HIV/AIDS committee worked separately with their respective community initiatives.

In other instances, the separation of official CSI and CSR from below was less dramatic, though nevertheless as complete. In Deco, divisional

HIV/AIDS committees had supported the company's sponsorship of a high-profile AIDS orphanage. In 2001, the CSI unit had handed over a large cheque to fund equipment for the kitchen which was to be named the Deco Kitchen. A number of the Corporate HIV/AIDS Forum members then organised collections of clothes, toys, blankets, soap and towels within their own workplaces, which they delivered to the orphanage, more than 70 kilometres from the nearest Deco site. Initially, progress at the orphanage was closely followed by members of the Corporate Forum but this interest fell away, as other, closer, priorities became apparent. In late 2003, the chairperson of one Deco HIV/AIDS committee explained that she was making the last trip to the orphanage as they were shifting their attention to local projects. The orphanage, she explained, was now funded by other organisations, but there were estimated to be between 500 and 600 AIDS orphans in surrounding communities who were receiving little if any assistance.

In the much smaller Manco, the senior manager responsible for both the company's CSI and its HIV/AIDS response recognised the different outcomes his limited budget needed to achieve. On the one hand, he had to support projects that would provide publicity for the company and which his managing director expected. On the other hand, he recognised that 'ideally it should be [used] where the guys [workers] live'. In attempting to accommodate this, he split his CSI budget between a head office fund that would focus on publicity-attracting donations and a portion of funds that would be spent on suggestions solicited from workers via the HIV/AIDS committee. In practice, however, this proved difficult and the matter came to a head at an early meeting of Manco's HIV/AIDS committee, which included the senior manager.

As part of an awareness week, the company had bought twenty blankets that the committee was to take to an AIDS orphanage on the other side of Johannesburg. The action was intended to provide publicity for the company newsletter and act as a team-building event for the committee. While the visit went ahead, there were differences of opinion as to whether this was the right thing to do. The senior manager justified it on the grounds that the company had a relationship with the orphanage, having already donated materials for its construction. This particular argument was privately undermined by another manager who disagreed with the donations to the AIDS orphanage on the grounds that it was not going to benefit the company in any way – people didn't go out and buy Manco's products just because they saw CSI publicity, he said. Rather, he felt CSI should be more specifically focused on projects that could directly benefit the company. His suggestion in this regard was to offer short training courses to friends and relatives of existing employees. Those who did well in the course would provide a pool of already-assessed applicants when the company needed to recruit. Meanwhile, a peer educator on the committee felt that the blankets would be put to better use in the townships and informal settlements around the company, rather than travelling 30 kilometres to give them to an already well-supported institution.

The senior manager smoothed things over, saying that they could fund other, more local, projects in due course. What lay behind the argument, however, was frustration with the way that official CSI was being practised, which the formation of the HIV/AIDS committee had brought into the range of public criticism. As one member of the committee vented, '[HIV/AIDS] is not just about T-shirts and banners. We need to go out there and do it! [But] for the company it's about looking at what they can afford at the end of the month, writing a cheque, and then the issue goes away.'

HIV/AIDS, the company and the community
Issues of company and community
What emerges from these different perspectives about what companies should be doing regarding HIV/AIDS in the community is not so much about alternative tactics – though these were different – but about fundamentally different views of the relationship between the company and the community. This difference can be crystallised around two issues over which there were divergent understandings.

The first issue is the degree to which the company and the community can be understood as separate entities. Official CSI activity, operating within a managerially determined framework, sees a clear and legitimate separation between company and community. On this basis, the company chooses to act as a good corporate citizen by voluntarily supporting community-based projects. The nature of this relationship does not bind. It is based on a non-committal generosity on the one side and gratitude on the other. By contrast, CSR from below challenges the validity of this separation between company and community. The community is not just out there. In fact, the company itself is a community of those who work within it. A nurse in one of Healthco's hospitals explained how the company saw 'HIV/AIDS as something out there in the community . . . but there is a community here [in the hospital]'.

What HIV/AIDS has revealed to many of those responding to the epidemic at work is that this community of those who work alongside each other is fractured. There are employees who do not have access to medical aid, and there are subcontracted workers who are as much a part of the life of the workplace as anybody but who are employees of other entities who provide different, lower conditions of employment. There are first-, second- and third-class members of the workplace community. Moreover, from the perspective of CSR from below, this community of work is not an entity with defined boundaries. Each person within the community of the workplace is part of other communities, and what happens in these different communities cannot be isolated. Problems at home – divorce, alcoholism or HIV/AIDS – come into the workplace, and what the workplace provides for employees determines the resources on which families and communities survive or flourish – or flounder.

This leads into the second conceptual difference between official CSI and CSR from below. Official CSI implies that the problems are not in the company, but out there in the community. This is fundamental to the very concept of official CSI: that it is others that need help. By contrast, CSR from below does not see this division of need. Rather, the problems that are out there, are also in here. This assessment emanates from the realisation that the workplace community is fractured, with some more exposed to the effects of HIV/AIDS than others and because the impact of HIV/AIDS flows across the different but connected communities that people constitute.

This understanding of problems was frequently based on direct contact and experience. At Manco, a member of the HIV/AIDS committee talked about a machine operator at the company. 'You have to see the bigger picture. David has a wife and four children. You can't just concentrate on him. He earns R500 a week. If he can't work [because he's ill] his children still have to eat.' She went on to explain that she would like to see the company put a collecting box in the reception area for donations of cans of food and clothing that could be used to support employees in difficulty. Her empathy for people struggling to make ends meet was, in part, informed by her own situation. As a staff member she was on the company's medical aid scheme, something that the majority of employees could not afford. However, the benefits provided by the scheme were not enough for her and her two children. By September each year her cover was exhausted and she had to pay the full cost of any prescription, something that could be difficult.

Two conceptions of company and community

We can see two different conceptions revealed through the lens of HIV / AIDS and the question of how companies and communities were and should be connected. Volunteer members of HIV / AIDS committees see an organically-structured society in which communities interlock as a result of overlapping memberships and within which problems are shared. This is rooted in their experience, but it is also a normative view of how they think the world should be. An administrative worker at a Healthco hospital outlined what she would like to see done at the company in the context of HIV / AIDS: 'I'd like to see us as a community. That's what makes a hospital. I'd like to see management stand up for staff and for staff to reach out to the [external] community. It'd be a chain reaction.' By contrast managers, while formally supportive of the actions of their HIV / AIDS committees, maintained a different view. In this, the role of the company was functionally defined by its operations and profitability. It was separate from the community, whether internal or external. This separation meant that the company did not share problems, but should rather position itself so that it could at least contribute to solving the problems of others.

These two perspectives of the relationship between company and community in the era of AIDS should not, of course, be regarded as absolute definers of the different positions of managers and volunteer members of HIV / AIDS committees. Rather, they represent Weberian ideal types (Gerth and Mills 1985). In practice, these two conceptions did not operate in complete isolation or without some compromise. The need to work together on workplace programmes meant that these two conceptions were inevitably brought into contact. As we have seen, at Manco the senior manager conceded the principle of who should benefit from company donations. In a number of Healthco hospitals it was clear that management was turning a blind eye when members of the HIV / AIDS committee manoeuvred the system to access treatment for subcontract workers without medical aid. In one of Deco's divisions there was an open discussion between managers and HIV/AIDS committee members as to the ideal balance between capitalism and caring in the company. Both sides in this discussion made compromises, acknowledging the importance of business objectives on the one side, and the importance of dealing holistically with people on the other. This discussion drew on concrete examples, with sub-units of the division used to illustrate disequilibrium between the objectives of responding to HIV/AIDS in the interest of the business and for the benefit of people. In terms of the community, the senior manager present conceded that the company would not be judged by whether nearby Decoville was the tidiest town in the province because of the number of flowers on the sidewalks, but by 'how we deal with this monster in our midst'. Agreement was cemented in terms of having to sell the division's HIV/AIDS response to higher managerial structures.

This reaching of agreement, implicit or explicit, between the two approaches to the relationship between company and community mediates the two positions, but also confirms their distinct perspectives. The need to reach agreement and strike compromises illustrates the difference in approach. It also demonstrates that CSR from below constitutes a social force operating within companies independently of management and official CSI.

Corporate social responsibility from below: Subversive, socially cohesive and politically charged

Stripped of their particular contexts, these different approaches to society – an interwoven community for which all are responsible versus an unencumbered arena for opportunity – are not new. What appears to have happened is that the magnitude of the AIDS epidemic and the relative failure of the most powerful agents in society – state, business and unions – to act has seen independent mobilisation of employees in response to the epidemic. One element of this has been their approach to the community, an approach that differs in conception and action from that of the managers to whom they report.

What are the implications of this? If nothing else, CSR from below is likely to pressurise managers and official CSI units to think more carefully about how they give, and to whom. There may also be the opportunity for institutional-level partnerships within companies that combine the available resources of official CSI to the informational and distributional advantages of CSR from below. Such partnerships are not without precedent – a number of South African companies encourage employees to identify good causes for corporate support. However, what seems to be little appreciated is that the assumption that employees and employers are aligned over the relationship between the company and community cannot be taken for granted. In contrast to the comfortable view of employers and employees uniting to help those less fortunate, the very existence of CSR from below exposes the extent to which the corporate response to HIV/AIDS has been found wanting by their own employees. The gap is further illustrated by the grey zone within which CSR from below generally operates. Despite a strong claim to the moral high ground, it frequently works in spaces created by employees rather than managerially-sanctioned terrain. It is fundamentally subversive to company decision making, frequently in approach and sometimes in action. At its extreme it assumes a Robin Hood type of form in taking from rich corporations to give to poor communities. Yet, this subversion of corporate norms and property is also socially cohesive. It helps to hold together the strained and threadbare fabric of South African society as the gale-force winds of the AIDS epidemic rip across the landscape.

But the recipients of help are not the only subjects in this process. Participation in CSR from below exposes employees to the poverty within society – something that the segmented nature of South African life allows them otherwise to avoid. The discovery that poverty flows strongly in their workplace and seeps into their own lives raises difficult questions. The idea of companies collecting tins of food at receptions so that the children of employees can eat poses fundamental questions about the distribution of income and whether official CSI justifies rather than challenges this inequality.

Notes

1. In this volume we have preferred the more explicit term corporate social and environmental responsibility (CSER) and used it interchangeably with the concept of corporate social responsibility (CSR). In this chapter the author develops the concept 'CSR from below'. In this case we have chosen not to change this to 'CSER from below'.

2. The voluntary nature of CSI as envisaged in this second narrative should not be underestimated. Ideologies of business put a premium on managerial freedom. Without this, a key justification for the private sector – its much-vaunted ability to make decisions and act on them – falls away.

3. See Meintjes, Giese and Chamberlain (2004) for a discussion of the complexities and over-use of the term AIDS orphan.

4. This refers to the combination of physical workplace layout, occupational hierarchies, social and racial backgrounds, and operational functions that create strongly segmented spaces within often relatively small physical locations.

5. Most, but not all, Deco employees had medical aid which allowed them to access anti-retroviral drugs if HIV-positive. Approximately a year after my first set of interviews at Deco, the company introduced an anti-retroviral drug scheme for employees without medical aid. The difficulty of dealing with HIV-positive, uninsured workers – with the government roll-out of anti-retroviral drugs still a long way from the company's industrial sites – appeared in the form of subcontracted workers who frequently found their way into company clinics.

6. Holding meetings outside work hours is difficult in any organisation where shift systems operate and, as in the case of hospitals, services are provided every day of the year. Realistically, a quorum requires the use of work time. During one interview, it struck the interviewee that the HIV/AIDS committee meeting needed to be placed within the monthly meeting morning in which a series of meetings – on infection control and health and safety, for example – were held one after the other, maximising attendance and minimising disruption. Of course, achieving this required the HIV/AIDS committee to be given official status by hospital management, something it did not have.

References

Barnett, T. and A. Whiteside. 2002. *AIDS in the Twenty-first Century: Disease and Globalization*. Basingstoke: Palgrave Macmillan.

Bezuidenhout, A. et al. 2003. 'A Political Economy of Corporate Social and Environmental Responsibility in South Africa'. Paper presented at the Corporate Social and Environmental Responsibility in South Africa Symposium, Johannesburg, 22 May.

Brink, B. 2003. 'Response to HIV/AIDS in South Africa: A Business Perspective'. *Labour Markets and Social Frontiers* 4 (October).

Brink, B. and L. Clausen. 1987. 'The Acquired Immune Deficiency Syndrome'. *Journal of the Mine Medical Officers Association of South Africa* 63: 433.

Clarke, E. and K. Strachan. (eds.). 2000. *Everybody's Business: The Enlightening Truth about HIV/AIDS*. Cape Town: Metropolitan.

Cohen, D. 1999. *Poverty and HIV/AIDS in Sub-Saharan Africa*. New York: United Nations Development Program (UNDP HIV and Development Programme Issue Paper, 27).

Dickinson, D. 2003. 'Managing HIV/AIDS in the South African Workplace: Just Another Duty?' *South African Journal of Economic and Management Sciences* 6 (1): 25–49.

———. 2004a. 'Corporate South Africa's Response to HIV/AIDS: Why So Slow?' *Journal of Southern African Studies* 30 (3): 627–50.

———. 2004b. 'Narratives of Life and Death: Voluntary Counselling and Testing Programmes in the Workplace'. Paper presented to the Life and Death in a Time of AIDS: The Southern African Experience Symposium. WISER/CRESP, University of the Witwatersrand, Johannesburg, 14–16 October.

———. 2005a. 'AIDS, Order and "Best Practice" in South African Companies: Managers, Peer Educators, Traditional Healers and Folk Theories'. *African Journal of AIDS Research* 4 (1): 11–20.

———. 2005b. 'Neither Management nor Union, but for the Love of People: HIV/AIDS Workplace Peer Educators in South Africa'. Paper presented to the *British Journal of Industrial Relations* Symposium on New Industrial Relations Actors, London School of Economics, 22–23 September.

Dickinson, D. and M. Stevens. 2005. 'Understanding the Response of Large South African Companies to HIV/AIDS'. *Journal of Social Aspects of HIV/AIDS* 2 (2): 286–95.

Fakier, A. 2004. 'Perceptions of Stakeholders on the Relevance of the Global Reporting Initiative on HIV/AIDS'. Paper presented to the HIV/AIDS in the Workplace Research Symposium, University of the Witwatersrand, 29–30 June.

Gerth, H. and C.W. Mills. 1985. *From Max Weber: Essays in Sociology*. London: Routledge & Kegan Paul.

Global Business Council on HIV/AIDS. 2001. 'Employees & HIV/AIDS: Action for Business Leaders'. Available at www.businessfightsaids.org. Accessed 10 October 2002.

International Labour Organisation (ILO). 2001. *An ILO Code of Practice on HIV/AIDS and the World of Work*. Geneva: ILO.

Johnson, L and D. Budlender. 2002. *HIV Risk Factors: A Review of the Demographic, Socio-economic, Biomedical and Behavioural Determinants of HIV Prevalence in South Africa*. Cape Town: Centre for Actuarial Research, University of Cape Town.

Marks, S. 2002. 'An Epidemic Waiting to Happen? The Spread of HIV/AIDS in South Africa in Social and Historical Perspective'. *African Studies* 61 (1): 13–26.

Meintjes, H., S. Giese and R. Chamberlain. 2004. '"We Are All Orphans Here:" Considering the Concept of "Orphanhood" in South Africa'. Paper presented to the Life and Death in a Time of AIDS: The Southern African Experience Symposium. WISER/CRESP, University of the Witwatersrand, Johannesburg, 14–16 October.

Nattrass, N. 2004. *The Moral Economy of AIDS in South Africa*. Cambridge: CUP.

Phillips, H. 2004. 'HIV/AIDS in the Context of South Africa's Epidemic History'. In *AIDS and South Africa: The Social Expression of a Pandemic*, edited by K. Kauffman and L. Lindauer. Basingstoke: Palgrave Macmillan.

Randall, C. 2002. 'Impacts and Response of Industries, Workplaces and Sectors of the South African Economy'. In *HIV/AIDS, Economics and Governance in South Africa: Key Issues in Understanding Response*, edited by the Joint Center for Political and Economic Studies. Washington: Cadre/USAID/Joint Center for Political and Economic Studies.

Rosen, S. et al. 2000. 'Care and Treatment to Extend the Working Lives of HIV-positive Employees: Calculating the Benefits to Business'. *South African Journal of Science* 96 (6): 300–34.

South Africa, Department of Health. 2003. *Cabinet's Decision on the Operational Plan for Comprehensive Care and Treatment of People living with HIV and AIDS*. Press Release, 19 November. Available at www.doh.gov.za.

———. 2005. *Report: National HIV and Syphilis Antenatal Sero-prevalence Survey in South Africa 2004*. Pretoria: Department of Health.

Trialogue. 2004. *The CSI Handbook*. Cape Town: Trialogue, 6th ed.

Truth and Reconciliation Commission. 1998. 'Institutional Hearing: Business and Labour'. In *Truth and Reconciliation Commission of South Africa Report: Volume Four*. Cape Town: CTP Books.

UNAIDS. 2000. *The Business Response to HIV/AIDS: Impact and Lessons Learned*. Geneva and London: UNAIDS, The Global Business Council on HIV/AIDS and The Prince of Wales Business Leaders Forum.

———. 2003a. 'UNAIDS Fact Sheet: Sub-Saharan Africa'. Available at www.unaids.org.

———. 2003b. UNAIDS Questions and Answers: Basic Facts about the HIV/AIDS Epidemic and Its Impact. Available at www.unaids.org.

Whiteside, A. and C. Sunter. 2000. *AIDS: The Challenge for South Africa*. Cape Town: Human & Rousseau, Tafelberg.

8

Afterword
Getting below the bottom line

Edward Webster

Social pressures on the triple-bottom-line

Under the impact of global corporate restructuring it is becoming increasingly necessary for investment analysts, when assessing the prospects of a company, to go below the financial bottom line and examine the social and environmental policies and practices of the enterprise. This is now frequently referred to as the triple-bottom-line, a concept that received great attention in the period around the World Summit on Sustainable Development (WSSD) in 2002. Such an assessment provides insight into the quality of management and any hidden costs the company may face. This book is the first research-based attempt in the developing world to provide the analyst with both the concepts and the evidence to make such an assessment. Its findings suggest that much of the discourse on corporate social and environmental responsibility (CSER) is designed as a public relations exercise, rather than a concern for the needs of company stakeholders. The authors demonstrate the need for a more rigorous approach to CSER, one that recognises the contradictory forces that face management. These include the need to become more competitive in the context of increased global trade; and adhere to global labour, social and environmental standards while responding to local pressures from the state and society to address the legacies of the past.

At the core of such an approach is the notion that in recent years a global norm of labour standards has emerged. This is being promoted actively by the International Labour Organisation (ILO), by non-governmental organisations (NGOs), and by the international labour movement. Such standards establish rights including freedom of association, collective organisation and bargaining; and protection from forced labour, exploitative forms of child labour, and discrimination in employment and occupation. A number of social forces are shaping the idea of a global norm of labour standards. These include multinational bargaining, codes of conduct, and ethical trading and consumption.

Multinational bargaining

More and more multinational companies are being exposed to bargaining pressures from a more internationally coordinated labour movement. In September 2002 the International Federation of Chemical, Energy, Mine and General Workers' Unions (ICEM) signed an agreement with AngloGold, in which the parties affirmed the principles of internationally-accepted human resource and labour relations practices. The ICEM expressed its intention to sign global agreements with as many multinational companies as possible (Scott 2002).

Indeed, the widespread supply chains inherent in global production introduce new vulnerabilities in enterprises, exposing them to international campaigns. Furthermore, the technological revolution brought about by globalisation can be used to activists' advantage – email, web sites, databases and many other computer applications are being widely used around the world to find, store, analyse and transmit information.

Codes of conduct

Codes of conduct are re-emerging as responses to these global pressures. Indeed, they have spawned an entire new industry of consultants and enterprises offering social accountability services to companies. Of course, codes of conduct are not new for business in South Africa – they were first introduced in the 1970s by the international community to put pressure on companies to remove racial discrimination in the workplace, as Bezuidenhout, Fig, Hamann and Omar show in their overview in Chapter 2. However, concern over the negative effects of globalisation has led to renewed interest in, for example, the Organisation for Economic Cooperation and Development (OECD) Guidelines, which were revised in 2000. Among the changes has been a strengthening of the follow-up mechanism and the extension of their application to OECD-based companies operating in non-OECD countries.

Ethical trading and consumption

Branding has become central to the new global economy. Scott Bedbury, Starbucks' vice-president of marketing, openly recognised that 'consumers do not believe there's a huge difference between products', which is why brands must 'establish emotional ties' with their customers through 'the Starbucks Experience'. The people who line up for Starbucks, writes CEO Schultz, are not just there for the coffee; 'they are there to experience the feeling of warmth and community people get in Starbucks stores' (Klein 2000: 20).

The key point to this marketing renaissance is that companies are no longer selling products as commodities, but as concepts – the brand as experience, as a lifestyle. Nike was the first to change the rules of the game when it decided to abandon its role as manufacturer by outsourcing production to subcontractors in the Third World, leaving its headquarters free to focus on the real business at hand – creating a corporate mythology powerful enough to infuse meaning into these raw objects just by signing its name. As Nike's Phil Knight explains:

> For years we thought of ourselves as a production-oriented company, meaning we put all our emphasis on designing and manufacturing the product. But now we understand that the most important thing we do is market the product. We have come around to saying that Nike is a market-oriented company, and the product is our most important marketing tool (Klein 2000: 22).

However, the flip side of the power of a brand is its growing vulnerability. Because it is so valuable to a company, a brand must be sustained and protected. Indeed, protesters, including anti-globalisation supporters, can use the power of the brand against companies by collecting, for instance, evidence of ill-treated workers or polluted rivers. And thanks to globalisation, with email and satellite television such as CNN, it is possible to communicate instantly across the globe. In this way a small group of activists can, in short order, have a world-wide impact. Indeed, this is what happened at Seattle in November 2000.

In recent years consumers in Europe and North America have shown increased concern for the social and environmental conditions under which the goods they buy are produced. Essentially, ethical consumption aims to ensure that conditions within mainstream production chains meet basic minimum standards and to eradicate the most exploitative forms of labour such as child, bonded labour and sweatshops. These demands have led to campaigns, such as the Clean Clothes Campaign, that have occurred on such a significant scale that they can be seen as one of the most significant social movements of the 1990s. Retailers in the garment and sports shoe industries have been particular targets of campaigns. A common reaction by many targeted companies has been to produce a code of conduct.

The discourse of corporate social responsibility

In response to these pressures, a new discourse on the need for greater CSER has emerged. Increasingly, the private sector finds it more difficult to argue that their sole responsibility is the pursuit of profit on behalf of shareholders. They have to respond to a much broader range of stakeholders and, as corporate citizens, they are expected to assume responsibility for their actions. This has led to what could be described as a stakeholder approach to the firm.

Stakeholders go well beyond the traditional players – such as shareholders, employees and customers – and include the new social movements and special interest groups that have emerged over the past 30 years and are concerned with worldwide labour conditions. In short, a stakeholder is any group or individual that can affect, or who is affected by, the achievements of the firm's objectives (see Figure 8.1). In 1992 in Rio de Janeiro and again in 2002 in Johannesburg, the United Nations brought together a broad network of environmental and developmental organisations, unions and other labour-related organisations to discuss sustainable development. This includes issues related to ethical production and consumption. These initiatives are formidable challenges to the traditional notion of the firm's responsibilities.

Increasingly, the business community is recognising that there is a strong interrelationship between good CSER practice and long-term shareholder value. 'This is not an esoteric debate', argues Nicky Newton-King, then general counsel and director of new business of the JSE Securities Exchange (she has since been elevated to Deputy CEO of the JSE). 'Investors are actively seeking out companies with good CSER records, and this is leading to a rise in socially responsible investment (SRI) and SRI funds' (Wilson 2002).

Linked to these initiatives has been the global trend towards what has become known as shareholder activism. As opposed to other interest groups who protest externally, shareholder activists utilise their position within a corporation in order to effect change. One of the emerging topics of debate within, for example, the Shareholder Project in Australia is the concept of ethical investment. In some cases, it is argued, companies should be excluded (negative screening) if they invest in gambling, alcohol, tobacco and uranium mining (Catherine Brown and Associates 2001: 11).

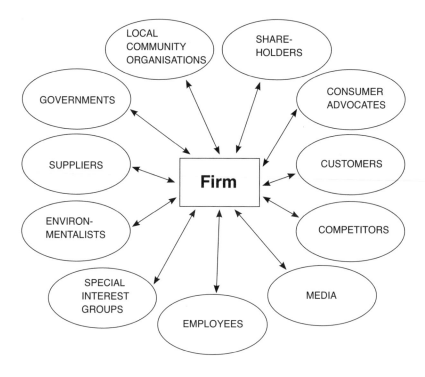

Figure 8.1: Stakeholder view of the firm.

The King Report on Corporate Governance, both in 1994 and 2002, placed South Africa at the cutting edge of debates on corporate governance. The approach adopted in the King Report is as follows: 'for a board to identify the company's stakeholders, including its shareholders, and to agree on policies as to how the relationship with those stakeholders should be advanced and managed in the interests of the company (King Committee 2002: 7).

A recent example is the corporate citizenship report for 2001 produced by Old Mutual, where the company has 'taken the initiative in stakeholder accountability through non-financial measurement and reporting of its social and business activities' (Old Mutual 2001: 3). In the words of the managing director:

There is an argument that businesses should concentrate on making profits and not engage in the social issues of the countries where they operate. Most leading companies, including Old Mutual, believe that this is too narrow a view of their role and that the only truly successful businesses of the future will be those which achieve a sustainable balance between their own interests and those of society. And that commercial success can be maximised by embracing social responsibility, neatly defined as corporate citizenship (Old Mutual 2001:3).

Conclusions

As a research unit striving to conduct high-quality research on the world of work, the Sociology of Work Project is very pleased to have housed this pioneering project. We have now extended our research focus to include comparative work on the Southern African region. In particular, we shall be concerned with examining the extent to which the rhetoric of CSER is being practised in Southern Africa. If we are to understand the real world of work, we have to get below the bottom line.

References

Catherine Brown and Associates. 2001. 'Shareholders' Project: An Examination of the Future of Shareholder/Corporation Relationships in Australia'. Background briefing paper. Melbourne: Catherine Brown and Associates.

King Committee on Corporate Governance. 2002. *King Report on Corporate Governance for South Africa, 2002*. (King II Report). Johannesburg: Institute of Directors.

Klein, N. 2000. *No Logo*. London: Harper Collins.

Old Mutual in South Africa. 2001. *Corporate Citizenship Report*. Cape Town: Old Mutual.

Scott, J. 2002. 'Gold Major Signs Pact with Global Labour Union'. *Mining Weekly* September 27.

Wilson, D. 2002. 'Social Responsibility not an Esoteric Debate'. *Business Report* 3 November.

Index

AA 1000 Standard   46, 187
Accelerated Leadership Development
   Programme (ALDP)   163
AccountAbility (UK)   32, 185
Accountability Institute   32
Ackerman Foundation   190
Ackerman, Raymond   26, 185–186
Advtech   219
AECI (chemical industry)   142, 170
affirmative action   208
affirmative procurement   165–166
AfricaBio   197, 198
African Institute of Corporate Citizenship
   (AICC)   32, 61, 105, 211
African National Congress (ANC)   3, 15,
   23, 208
African renaissance   70
African Union (AU)   70
Agriculture Portfolio Committee   198
agri-sciences   142
AIDS   33, 84
   orphanage   225
   see also HIV / AIDS
AIDS-orphan fostering projects   189
air pollution   30, 174
Air Quality Act   160
AKA Capital   229
Amalgamated Beverage Industries (ABI)
   180
American Growth and Opportunities
   Act   44
Anglo American Corporation   19, 42, 97,
   101, 107, 108, 118
anti-retroviral (ARV) drugs   242
share prices   119
AngloGold   64
Anglo Platinum   128, 131
Anglovaal   97, 141
Angola, war in   15
Annan, Kofi   45

anti-globalisation movements   13
Anti-Privatisation Forum   33, 82
anti-retroviral (ARV) treatment   33, 63,
   64, 76, 162, 241
apartheid   2–5, 141
   mining companies' role   98
   political economy of   14–16
Appletiser   180
Aquarius Platinum company   128
asbestos sufferers   117
audit procedures   147

Bafokeng Tribal Authority   130
beer industry   180, 184
beverage industry   179–180
Bhopal disaster (India)   7, 44, 144, 149
BHP Billiton   103, 107, 108
Bill of Rights   24
biodiversity   29
biotechnology   29, 174
Biowatch South Africa   197
black economic empowerment (BEE)
   4, 6–7, 39, 61, 62–63, 85
   company control BEE   215–216
   corporate social responsibility
      208–213
   criticism of   86
   equity targets   120
   firms and corporate social
      responsibility   222–236
   food industry   182, 184, 187
   mining companies   109, 118
   role of state   115–123
   SASOL's obligations   153
   scorecard   120–123, 131–132, 132,
      135, 209
   South African corporates   213–222
Black Economic Empowerment Act
   210, 215

Black Economic Empowerment
  Commission (BEE Com)
  62, 208, 227
black-owned companies   224
black-owned pension funds   226–231
black unionism   101
BoE Asset Management   229
Botha, P.W.   20
bovine spongiform encephalitis (BSE)
  173–174
BP   51
branding   267–268
Brimstone Investment Corporation   235
British American Tobacco of South Africa
  (BAT-SA)   6, 180, 187, 192,
  195–196
broad-based BEE   208
Broad-based Socio-economic
  Empowerment Charter   120–123
Brundtland Commission   40–41
Bushveld Complex   128
Business Council on Sustainable
  Development (BCSD-SA)
  29–30, 31

Cadbury-Schweppes   180
Caltex Oil SA (now Chevron)   218
Cape Action Plan for the Environment
  28
capital concentration   184
Cartagena Biosafety Protocol   198
Carte Blanche (MNet)   36
casualisation   123
Centre for Development and Enterprise
  (CDE)   32, 56, 222
Centre for Policy Studies   33
certification   47–50
Chamber of Mines   30, 31, 74, 75
charitable trusts   19
Charities Aid Foundation (CAF)   32
Charter on Financial Services   79
Chemical and Allied Industries'
  Association (CAIA)   30, 31, 44,
  74, 150, 151

Chemicals, Energy, Paper, Printing,
  Wood and Allied Workers' Union
  (CEPPWAWU)   34, 77–78,
  150–151, 164
chemicals industry
  health and safety   143
  multinationals   142
  regulation and self-regulation
  143–144, 146–147
  workers   142, 144
childhood development projects   188
child labour   175, 195
Chinese producers, competition from   7
cholera   82
chrome mining   128–133
Circle Labour and Accommodation   127
civil society organisations (CSOs)
  conservation paradigm   27
  influence on firms   74–78
Claus Daun   126
Clean Clothes Campaign   268
Clean Development Mechanism (CDM)
  51, 71, 81
climatic changes   174
coal
  carbon emissions   159
  conversion into petroleum   141,
  151–152
  deposits   151
Coca-Cola   175, 180
  Promise   185
Code of Corporate Practices and Conduct
  187
Code of Good Practice on Key Aspects of
  HIV / AIDS and Employment   64
codes of conduct   53–47, 266
  international   5
  pressure on corporates   69
commercial farmers   175
Commission for Conciliation, Mediation
  and Arbitration (CCMA)   127
Commission of Inquiry into Safety and
  Health in the Mining Industry
  106
commodification of food   173
Commonwealth Business Council

Working Group on Corporate
    Citizenship   187
community
    engagement guidelines   108–109
    helping initiatives   250–252
    involvement in environment   108
    projects   253
    reaching of   252–253
community feeding programme
    (WARMTH)   189
Community Growth Fund   60–61
company-community relations   109
Compensation Commissioner   147
Compensation Fund   178
Competition Tribunal   165
Confederation of the Food and Drink
    Industries of the European
    Community (CIAA)   202
Congress of South African Trade Unions
    (COSATU)   19, 34, 60, 76, 77, 78,
    82, 230, 232, 236
    Kopano Ke Matla   231
    policy statements   233
    September Commission   230
Constitution (1996)   23–24, 28, 41, 107
Consultative Business Movement   30
Consultative National Environmental
    Policy Process (CONNEPP)   31,
    58–59
consumers, role of   78
contract system in mining   124
co-regulatory approaches   144
Coronation Fund Managers   229
corporate accountability   68
Corporate Accountability Week   73
Corporate Accountability Working
    Committee   191
corporate citizenship   104–105
corporate environmental responsibility
    25–30
corporate food sector   174
corporate HIV/AIDS forum   162
corporate policies   114–115
corporate reports   115
corporate social and environmental
    responsibility (CSER)   vi

broad definition   8–9
context   1–2
evaluation of   82–87
food industry   184–191
mining   102–113
sectors and companies   64–66, 67
shifting meanings   43
corporate social investment (CSI)
    8, 37–39
    average contributions   56
    HIV/AIDS   242–245, 245
    philanthropy   55–58
    redress   86–87
    spending of selected companies
        57, 213
    strategies 38
corporate social responsibility (CSR)
    38–39
    criteria of companies   65
    discourse   268–270
    emergence of   16–17
    HIV/AIDS   242–245, 245, 259–260
    mining   101–102
    peer pressure   74
Corpwatch   73
corruption   5, 36
Cotlands   225
Cyanide Code   1, 34

De Beers   50, 64
De Klerk, F.W.   20
Democratic Alliance (DA)   24
Democratic Party (DP)   24
Department of Agriculture   198, 201
Department of Environmental Affairs
    and Tourism (DEAT)   160, 198
Department of Trade and Industry (DTI)
    210
    Codes of Good Practice   210
    Empowerment Strategy   210
depatriation   190–191
desertification   174
destabilisation operations   15
Development Bank of Southern Africa
    230

diamond industry   50, 97
discrimination   2, 8, 208, 211
diversity
   management   187
   promotion of   211
Dow Chemicals   142
Dow Jones Sustainability Index   160,
   186, 191
drought   174
Durban Declaration   51
Durban Roodepoort Deep (DRD)   125,
   214

Earthlife Africa   27, 34
Earthyear   28, 36
East Rand Proprietary Mines (ERPM)
   case study   125–128
EcoLink   33, 189, 200
ecological modernisation   85
eco-modernisation   134
economic liberalisation   7
education   57, 102
Ehrenreich, Tony   76
employment
   chemicals industry   142
   equity   135, 153, 187, 211, 216
   food industry   177–178
   mining   135
Employment Equity Act   215
Endangered Wildlife Trust   27
Energy Africa   219
environmental court   81
environmental, health and safety
   regulation   7
environmental justice movement   144
Environmental Justice Networking
   Forum   27, 33
Environmental Management Co-
   operative Agreements (EMCAs)
   29, 77, 154
Environmental Management Programme
   Report (EMPR)   105–106
Environmental Monitoring Group   75
environmental pressure   34–37, 174
Environmental Protection Agency (EPA)
   see under United States

environmental sustainability   174, 211
Eskom   6, 26–27, 31, 83
Ethical Trade Forum   55
Ethical Trade Initiative (ETI) (UK)   32,
   48, 55
   Base Code   55
ethical trading and consumption   267–
   268
European Union (EU)   41
   White Paper on Chemicals   154

fair trade   54–55
Fair Trade in Tourism programme   54
farm workers, minimum wage of   175
fast-food industry   174
Fifth Quadrant Consultants   230
Financial Mail
   BEE ranking   *219–221*
   empowerment index   214, 218, 221
Financial Services Board   229
Financial Services Charter   229
FirstRand   229
fiscal discipline   23
Fischer Tropsch technology   141, 151
fishing companies   192
food
   preservation   175
   price inflation   173, 200
   pricing   199–200
   safety regulations   193
   security   173, 198–199, 201
Food and Agricultural Organisation
   (FAO)   201
Food and Allied Workers' Union (FAWU)
   34, 198, 199–200
   Ikwezi company   231
Food and Trees for Africa   33
Food Monitoring Committee (FMC)   199
food sector
   commercial benefit   187–188
   empowerment   191–192
   industry dimensions   176–177
   ownership structure   182–183
   productive activities   179–181
   regulation of   192–196

foot-and-mouth disease 173–174
foreign investors 101, 175
foreign wholly-owned subsidiaries 182, 191
Forest Stewardship Council (FSC) 5, 49–50
Freedom Charter 3
free trade agreement 44
Friends of the Earth International 73
FTSE4Good Index 61, 113, 215
FTSE/JSE share index 213–214
FutureGrowth 61

G20+ 70
gangsterism 5
gang subcontracting 124
Gencor 97
genetically engineered (GE) foods 196–199
genetically modified (GM) foods 78, 174
genetically modified organisms (GMOs) 185
Genetically Modified Organisms Act 78, 198
Genfoods-Premier 183
Global Compact *see under* United Nations
Global Environmental Facility (GEF) 26, 81
Global Exchange 54
globalisation 68–69, 232, 267
Global Reporting Initiative (GRI) 46, 52–53, 69
  food industry 187, 191
  guidelines 109
  SA companies *52–53*
  SASOL 154
Global Sullivan Principles 46, 187
Global Sustainability Services 32
Gold Fields 97
gold mining 97
Government of National Unity (GNU) 23
government pressures 79–81
grain milling 183

greenhouse gas emissions 51
Green Scorpions 51, 80–81, 160
Green Trust Awards (Nedbank) 27
greenwash perspective 115
Gross Domestic Product (GDP)
  chemicals industry 142
  food sector 176
  mining sector 97
GroundWork 34, 51, 73, 75, 159, 168
  Corpse Awards 34, 168
Group for Environmental Monitoring (GEM) 27, 75–76
Growth and Development Summit 200
Growth, Employment and Redistribution (GEAR) 3, 23, 25, 29

hazardous chemicals 161
health care
  private system 248
  unequal access to 243
HIV/AIDS 6, 39, 76, 194
  antenatal sero-prevalence surveys 241
  case studies 246–256
  community-focused activity 244
  company and community 256–259
  company-based activity 244
  corporate responses 63–64
  mining companies 46, 109–112, 242
  policies 212, 242
  SASOL strategy 153, 161–163
  housing equity 135
human rights 211
  mining companies 108
  violations 3

Impala platinum company 128
import-substitution industrialisation 15
import(s)
  competitive 173
  tariffs 21
income inequality 243
indentured labour 175
Industrial Development Corporation 125, 197, 230

Industrial Environmental Forum (IEF)
6, 81 *see also* Business Council on
Sustainable Development
industrialisation   15
import-substitution   141
inequality   1, 243
informal sector workers   180
informal settlements   130
Inkatha Freedom Party (IFP)   23
integrated development plans (IDPs)   28
Integrated Food Security Strategy   201
International Convention on Corporate
Accountability   73
International Council of Minerals and
Metals   133
International Federation of Chemical,
Energy, Mine and General
Workers' Unions (ICEM)   144,
266
International Federation for Alternative
Trade   54
International Labour Organisation (ILO)
70, 265–266
International Monetary Fund (IMF)   13
international organisations   69–71
International Research Network on
Business, Development
and Society   9
International Standards Organisation 146
international treaties   69–71
International Union for the Conservation
of Nature and Natural Resources
(IUCN)   *see* World Conservation
Union investor(s)
confidence   107
role of   78
ISCOR   83
ISO 14000   5, 47, 69, 146, 155, 187, 191
South African plants   47

Johannesburg Child Welfare Society   225
Johannesburg Consolidated Investments
97
Johannesburg Plan of Implementation
71–72, 73

Johannesburg Securities Exchange (JSE)
61, 62, 66, 113, 182
Social Responsibility Investment
Index (SRII)   61, 210–211, 212,
218
Joint Education Trust (JET)   21–22, 30, 40
Jubilee South Africa   33
Jubilee 2000   86
Just Exchange organisation   54

Kagiso Asset Management   229
Kagiso Trust Investments   229
Khulumani   86
Khumo Bathong Holdings   125, 126
Kimberley process   5, 50
King Committee   69
King Report on Corporate Governance
for South Africa (King 2)   5, 46,
69, 269
and BEE   211, 229
chemistry industry   153, 154
food industry   183, 186
mining industry   112
Koeberg Alert   27
KPMG   32, 53
Kumba Resources   64
Kyoto Protocol   51, 70

labour
brokers   126–128, 177
contractors   128
core standards   212
flexibilisation   7, 23
inequitable ownership   173
inspectorate   143
international movement   266
legislation   22–25
standards   265–266
tenancy   175
Labour Research Service   60–61
land
ownership   175
use   15
Land Bank   197
Landless People's Movement   33

Legal Resources Centre   34
legislation
   chemicals industry   143–144
   food safety   193
   labour   22–25
Leon Commission   147
Lesotho   44
liberal school of thought   16
Liberty Life Foundation   21, 54
Liquid Fuels Charter   164
Liquor Act   192
listed firms   183
local economic development (LED)
   projects   28
London Stock Exchange   101, 190, 191
Lonmin platinum company   128

MacArthur Foundation   viii
macroeconomic policy   9
   RDP to GEAR   22–25
Macroeconomic Research Group (MERG)
   20
Mail & Guardian   28, 36
maize, staple food crop   174
Makana Investments   225
Makhatini cotton experiment   197
malpractice   5
management practice standards (MPSs)
   150
Mandela, Nelson   20
Manto Tshabalala-Msimang Healthcare
   Bursary Trust   225
market
   conditions and incentives   81–82
   liberalisation of   192
market-based incentives   *113*
Mbeki, Thabo   29, 31, 70, 208–209
   International Investment
      Council   189
   International Marketing
      Council   189
   State of the Nation address   209
media, role of   36
medical aid   248
mercury exposure   147
Middelbult Colliery   147

migrant labour   15–16, 95, 96, 99, 130,
   175, 243
Mine Health and Safety Act   106
Mineral and Petroleum Resources
   Development Act   118
Minerals Act   105
Mineworkers' Investment Company
   (MIC)   231, 234
Mining Charter   79, 209
mining companies
   concept of CSER and CSI   102–104
   corporate citizenship   104–113
   historical context   97–101
   implementation gap   114–115
   legislation   116, *116*
   litigation against   99–100, 117
   social problems   133–134
   subcontracting   123–133
Mondi   6, 50
Monsanto Pledge   199
Monsanto South Africa   196, 198
Mozambique   152, 168
   Beira Industrial and Commercial
      School   168
   natural gas   159
MTN   218
multinational bargaining   266
multinational corporations (MNCs)   13,
   65
multi-stakeholder agreements   60, 144
Mvelaphanda Holdings   224–225
Mvelaphanda Sports Investments   225

National Business Initiative (NBI)
   30–31, 38, 74, 81, 84
   Big Business Working Group   31
   Business Trust   31
   Sustainable Futures Unit   31
National Committee on Climate Change
   70
National Council of Trade Unions
   (NACTU)   19
   Investment Holdings   231
National Economic Development and
   Labour Council (NEDLAC)   22,
   34, 64, 77, 79

national democratic revolution (NDR)
    223
National Environment Action Campaign
    27
National Environmental Management
    Act (NEMA)   7–8, 28–29, 50, 79,
    143, 144
National Federation of Chambers of
    Commerce (NAFCOC)   62–63
National Labour and Economic
    Development Institute (NALEDI)
    78
National Occupational Safety Association
    (NOSA)   146, 147
National Party (NP)   23
National Skills Fund   217
National Strategy for Sustainable
    Development   42
National Union of Metalworkers of South
    Africa (NUMSA)   234–235
    Investment Company   231
    Investment Trust   235
National Union of Mineworkers (NUM)
    34, 101, 126
    Mineworkers' Development Agency
    34
National Waste Management
    Strategy   50
National Water Act   79
nature conservation   16, 25
Nelson Mandela Scholarship project
    189
neo-Keynesian approach   20
neo-liberal economic policies   13, 29,
    144, 232–233
Nestlé   180, 189
New African Investments Limited   225
New National Party (NNP)   24
New Partnership for Africa's
    Development (NEPAD)   70, 212
New York Stock Exchange   152, 153
non-governmental organisations (NGOs)
    vi, 24, 266
    conservation   27
    environment   26, 33

Noseweek   36
nuclear industry   27
    laws   29
Nutrition Society of South Africa   194

occupational disease   161
Occupational Health and Safety Act
    (OHSA)   143
    OHSAS 18000   187
occupational health and safety training
    147
occupational injury claims   178
Old Mutual   218, 270
Oppenheimer, Ernest   101
Oppenheimer, Harry   19, 81, 101
oppositional environmentalism   27
oppression, class-based   2
organic farming methods   185
Organisation for Economic Co-operation
    and Development (OECD)   vi,
    266
Organisation of African Unity (OAU)
    70, 71
outsourcing of services   142–143, 177

Parmalat dairy enterprise   188
partnerships   39–40, 191–192
    multi-stakeholders   58–60
    public-private   84
patenting of life forms   174
patriotism   223–224
Peace Parks Foundation   26
peer educators   249
pension fund
    industry   227–228
    investments   61–62
    scandals   229
Pension Funds Act   226, 227
Pepsico   180
performance
    questionnaires   150
    targets   143–144
Petronas (Malaysian oil company)   164
philanthrophy   5
    add-on strategy   39

corporate social investment   55–58
   mining companies   133
Pick 'n Pay   192
   community initiatives   190
   philosophy   185–186
Pioneer Foods   183, 187, 201
Plastic Bag Agreement   145–146
platinum mining   97, 128–133
   map of areas   *129*
political economy
   apartheid   14–16
   approach   96–97
   deracialisation of   208
poultry food tests   193
poverty   4–5, 9
   alleviation   84
   eradication   42
   and HIV/AIDS   241, 243
Power Station Project   54
Practice in Place (PIP) standards   155
price inflation   217
privately-owned BEE companies
      224–226
privatisation   19, 23, 40, 82
Proctor & Gamble (P&G)   186
   Principles, Values and Statement of
      Purpose   186
procurement   217–219, 221–222
   preferential   210
publicly-owned companies   65
public reporting   52–54

quantitative indicators of performance
   (QIP)   150

race/class debate   16, 98
racial inequality   223
Ramaphosa, Cyril   208–209, 229
   Millennium Consolidated
      Investments   229
Rand Mine   97
Reckitt & Colman   175
Reconstruction and Development
      Programme (RDP)   3, 20, 23,
      208, 227

Recordable Case Rate (RCR)   155
Rembrandt   19
reportable injuries   154–155
reputation assurance   107
respiratory diseases   16
responsibility
   before-profit and after-profit   38–39
   understanding of term   9
Responsible Care Codes of Practice   155
Responsible Care Product Stewardship
      code   155
Responsible Care programme   5, 30, 31,
      44, 69, 146, 147
   chemicals industry   149–151, 169
   SASOL   154
retail activities   181
retirement funds   230–231
revisionist approach   16
Rio+10 Summit (WSSD)   36
Rio Tinto   118
   share prices   *119*
risk management   107
Rothmans International   180–181
Rupert, Anton   19, 26, 181

SA 8000   48, 187
SAB Limited   180
SABMiller   180, 184, 185, 191
SAB plc   190, 192
Safcol   50
safety audits   169
safety, health and environment (SHE)
      77–78, 105, 107
   chemicals industry   153–154
   Corporate Governance Committee
      154
   mining companies   131
Samancor chrome mine   128
sanctions against apartheid   15, 141
SAPPI   6, 27, 50
Sasfin Frankel Pollak Securities   61
SASOL   50, 51, 83, 141, 142, 147
   Air Quality Monitoring Committee
      168
   case study   151–155, 159–163

CSER contributions   166, *166–167*,
       168–169
CSER spending   *167*
   designated groups   *163*
   Employment Equity Plan   163
   environmental record   153
   HIV/AIDS Response Programme
       (SHARP)   162–163
Save St Lucia   27
Sector Education and Training
       Authorities (SETAs)   217
Secunda
   plant explosion   159
   Voice of the Voiceless   168
Sekunjalo   225
Sentrachem   142
sexually transmitted diseases (STDs)   64
Sexwale, Tokyo   224–225
sharecropping   175
shareholder(s)
   activism   183, 269
   long-term value   268
   role of   78
   view of firm   *269*
Shell Southern Africa   51, 218
single-sex housing compounds   130
skills and training   217
Skills Development Act   215, 217
slavery, legacies of   175
small, medium and micro enterprises
       (SMMEs)   143, 190, 210
social certification schemes   48–50
social investment   187
socially responsible investment (SRI)
       60–62, 112–113
Socially Responsible Investment Index
       (SRII)   182–183, 191, 211
Social Movements Indaba   33
social philanthropy   83
social pressure   34–37
Social Responsibility Index   *see under*
       Johannesburg Securities
       Exchange
socio-economic status and HIV   249
soil degradation   174

South Africa Foundation   23, 84, 222
South African Breweries   *see* SABMiller
South African Broadcasting Corporation
       (SABC)   201
South African Business Coalition on
       HIV/AIDS (SABCOA)   64
South African Chambers of Business
       (SACOB)   63
South African Clothing and
       Textile Workers' Union
       (SACTWU)   234, 235
   Investment Holdings   231
South African Democratic Teachers'
       Union (SADTU)
   Investment Holdings   231
South African Federation of Chambers of
       Commerce (SAFCOC)   44, 74, 75
South African Futures Exchange   199
South African National Parks Trust   26,
       80–81
South African Railway and Harbour
       Workers' Union (SARHWU)
       234–235
   Investment Holdings   231
   Investments Trust   235
South African Revenue Services   193
South African Sugar Association   188,
       192, 194, 201–202
South Durban Community
       Environmental Alliance   75
Southern African Customs Union   44
Southern African Development
       Community (SADC)   15, 70
Southern African Grantmakers'
       Association (SAGA)   23, 32, 37,
       74, 81
   food industry   182, 185
Southern African Nature Foundation
       (SANF)   26
Southern African Wildlife College   28
Southern Sun   218
Soweto
   Electricity Crisis Campaign   33
   uprising   16, 19, 102
Special Assignment (SABC3)   36, 193

stakeholder(s)
    accountability 270
    engagement mechanisms 160–161
    relationships 211
Standard Industrial Classification System 177
state-owned corporations 15
Steel and Engineering Industries'
    Federation of South Africa
    (SEIFSA) 47, 74–75
Steve Biko Foundation 225
stock exchange 106
    listing requirements 115
Stockholm Convention on Persistent
    Organic Pollutants 153
strikes 16
    anti-privatisation 127
    mining 125
subcontracting 85–86
    mining sector 123–125
subjugation, racial and gender 2
subsistence economies of rural
    communities 96
sugar 193–195
Sugar Act 192
Sullivan Code 2
Sullivan Principles 17–18, 19, 38, 43, 212
    companies engaged in *18*
sustainability index 113
sustainable development 13, 39, 107
    Brundtland definition 186–187
    discourse of 40–42
    international discourse 134
    SASOL's strategy 153
sustainable growth 41–42

Table Mountain Fund 28
tariff reform 19
tax incentives 81
technology, cleaner 50
Telefood concert 201
Telkom 218, 219
Terra Nova Awards (Audi) 27
Thor Chemicals factory 27, 147–149
Timberwatch Coalition 50
titanium mining 97

tobacco industry 174, 180–181, 192–193, 195–196
Tobacco Institute of South Africa 193
Total BEE Score 218–219
tot system 175
trade liberalisation 23
Trade Policy Network 34
trade, terms of 173
trade unions 19, 60–61
    ANC-aligned 20
    investment companies 231–236
    retirement funds 230
transformation 215
transition, process of 19–22
transnational corporations (TNCs) vi, vii, viii
Transparency International South Africa 34
Treatment Action Campaign (TAC) 33, 63, 76
triple-bottom-line 107–108
    accounting 68, 82–83, 128, 182, 183
    management 48–49
    social pressures on 265–266
Truth and Reconciliation Commission
    (TRC) 4, 8, 99, 242
Tshwarisano (liquid fuels business) 165

Uhambo (liquid fuels business) 165
Umkhonto we Sizwe Military Veterans
    Association 225
unemployment 173
    levels and HIV/AIDS 162
    rates 83–84
unfair labour practices 4
Unilever 175, 188–189
    Code of Business Principles 184–185
    Foundation for Education and
    Development 189
    sustainable agriculture initiative 185
United Nations (UN) vi
    Commission on Sustainable
    Development 41
    Conference on Environment and
    Development 25–26, 41

Conference on Trade and
  Development 70
Convention on Biological Diversity
  71
Framework Convention on Climate
  Change 70, 153
Global Compact 5, 6, 45, *45–46*, 69,
  73, 154, 169, 187
Universal Declaration of Human
  Rights 215
United Nations Research Institute for
  Social Development (UNRISD)
  viii, ix, 33
United States
  Business for Social Responsibility
    185
  Communities for a Better
    Environment (CBE) 159
  Comprehensive Anti-apartheid Act
    164–165
  Environmental Protection Agency
    (EPA) 146, 154
  High Production Volume Chemicals
    Program 154
  Occupational Safety and Health
    Administration (OSHA)
    154–155
  Sugar Association 194
United Tobacco Corporation 180–181
University of Cape Town 32
  Graduate School of Business 32, 33
University of Johannesburg 51
University of KwaZulu-Natal 33
  Centre for Civil Society 33, 34, 83,
    168
University of Pretoria 32
University of South Africa (UNISA)
  Centre for Corporate Citizenship
    32–33
  Southern African Symposium on
    Corporate Citizenship 33
University of Stellenbosch 33
  Sustainable Institute 33
University of the Witwatersrand 33
  Sociology of Work Unit (SWOP) 33
unlisted firms 183

Urban Foundation 19, 30, 102
urban reform 2–3

Vaal Environmental Justice Alliance 169
Voluntary Advisory Forum 151, 170
voluntary agreements 144
voluntary initiatives
  chemicals sector 155–159
  corporate behaviour 43–58

water contamination 174
Widows of African National Congress
  Veterans 225
Wildlife and Environment Society 28
wine industry 179–180
Wipcapital 229
Women's Development Bank Investment
  Holdings (Wiphold) 225
Woolworths 193
workers' compensation 144
workplace
  discrimination 8
  equity 216
World Bank 13, 24, 26, 41
World Business Council for Sustainable
  Development (WBCSD) 26, 41,
  199
  Charter 45
World Commission on Environment and
  Development (WCED) 40 *see
  also* Brundtland Commission
World Conservation Union 54
World Health Organisation 194
World Summit on Sustainable
  Development (WSSD) 25, 107,
  212, 265
  Civil Society Secretariat 42
  impact of 71–73
World Trade Organisation (WTO) 13,
  70, 81, 192, 198
  Doha round 70
Worldwide Fund for Nature – South
  Africa (WWF-SA) 26, 28

Xstrata chrome mine 128